THE LONG WEEKEND

THE LONG WEEKEND

Life in the English Country House Between the Wars

Adrian Tinniswood

JONATHAN CAPE
LONDON

BY THE SAME AUTHOR

Historic Houses of the National Trust

Country Houses from the Air

Life in the English Country Cottage

Visions of Power: Ambition and Architecture

The Polite Tourist: A History of Country House Visiting

The Arts & Crafts House

The Art Deco House

His Invention So Fertile: A Life of Christopher Wren

By Permission of Heaven: The Story of the Great Fire of London

The Verneys: A True Story of Love, War and Madness in Seventeenth-Century England

Pirates of Barbary: Corsairs, Conquests and Captivity in the Seventeenth-Century Mediterranean

The Rainborowes: Pirates, Puritans and a *Family's Quest for the Promised Land*

People who formerly lived in very large houses are now getting out of them. As to who goes in is another matter.

Country Life, 25 October 1919

'It's rather sad,' she said one day, 'to belong, as we do, to a lost generation. I'm sure in history the two wars will count as one war and that we shall be squashed out of it altogether, and people will forget that we ever existed. We might just as well never have lived at all, I do think it's a shame.'

Nancy Mitford, *The Pursuit of Love* (1945)

3 5 7 9 10 8 6 4 2

Jonathan Cape, an imprint of Vintage Publishing,
20 Vauxhall Bridge Road,
London SW1V 2SA

Jonathan Cape is part of the Penguin Random House group of companies
whose addresses can be found at global.penguinrandomhouse.com.

First published by Jonathan Cape in 2016

www.vintage-books.co.uk

A CIP catalogue record for this book is available from the British Library

ISBN 9780224099455

Designed by Peter Ward
Typeset by Palimpsest Book Production Ltd, Falkirk, Stirlingshire
Printed and bound by Firmengruppe APPL, aprinta druck, Wemding, Germany

Penguin Random House is committed to a sustainable future for our business, our readers
and our planet. This book is made from Forest Stewardship Council® certified paper.

CONTENTS

For my friend
Godfrey Napthine
1954–2015

PREFACE AND ACKNOWLEDGEMENTS

THERE IS NOTHING QUITE AS beautiful as an English country house in summer.

And there has never been a summer quite like that Indian summer between the two world wars, a period of gentle decline in which the sun set slowly on the British Empire and the shadows lengthened on the lawns of a thousand stately homes across the nation.

At least, that is the conventional view of a period which has always been seen as witnessing the end of the country house. One by one, so the story goes, the stately homes of England were deserted and dismantled and demolished, their estates broken up, their oaks felled and their parks given over to suburban sprawl.

There's certainly truth in that. But it masks an alternative narrative which exists side by side with the familiar tale of woe. A narrative which saw new families buying, borrowing and sometimes building themselves a country house; which introduced new aesthetics, new social structures, new meanings to an old tradition. A narrative, in fact, which saw new life in the country house. That is what I have tried to explore in *The Long Weekend*.

My title is borrowed from Robert Graves and Alan Hodge, who in 1940 published a social history of Britain beginning at the Armistice and ending with Neville Chamberlain's broadcast to the nation at 11.15 on Sunday, 3 September 1939, in which he explained that he had asked Germany to undertake to withdraw her troops from Poland: 'I have to tell you now that no such undertaking has been received, and that consequently this country is at war.' Graves and Hodge called their book *The Long Weekend*, a phrase that seemed peculiarly appropriate for a study of the country house between the wars, conjuring up – for me, at least – a transitional moment of leisurely uncertainty, a pause.

I have had so much help in the writing of this book – from

Right: *Edwina Mountbatten and the Duke of York, 1920.*

friends, from colleagues and from complete strangers who commented with kindness on items in my sporadic *Long Weekend* blog or offered ideas and enthusiasm at country houses and archives and libraries all over the country. I can't mention them all by name: indeed, there are many whose names I don't even know, like the staff at Bath Central Library who retrieved endless quantities of heavy bound volumes of *Country Life* from deep in the stacks for me, staggering under the weight with unfailing cheerfulness. But they all have a place in my heart. I am grateful to them.

I do want to thank by name Jean Appleton, Gavin Johns, Patricia Lankester, Katherine Ponganis and Nerys Watts. They know why.

And I want to thank Helen. She knows why, too.

Adrian Tinniswood
Bath, October 2015

THE LONG WEEKEND

INTRODUCTION

Everyone Sang

Everyone suddenly burst out singing;
And I was filled with such delight
As prisoned birds must find in freedom . . .

Siegfried Sassoon, 'Everyone Sang' (1919)

Sir Henry and Lady Alda Hoare with their son Harry at Stourhead, 1912.

JUST BEFORE LUNCH on Christmas Eve 1917, a telegram arrived at Stourhead in Wiltshire.

Over the previous five weeks a flurry of messages had flown back and forth between Stourhead, the ancestral seat of the Hoare family, and the Middle East. On 17 November Sir Henry and Lady Alda Hoare's son Harry was shot through the lungs while fighting the Turks at Mughar Ridge in Palestine; after a night lying out on the battlefield he had been taken to a dressing station and then moved to the small British Army hospital at Ras el-Tin, overlooking the harbour of Alexandria. He was now on the mend, his parents had been told, and coping with his injury 'with patience, cheerfulness and pluck'. A few days earlier Harry's doctor had wired to say the boy's condition was improving, and a West Country neighbour who was stationed in Alexandria followed this up with another telegram: 'Saw Harry yesterday – progressing satisfactorily'. Alda Hoare recorded their relief in her diary: 'we knelt and humbly thanked God for His unspeakable mercy'.[1]

But Harry Hoare was dead. His wound had haemorrhaged and he had died. This was the news that the Christmas Eve telegram brought for his parents.

They didn't cry. Instead Alda fell on her knees and prayed, 'O God, for strength to us, in our shattered lives'. Then together the couple walked through the great old house and stood looking at the full-length portrait of Harry, painted when he was twenty-one. 'Our only and the best of sons,' wrote Sir Henry a little later. 'He never grieved us by thought, word or deed.'[2]

Harry Hoare's death was a blow from which his parents never recovered. Sir Henry's reaction was an urge to get away from the Wiltshire estate where his family had lived for nearly 200 years. It held too many memories. His wife was determined to stay at Stourhead, and for exactly that reason. 'I cannot bear to leave my son I everywhere see here,' she confided to her diary.[3]

So they stayed. For another thirty years the couple managed Stourhead, living the life of country gentry. Sir Henry wrote letters to *The Times* and entered his hunters in local horse shows; Lady Alda opened the house at a shilling a time in aid of the Queen's Institute of District Nursing, and ran the household with three housemaids, a cook, a kitchen maid and scullery maid and three or four other staff.

Harry remained in Egypt, in the Hadra War Cemetery at Alexandria. Back at Stourhead, his name topped the list of local men commemorated in a roll of honour at the little medieval church of St Peter, with an epigraph from Ecclesiasticus: 'A good life hath but a few days: but a good name endureth for ever.'

His parents' grief endured, too. It defined them, it engulfed them. And since Harry had never married, it left them uncertain for a future without a direct heir. In 1925 Sir Henry went down to Bryanston in Dorset, where the 4th Viscount Portman was selling up to pay the estate duties resulting from the death of his predecessor. Sir Henry was shocked to see family paintings, photographs, even the 3rd Lord Portman's personal effects, all coming under the hammer. 'It brought home to me what may happen when we are gone,' he wrote.[4] 'Oh, had he married, and given us a grandson to love,' said Alda.[5]

Perhaps Siegfried Sassoon was right. Perhaps everyone sang when the war was over. But so many of those songs were shot through with sadness.

If all the peers in Britain came together to celebrate the Armistice at the end of 1918, the resulting group portrait would fill a large canvas. There would be 746 of them arranged, no doubt, in order of precedence: dukes in front, then marquesses, earls, viscounts and barons (not to mention two archbishops, thirty-nine bishops and two dozen women, peeresses in their own right). Long-lineaged nobles like Charles Chetwynd-Talbot, 20th Earl of Shrewsbury, whose ancestor had fought with Henry V in the Hundred Years War, would rub shoulders with nouveau-riche press barons like Viscount Northcliffe and Lord Beaverbrook as they raised their glasses to victory. The 5th Baron Headley would have given the champagne a miss: he had converted to Islam in 1913 and, as Lord Headley el-Farooq, was president of the British Muslim Society and a staunch believer in the ability of Islam to arrest the decline of Western civilisation and put a stop to suffragettism and short skirts. The 12th Viscount Taaffe, whose forebears had fought for James II at the Battle of the Boyne, might have found the toasts rather awkward, since he was currently a serving officer in the defeated Austrian Army with a castle in Bohemia. In March 1919 he was one of four 'traitor peers' to be deprived of their titles for 'adhering to the king's enemies during the war'; the others were the dukes of Cumberland, Albany and Brunswick, three high-ranking German nobles whose British titles came to them through their descent from George III or Victoria and Albert.*

There were some who wouldn't have been at this imaginary gathering at all if it hadn't been for the war. When the fighting started, the middle-aged Walter Beresford Annesley had no expectation of succeeding his young cousin as 7th Earl Annesley: then came the day in November 1914 when the 6th earl climbed into a Bristol biplane and set off across the Channel, never to be seen again. George Amias Fitzwarrene Poulett, 8th Earl Poulett, was nine years old when he succeeded to his title; his father, the 7th earl, had survived three years in France before being transferred back to Yorkshire, only to fall victim to the Spanish influenza pandemic in July 1918.

* Taaffe, who was also a Count of the Holy Roman Empire, was doubly unfortunate: four weeks after losing his Irish titles, he learned that the newly established Austrian republic had abolished the nobility altogether, and with it his remaining title. Land reform in the new Czechoslovakia then took away most of his Bohemian estates, and plain Mr Henry Taaffe died in debt in Vienna in 1928.

Altogether a dozen British peers died on active service, and one British prince: Queen Victoria's youngest grandchild, 23-year-old Maurice of Battenberg, who was killed at Ypres at the beginning of the war while serving with the King's Royal Rifle Corps. Viscount Hawarden died in France in August 1914, three weeks after war was declared. Marquess Conyngham was killed forty-eight hours before the Armistice.

But the psychology of loss went much deeper. It involved uncertainty about the future, the break-up of estates, perhaps even the prospect of financial ruin. One in ten titled families lost heirs in the war. Tommy Agar-Robartes, whose family owned Lanhydrock in Cornwall and Wimpole Hall in Cambridgeshire, died at Loos after being hit by sniper fire while he was bringing in a wounded private from no-man's-land. Nineteen-year-old Denis, the only son of Viscount Buxton and a second lieutenant in the Coldstream Guards, disappeared in Flanders in October 1917; all that remains of him is his name on a memorial to the missing on the Ypres Salient. Lord and Lady Desborough's eldest boy, Julian Grenfell, was hit in the head by a shell splinter at Ypres; the day after he died *The Times* published his poem 'Into Battle', with its prophetic final stanza beginning 'The thundering line of battle stands, / And in the air Death moans and sings'. When she heard of his death, his ten-year-old sister Imogen wrote, 'I am glad that he is at peace and did his duty.'[6] Two months later the next in line, Billy Grenfell, was killed leading a charge within a mile of where Julian had been hit.

And the roll of horror rolls on. At St Michael's Mount, Lord St Levan lost his brother and heir, drowned in the Mediterranean in 1916. The De Blaquieres of Brockworth Manor in Gloucestershire lost their elder son in France in the spring of 1915, and their younger two years later; with the death of Lord De Blaquiere in 1920 the male line ended and the title, an Irish barony created in 1722, became extinct.

The survivors coped in different ways, selling up or soldiering on or, occasionally, taking control of their lives in a way which would have been unthinkable before the war. In September 1915, for example, Kathleen Cuthbert's husband James, a captain in the Scots Guards, was reported wounded and missing at Loos. At twenty-nine she was left a widow with three children under the age of five and a fourth on the way.

It wasn't until 1917 that Kathleen found out for certain that James was dead, so that for nearly two years a cloud of uncertainty hung over her future and the future of the 4,000-acre Cuthbert estate in Northumberland, at the heart of which was Beaufront Castle, a 'domestic castellated' mansion of 1836–41, designed by the prolific Co. Durham architect John Dobson.* Beaufront was held in trust for their eldest boy. Their land agent had gone off to the war at the same time as Kathleen's husband; and even before Cuthbert's death was confirmed there were rumblings in the family that someone – some *man* – should be brought in to run the estate on Kathleen's behalf.

She wouldn't have it. She insisted on managing the entire estate by herself, paying the men every week, letting the farms and cottages. If she needed advice, she went to her father, a landowner and mine owner whose estate bordered Beaufront. For a short time she had a bailiff, but he was dismissed after an incident which demonstrated her drive and determination. Late one night she was coming home from a party when she was puzzled to see one of her shepherds, a man named Beatty, driving some sheep out of the park gate.

Beatty's family had worked for the Cuthberts for generations. Even so, it was past midnight – a funny time to be moving stock. Kathleen ordered her chauffeur to stop the car, got out and demanded to know what the man was doing. 'Moving sheep,' he told her. So she asked him to come up to the house the next morning.

When Beatty arrived, she accused him of selling sheep at market on his own account (having first telephoned the mart to check that he was indeed doing just that). Then she dismissed

* Beaufront was the scene of a gruesome tragedy in 1907. Captain Cuthbert and his first wife Dorothy were out with a shooting party in woodland on the estate when he tripped and accidentally discharged his gun, hitting his wife in the head at point blank range. She died instantly.

him without a reference and evicted him and his wife from their tied cottage. When her father asked her if she wouldn't have been better to give him a second chance she answered, 'As a woman I've got to behave like that. If I was a man, I could go and rant at him . . . But all I can do is to give him notice to get off the place.'[7] She suspected that her bailiff had known about Beatty's tricks, although she couldn't prove it. She dismissed him as well.

In February 1917 Henry Cubitt's father died and he inherited the Cubitt family estates, which included Denbies in Surrey, a vast Italianate mansion designed by his grandfather, the famous London master-builder Thomas Cubitt; and Fallapit, a slightly more modest neo-Tudor country house in south Devon. He also inherited a title, becoming the 2nd Baron Ashcombe. His eldest son Henry, a captain in the Coldstream Guards, was already dead, killed on the Somme in September 1916. His second son, Alick, died in the Battle of Cambrai in November 1917; he was buried in an unmarked grave.

Four months later the Ashcombes lost their third son, William, a lieutenant in the Royal Dragoons who died of wounds in northern France. All three boys were in their early twenties. The Ashcombes were well supplied with sons – they had six in all – but that can have been of little comfort to them. In November 1920 their fourth, Roland, married Sonia Keppel, whose mother had been the mistress of Edward VII and whose sister Violet was currently the lover of Vita Sackville-West.* In a reminder that death was not the only outcome for casualties of war, *The Times* pointed out that the wedding decorations were all being carried out by a nephew of the Keppels from the Scots Guards, 'who lost the sight of both eyes during the war in trying to save his sergeant, and who has now a Victory florist shop in the Piccadilly-arcade'.[8]

* The genealogically minded will already have noticed that Roland and Sonia were the grandparents of the present Duchess of Cornwall.

Of course they all had stately homes – the quick and the dead, the brash profiteer and the bereaved earl, the survivors and the scarred. Wasn't the ownership of a grand mansion a defining characteristic of a British aristocrat? It might be a baroque pile, like the Marlboroughs' Blenheim Palace and the Devonshires' Chatsworth, or a rambling romance like Broughton Castle, home to the Fiennes family since the 1440s; a modest Georgian block or an outrageous piece of pathologically earnest Gothic Revivalism brimming over with turrets and battlements. Style wasn't the point. Taste wasn't the point. Big or small, elegant or ugly, a country house was a necessary adjunct to membership of that most elite of elites, the nobility of Britain. Wasn't it?

Up to a point. The 1919 edition of that great directory of the traditional landed classes and their pedigrees, *Debrett's Peerage, Baronetage, Knightage, and Companionage*, shows that the vast majority of peers of the realm owned, leased or otherwise lived in at least one country house. A quarter of all peers boasted two, and several had a string of them. The main residence of Hugo Charteris, 11th Earl of Wemyss and March, was Gosford in East Lothian, designed in the 1790s by Robert Adam, and remodelled for the earl's father a century later. After he succeeded to the title in 1914 he chose to live there with his mistress, the original forces sweetheart Lady Angela Forbes. His wife understandably preferred to live in their Cotswold home, the breathtaking sixteenth- and early seventeenth-century Stanway House in Gloucestershire. She supplemented her income by renting Stanway each summer to J. M. Barrie for the considerable sum of 200 guineas. 'Lady Wemyss [has] a very clear understanding of the things that matter in life,' wrote Lady Angela in her autobiography – an unnecessarily waspish comment, considering she was sleeping with the woman's husband.[9]

As well as Gosford and Stanway, the Wemyss family, whose ancestors claimed descent from Charlemagne the Great, also owned Neidpath Castle, a severe tower house in the Scottish Borders; and Hay Lodge on the banks of the River Tweed at Peebles. And Amisfield House, Haddington, designed in the 1750s by Isaac Ware, and one of the most significant Palladian

Stanway House in Gloucestershire, one of the 11th Earl of Wemyss and March's six country houses.

buildings in Scotland. And Elcho Castle, a rather lovely fortified mansion of the sixteenth century. There was also a town house in Cadogan Square, designed in 1887 by Richard Norman Shaw.

Wemyss was unusual in the size of his property portfolio, but not unique. The Duke of Buccleuch also owned six country houses, and like Wemyss's, five were in Scotland. As well as Wentworth Woodhouse near Rotherham, claimed as the largest private house in the United Kingdom by the *Guinness Book of Records*, William Charles De Meuron Wentworth-Fitzwilliam, 7th Earl Fitzwilliam, owned two estates near Doncaster, a Jacobean lodge on the outskirts of the Yorkshire town of Malton, and two houses in Co. Wicklow, Ireland: Coolattin, built for his great-grandfather by John Carr of York at the beginning of the nineteenth century; and nearby Carnew, a ruined castle which was restored and reroofed in about 1817. He was also the patron of no fewer than eighteen livings.

At the other end of the scale, one in nine peers had no country house at all in 1919. A few were living in very modest circumstances. The 3rd Lord Magheramorne, for example, gave his residence as 37 Knyveton Road, Bournemouth; and Lord Strathspey, 31st Chief of the Clan Grant, lived not in a palace but in Putney. But most of the eighty-eight British nobles without a place in the country at the end of the war had prestigious London homes in Mayfair or Park Lane or Regent's Park. Their decision to do without a rural residence was a matter of choice rather than straitened circumstances, a reflection of the declining importance of the country house, and perhaps of the growing appeal of metropolitan life. By the 1920s many who *did* own country houses, especially among the recently ennobled and those who aspired to aristocracy, did not have the links with the land which their predecessors in earlier centuries would have taken for granted. For them, a country house, no matter how grand, was a weekend retreat rather than a home.

The *Debrett's* list is the roughest of rough indications of trends in country-house ownership after the war, and no more than that. It isn't always reliable: only one country residence was listed for the

2nd Duke of Westminster, Eaton Hall in Cheshire, even though he owned several more. And more importantly, those 746 peers of the realm were the tip of the iceberg, a fraction of what their Victorian parents used to call the Upper Ten Thousand. What about the baronets, the knights, the country squires? The press barons and the brewers and bankers? The Americans?

Some of these bought and sold mansions with the same ease with which they bought and sold companies or racehorses. For others, though, the country house was a home and more – something woven into the fabric of society, a symbol of continuity which held out the hope of a return to normality after the slaughter.

This feeling was strong among those who came home from the war confused, uncertain about the point of it all. The author John Buchan, although he was never fit enough for active service and spent the war as a correspondent, an intelligence officer and eventually as director of information under Beaverbrook, wrote movingly of his first excursions into the English countryside after being demobbed; of how throughout the war he found it impossible to respond to nature without recalling the scent of hawthorn and lilac vying with the stench of poison-gas, or the sound of birdsong signalling a lull in an artillery barrage. As he tramped along the lanes of Warwickshire and Oxfordshire in the cold, wet April of 1919, he recovered the past, he said, and with it some hope for the future.

Finding in country life a delight 'in the rhythm of nature, and in small homely things after so many alien immensities',[10] Buchan and his wife Susan sold their London house and moved with their four young children to Elsfield in Oxfordshire, where they bought an attractively unassuming early eighteenth-century stone manor house with deliciously haphazard additions. Here Buchan threw himself into the life of 'a minor country gentleman with a taste for letters', as he wrote with rather deliberate self-deprecation.[11] The family employed a small staff from the village, and sat in the front pew at church every Sunday. John always read the lesson; Susan founded a branch of the Women's Institute and dispensed tea on Sunday afternoons to visiting Oxford undergraduates. She also presided over house parties where visitors might include the poets John Masefield and Walter de la Mare, Robert Graves, who lived nearby, or T. E. Lawrence, who used to turn up at Elsfield at odd times on Boanerges, his 1,000 cc Brough Superior motorcycle, and talked for hours about the Arabs, the war, his muddled masochism and his powerful sense of disillusion. On weekdays Buchan commuted to his office in London, but from Friday evening until noon on Monday he was a country squire, riding out each morning, revelling on winter evenings in the smell of woodsmoke and the hooting of owls in the spinneys and copses.

There were alternative and sometimes competing narratives to the kind of rural idyll in which Buchan chose to lose himself. December 1920 saw the posthumous publication of *Poems by Wilfred Owen*: Owen's portrayal of the soldier as victim and, in the words of one reviewer, his 'sternly just and justly stern judgement on the idyllisers', shifted the emphasis away from Buchan's conviction that the way of life epitomised by small manor houses like his own was what England had been fighting for.[12] And two years later T. S. Eliot's *The Waste Land* replaced old certainties with a kaleidoscope of fragmented and bewildering realities, turning gardens into graveyards and teaching that far from offering hope for the future, April was the cruellest month.

But the rural idyll, bred by the Romantics in the nineteenth century, nurtured by the Edwardians' quest for the heart of England and brought to full maturity by the war, is crucial to the conception of country-house life in the 1920s and 1930s. In the mansions and manor houses of post-war England it was Buchan's view which triumphed, not Owen's bitter sacrifice or Eliot's message of despair and redemption. That isn't surprising – Buchan's was a view which placed those mansions and manor houses at the heart of the nation, gave them a leading role in the culture. *They* were the country in 'king and country'. A house in the country, rambling, ancient, oozing tradition, with an estate which was small enough not to be an encumbrance but big enough for some riding and rough shooting, was the *beau idéal*. Those who already possessed such a thing buckled down and buried their sons, or at least memorialised them in a new stained-glass window for the local church, where St Georges slew dragons and knights in gleaming armour gazed proudly, poignantly out at congregations whose losses might be just as great, but who lacked the resources and the social status to commemorate those losses quite so graphically. Those who had no country house to connect them to the land fit for heroes could always follow John Buchan's example and buy themselves a piece of the past.

CHAPTER ONE

It Is Ours

On 4 March 1930 the diplomat and journalist Harold Nicolson and his aristocratic wife, the author Victoria Sackville-West, heard that they were to have new neighbours. The couple had lived happily at Long Barn in the Kent village of Sevenoaks Weald, 'our own nestling home amid the meadows', for the past fifteen years, and neither could imagine leaving what Harold called 'our little mud pie, which we both love so childishly and which for both of us is the place where we have been so happy'.[1]

Now that was all changed. They discovered that Westwood, the farm next door, was being sold to 'poultry people'. The idea of a chicken farm on their doorstep appalled them, but neither wanted to leave Long Barn and they immediately contacted the vendor and asked if they could buy Westwood instead. But at £16,000 her asking price was too high for them; Vita suggested offering £13,000, but Harold didn't think it was worth it and by the end of March Vita was reconciled to the fact that they would have to move.

On the evening of 4 April Harold, who was on the staff of the *Evening Standard* and stayed up in London during the week, had a phone call from his wife. A local land agent had told her about Sissinghurst, a sixteenth-century castle outside the little town of Cranbrook, twenty miles south-east of Long Barn, which had been on the market for two years. She had gone down to see it that afternoon and fallen in love with it.

Harold took the train down the next day, a Saturday. Vita met him at the station and with their two teenage boys they motored over to Cranbrook, where Harold had his first sight of Sissinghurst – or rather, of the fragments that remained. The once-great courtyard house which had entertained Elizabeth I had all but disappeared during three centuries of neglect: in 1752 Horace Walpole had described seeing 'a park in ruins, and a house in ten

Sissinghurst, 'as personal and lively as anything in England'.

times greater ruins'; and it had gone downhill from there, serving as a prisoner-of-war camp during the Seven Years War, a workhouse and, finally, a sort of adjunct to the neighbouring farm, housing farm labourers, horses and bits of agricultural machinery.[2] Virtually all that survived intact was a low range of buildings and beyond it, a strikingly beautiful tower, four storeys high and built entirely of soft red brick.

Harold was non-committal, but the next day he and Vita went back for another look and half-decided to offer £12,000 for the castle, its grounds and the adjoining 400 acres. Still they dithered. Harold reckoned they would need to spend at least another £15,000 to put it in order. By the time they had finished, they wouldn't have much change out of £30,000 – a large sum, more than £4 million in today's money. For the same amount, he told his wife, they could have 'a beautiful place replete with park, garage, h[ot] and c[old], central heating, historical associations, and two lodges'.[3] On the other hand, Sissinghurst was in a part of Kent which they both liked. It had links, albeit tenuous ones, to Vita's family: Cecily Baker, whose father owned the place in Henry VIII's time, had married her ancestor, Sir Thomas Sackville, 1st Earl of Dorset. And, most decisively, 'we like it'.[4]

All through the middle of April they hummed and hawed. Harold's elderly mother advised them against it, saying it would cost too much to keep up. When they walked over it once more in icy winds and rain, it looked so big and dilapidated that Harold almost lost his nerve. 'I am terrified of socialist legislation, of not being able to let the fields, of finding that the place is a huge hole into which we pour money, of finding that the whole thing is far more bother than it is worth,' he confided to his diary, admitting that he and Vita were both depressed and worried about making the wrong decision.[5]

Finally they made an offer, and sat back to wait for an answer. After dinner one night at the beginning of May the telephone rang, and Vita took the call. It was from the land agent who was handling the sale. Harold described what happened next. '"Quite" . . . "Yes, of course" . . . "Oh naturally!" She puts down the receiver and says,

The Nicolsons at Sissinghurst, 1932.

"It is ours." We embrace warmly. I then go and get the plans and fiddle.'[6]

It would be another five months before the couple could even camp out at Sissinghurst. They moved in permanently in 1932, letting Long Barn to the film producer Sidney Bernstein and then, in 1936, to Charles Lindbergh and his wife Anne, who had left America in search of some privacy after the media frenzy that followed the kidnap and murder of their baby son. ('No, sir, we shall not stare at the poor people,' the village postmistress promised Harold when he told her the identities of Long Barn's new tenants.[7]) Sissinghurst's famous gardens were more or less complete by 1937. Even then, Harold was still looking to a future when the place would be finished. 'I really believe', he told Vita, 'that you will be able to make of that ramshackle farm-tumble something as personal and lovely as anything in England.'[8] As of course she did.

*

As buyers in 1930, Harold and Vita benefited from the fact that supply was outstripping demand as historic country houses poured onto the market in the wake of the Wall Street Crash of the previous October. That summer the Marquess of Lothian let Blickling Hall, the finest Jacobean survival in Norfolk, fully furnished to Major Gilbert Russell, a great-grandson of the 6th Duke of Bedford. One of the great mid-Georgian houses, Claremont in Surrey, built for Clive of India by the impressive triumvirate of Capability Brown, Henry Holland and Sir John Soane, came up for sale a few weeks later, as a business opportunity rather than a home: the agents said that the 210-acre estate, whose pleasure grounds included work by Brown, Vanbrugh and William Kent, was 'ripe for immediate development for building purposes'.[9] Broome Park in Kent, an extravaganza of cut and moulded red brick dating from the 1630s which had once been the home of Lord Kitchener of Khartoum, also came back on the market, having been sold only four months before. Claremont became a girls' school, Broome a hotel.

In the week that the sales of Claremont and Broome were announced, stories began to circulate that the Great Chamber of Gilling Castle in Yorkshire was off to America for a five-figure sum. Gilling had been bought the previous year and was being turned into a prep school. The Great Chamber, one of the finest Elizabethan interiors in the country and a riot of strapwork and inlaid flowers with a heraldic frieze containing no fewer than 443 coats of arms, had been bought by a wealthy American – William Randolph Hearst, who also obtained panelling from Gilling's Georgian long gallery.

That summer the president of the Auctioneers and Estate Agents' Institute lamented that 'the large family residences, especially of the older type, are practically unsaleable'. Some few country houses were being turned into schools, institutions and local authority offices, he acknowledged; 'but the demand for such purposes is very limited, and it is now found that even the moderately large house . . . is extremely difficult to dispose of'.[10] At the same time concern was voiced that there was a crisis coming

in the countryside. Landowners, said the Duke of Montrose, were impoverished, 'mostly living on capital which, sooner or later, must become exhausted'.[11] The time was coming, he argued, when the state should accept land in lieu of death duties, which since the 'tax on death' had been introduced back in 1894 had risen until now it stood at 34 per cent for estates valued between £500,000 and £600, 000, rising to a whopping 50 per cent on estates over £2 million. 'The continuance of the current burdensome conditions of private ownership', said Montrose, 'is quite impossible.'[12]

Not everyone agreed. *Country Life* applauded the fact that in the past decade big houses like Stowe in Buckinghamshire and Westonbirt in Gloucestershire had found new uses as schools, seeing their sale as evidence of an adaptable market. The magazine noted that the vast majority of sales were still to private individuals, and maintained that scores of country estates, some quite large, had found buyers over the past year. By the end of the year, though, even *Country Life*'s relentlessly optimistic estate market correspondent, 'Arbiter', was forced to admit that with property transactions £8 million or £9 million down on the previous year, 1930 was probably the worst since the great agricultural depressions of the 1870s.

How had it come to this? In 1918 the future looked bright for the country house and its estate. The volume of sales and prices had improved steadily right through the war, after a predictable and dramatic slump in the autumn of 1914. Farms were in particular demand: the shortage of labour as agricultural workers left for military service was more than offset by the absence of foreign competition and the fact that there was an assured market at fixed prices for every ounce of food that could be produced. True, there was a trend, first noticed before the war, for syndicates or individuals to buy up large estates and then break them up for resale, a practice which disadvantaged the tenant farmer who, if he or she wanted to own their farm, had to pay the speculators' profit on top of the market value or face the prospect of seeing it sold out

The Great Chamber at Gilling Castle in Yorkshire, one of the finest Elizabethan interiors in the country.

from under them. The elderly Marquess of Aberdeen came in for some mildly reproving comments in 1919 when he announced to his tenants that he had sold 37,000 acres of his 50,000-acre estates in Aberdeenshire to a shipbroker, Herbert Boret, who was busy buying up land in England as well as Scotland. The marquess, who kept his ancestral home of Haddo House (and who also owned a ranch in British Columbia), maintained that he was merely moving with the times, which were clearly in favour of substituting ownership for tenancy. The press reckoned he was escaping from his responsibilities as a landowner, and when he claimed that Boret intended to give tenants the opportunity to own their holdings, critics made pointed comments about the profit he would expect as middleman.

Although the spectre of the speculator remained throughout the 1920s, he proved less of a problem than commentators predicted. This was partly because landowners realised that they would get more for their estates by breaking them up themselves and selling them off in separate lots, offering farms to their tenants privately before going to auction; and partly because many believed quite sincerely that they owed a duty of care to their tenants, and were prepared to put their money where their mouths were. The politician Walter Long, for example, sacrificed a cool £20,000 by refusing an offer from a syndicate for his 15,000-acre Wiltshire estates and offering them instead to his tenants.

In 1918 the property market saw sales of £11.38 million, an increase of more than 25 per cent on the previous year. There was a strong demand for country houses, especially those which came without large estates. 'Today there are on the books of the leading agents scores of applicants for properties, who cannot get what they want at the moment,' wrote *Country Life*'s 'Arbiter' in his end-of-year round-up of sales. 'They are in themselves a guarantee of the coming year's auctions.'[13]

He was right. 1919 was the most remarkable year since estate records began, with more country houses bought and sold than ever before, and prices continuing to rise. Smaller country houses continued to be in demand, especially those within an hour's drive of London. The firm of Hampton & Sons, one of England's leading estate agents, reported that furnished country houses were being let for the summer at higher rents than recently, and that 'for country houses with several hundred acres prices have been distinctly on the upgrade, while for the house of medium size, with a home farm from 100 to 200 acres, the demand has been phenomenal'.[14] Another prominent firm of estate agents, Knight, Frank & Rutley, recorded sales of more than three-quarters of a million acres, and total combined sales for the year reached more than £30 million. Mansions and their estates played a huge part in this boom, particularly those with historical associations. 'It is striking', said *The Times*, 'how many places sold this year were visited by Queen Elizabeth'; and equally striking that not a few claimed 'a more or less authentic record running back to before the Norman Conquest'.[15]

But there were early signs of a coming storm, as big landowners moved to capitalise on the rising market and liquidise their assets. In the final weeks of 1918, land on the edges of half a dozen estates were sold off, including 1,000 acres of the Holme Hall estate near York, which realised £29,000; nine or ten of the best farms on Lord Pembroke's Wilton estate; and 8,000 acres on Earl Beauchamp's Madresfield Court estate. In fact the sale of 'outlying portions' – a phrase which referred to land on the margins of an estate or perhaps separated from it – crops up again and again in the property pages, suggesting rationalisation or consolidation, but not financial need. 'Arbiter' was at pains to point out that Lord Beauchamp's sale had nothing to do with Madresfield Court itself. 'The sale of 8,000 acres on an extensive estate like Lord Beauchamp's has, necessarily, no more connection with the mansion and its surroundings than it has with a town house.'[16] What 'Arbiter' couldn't know or refused to admit, was that the sale of 'outlying portions' would become a frequent precursor to the sale of a mansion and the departure of a family who, whether or not they had been living there since the Norman Conquest, could no longer make ends meet.

Several big Scottish sporting estates came on the market in late 1918 and early 1919. The 11,600-acre Castle Menzies estate in Perthshire was offered at a reduced price of £60,000 in a sale which included five miles of salmon and trout fishing and grouse moors yielding an average of 1,200 brace of birds each year; and nearly 92,000 acres of the Duke of Sutherland's Highland property, 'including Dornoch Castle', said the sale particulars, referring to a reputedly haunted sixteenth-century hunting lodge, 'but not the town of Dornoch'.[17] This was in addition to 237,000 acres which the Duke of Sutherland had sold earlier in the year.

A further sign that all might not be well in the country house market was voiced in January 1919 by a spokesman for Hampton & Sons, who remarked on 'the number of properties which have been disposed of together with the interior furnishings, a transaction which was comparatively rare in pre-war days'.[18]

In March 1919 *The Times* ran a story under the headline 'Ancestral Seats as Garden Cities'. The report centred on Lord Middleton's announcement that he intended to sell Wollaton Hall, perched in a remarkable hilltop setting on the outskirts of Nottingham, and that he had given first refusal to the city council. Wollaton was, and indeed still is, one of the most flamboyant Elizabethan country houses. A glittering palace of turrets and towers and mannerist decoration, it was built in the 1580s for Middleton's ancestor, Sir Francis Willoughby, and designed by the greatest of all Elizabethan architects, Robert Smythson, who was buried in the local church. Its future, declared *Country Life*, 'must be a matter of concern for all who have any admiration of the beautiful and any respect for the past'.[19]

Middleton was in his seventies and without children. The council was interested in his proposal – very interested indeed. But nothing came of the plan before Lord Middleton's death in 1922, when his estates and title went to his 75-year-old brother. The 10th Lord Middleton, a former major in the Indian Army, announced his intention to retreat to another family seat, Birdsall House in Yorkshire, remodelled in the 1870s; and to sell off his Nottinghamshire estates, including Wollaton. But he died in 1924

Wollaton Hall, Nottinghamshire.

and his son and heir was faced with a second set of death duties in the space of only two years. The 11th Lord Middleton sold land, some family pictures and a library from Wollaton which included important medieval manuscripts, hundreds of rare sixteenth- and seventeenth-century pamphlets and a First Folio Shakespeare.

The four-day sale at Christie's of 'one of the few remaining of the old and well-matured libraries, buried in a great country house and practically unknown to bibliographers',[20] raised over £8,300. But it wasn't enough, and he repeated the offer to give Nottingham first refusal on the Wollaton estate. The council unanimously agreed to buy the hall and 800 acres of parkland for £200,000.

And now it emerged that the council didn't want the mansion at all, no matter that it was one of the finest country houses in England. It wanted the park for development, and plans were swiftly unveiled to sell off the land that fronted the main Nottingham–Derby road 'as sites for houses of a good class'. This would enable the authorities to recoup most of the purchase price. Some land was set aside for municipal housing, for playing fields and for an eighteen-hole golf course, which was expected 'to improve the value of the adjoining building land by 2s. a yard'.[21] As for Wollaton Hall itself, the council didn't quite know what to do with it. The favoured option was to house the city's natural history collection there, and this was what eventually happened. 'The conversion of a park so charming as this into a mass of houses has its painful side,' commented *The Times*, 'but the process is inevitable, and if it is carried out with taste and skill the regret is reduced to very small proportions.'[22]

This tale of an unwanted masterpiece illustrates two sides to the country house in the 1920s. First, there was the obvious story of retrenchment and decline, as an established landed family was forced by death and taxes to break centuries-old links with its ancestral seat. This was sad, but hardly new: country-house-owning families had been selling up, going broke and dying out for centuries. More novel was the notion that it was really quite difficult to find a use for a historic mansion in post-war Britain; that while its grounds were worth something as a setting for suburbia, the mansion itself was no longer any use as a home. It was as dead as the stuffed birds and animals that stared out unseeing on Wollaton's halls and galleries, as much a thing of the past as the fossils in their glass cases.

*

At least Wollaton survived. Twenty miles north of Nottingham's new natural history museum and golf course, and just across the border in Derbyshire, lay Sutton Scarsdale, the grandest early Georgian house in the county. An enormous balustraded and rusticated mansion facing east – always a brave choice in the wind-whipped hills of Derbyshire – Sutton Scarsdale was the work of Francis Smith of Warwick, who remodelled it magnificently in the 1720s. It was bought in 1824 by Richard Arkwright, son of the inventor of the spinning jenny and one of the richest commoners in England; and for nearly a century the Arkwrights lived at Sutton Scarsdale without making any major alterations to the house. Then in 1918 William Arkwright, whose interests lay more with the breeding of pointers than architecture and elegant living, tried to let the house, having first astutely allowed the historian Margaret Jourdain to describe its beauties to possible buyers in a feature for *Country Life*. There were no takers. In June 1919 a notice appeared in the press announcing the auction of the entire Sutton Scarsdale estate, including the mansion, the local pub, thirty farms and seventy houses, cottages and shops. The sale, which took place on 6 November, made more than £100,000, but the mansion failed to sell and was withdrawn at £12,600. That figure, commented *The Times*, 'will have to be considerably improved upon before it reaches a reasonable estimate for so stately and historic a house'.[23]

But no one wanted Sutton Scarsdale – not as a country house, anyway. It was bought after the auction by a syndicate of local businessmen who gutted the place, stripped the lead from its roof and sold off its fittings to a London antiques dealer, Charles Lockhart Roberson, whose prospectus offered panelled rooms and old chimney pieces and declared that 'in these days when so many of the estates and country seats of the nobility are changing hands', his Knightsbridge gallery offered 'an ideal medium through which they may be brought to the notice of possible buyers'.[24] Roberson sold a stunning carved chimney piece from Sutton Scarsdale to William Randolph Hearst; and in 1928 the new Philadelphia Art Gallery announced that three rooms acquired from Roberson from

The entrance hall at Sutton Scarsdale, Derbyshire, shortly before the house was dismantled.

the Arkwrights' mansion, two panelled in deal and one in oak, were to form the setting for paintings by Gainsborough, Romney and Reynolds. Sutton Scarsdale itself was left to fall into decay, a sad roofless ruin.

An even more ignominious fate befell Nuthall Temple, which stood a few miles north of Nottingham, between Wollaton and Sutton Scarsdale. Nuthall was the last of a handful of eighteenth-century English country houses inspired by the Villa Rotunda, the domed place of entertainment on a hill outside Vicenza built by Andrea Palladio in 1566–71.* It was designed by Thomas Wright and built in 1754–7 for Sir Charles Sedley, a local MP and the grandson of the notorious Restoration rake of the same name.

By the 1920s Nuthall belonged to the Holden family. In November 1927, Robert Millington Holden, faced with falling rents and a bill for death duties, put the Temple up for auction. Advertising it as a 'wonderful Palladian mansion containing [the] finest specimens of Rococo decoration in the kingdom', the agents for the sale suggested first that it was 'eminently adapted for club house or residential hotel', and then that its 650 acres offered 'a splendid opportunity for creating a garden city'.[25]

It failed to sell. The contents, including some fine Georgian furniture, a Second Folio Shakespeare and a Zoffany of Charles James Fox, were auctioned off the following March; and in May 1929 the fixtures and fittings were sold as well – twenty-four carved marble and wood mantelpieces, 130 doors, the fittings of an Adam drawing room and all of that rococo work. The denuded carcase went to a local demolition contractor for £800, and at the end of July, in the presence of the local press and a crowd of onlookers, he set fire to it. 'A wonderful sight', reported the *Nottingham Evening News* the next day. 'What took only a few minutes to demolish by fire might have taken by the pick and shovel method a month or two.'[26]

The architectural salvage trade was booming, as the break-up of estates was followed by the break-up of the mansions that had been at their heart. Some of the casualties were surprisingly modern: Wood Norton near Evesham in Worcestershire, a big Victorian house which until 1900 had been the home of Prince Philippe, Duke of Orléans and pretender to the French throne, was offered for sale in the early 1920s. In spite of having been extensively remodelled by the duke in the 1890s it failed to find

* Others included Chiswick House in Middlesex (3rd Earl of Burlington for himself, 1725-9); and Mereworth Castle, Kent (Colen Campbell for John Fane, later 7th Earl of Westmorland, 1722-4).

a buyer, and in the summer of 1924 it was on the market again. Only this time it was offered for sale prior to demolition, and the auctioneers catalogued the house as so many thousand feet of oak panelling, so many oak doors, thirty-six oak mantelpieces and overmantels, and so on.

Wood Norton was saved from demolition at the last minute (it is now a hotel); but other houses weren't so lucky. Over the border in Wales, the Earl of Powis offered Lymore Hall near Montgomery, a timber-framed mansion dating from 1675, at a nominal rent of £1 a year to anyone who was prepared to repair and preserve it. It was in a poor state, and whoever leased it would have to spend around £20,000 on repairs. In 1921 there had been an unfortunate incident during a church fete at the house when the earl and twenty people fell through the floor of the Great Hall into the cellar. 'Without any audible premonitory symptoms, a knot of guests were observed to disappear outright,' reported the local paper.[27]

No one took the lease. So the earl offered Lymore as a free gift to the town of Montgomery. The town didn't want it. Nor did the Office of Works. Nor the National Trust. Not even when an anonymous donor came forward and offered £10,000 towards saving it.

With all other avenues exhausted, the earl sold Lymore at auction in October 1929. Bidders came to the sale from all over Britain; an unnamed American museum made a big private offer for a magnificent carved Elizabethan staircase. But eventually Lymore went as a single lot to a local antique dealer, Frederick Anderson, who paid £3,500 and announced that the staircase, the oak panelling and most of the other features were likely to go to America. (In the end the staircase only got as far as Yorkshire, where it was installed in another country house, Aldborough Hall.) The earl was too upset to attend the sale. Those who did were warned to be careful about putting too much weight on the floors.

More than 180 country houses were destroyed between the end of the war and that day in the spring of 1930 when Vita Sackville-West fell in love with Sissinghurst, and hundreds more in Scotland, Wales and especially Ireland, where the houses of the

Anglo-Irish were frequent targets for Republican gangs during the War of Independence and the civil war that followed. Casualties included Summerhill, the vast and magnificent Palladian mansion in Co. Meath where the restless Empress Elisabeth of Austria had found some peace in the 1870s, and which was burned by the Irish Republican Army in 1921; and the bizarre Gothic Revival chateau that was Roxborough Castle in Co. Tyrone, home of the earls of Charlemont and also burned down by Republican soldiers. 'Furniture vans engaged for nine months ahead are taking goods from the country to England,' wrote Lady Gregory in August 1922.[28]

Even in the comparatively peaceful rural landscapes of post-war England, fire was an ever-present danger. On Bonfire Night 1926, Little Bromley Hall in Essex was burned down along with all the furniture and silver, because a window was left open in the drawing room. The cause wasn't a stray rocket or a misfiring Roman candle, but a breeze which blew the curtains over an oil lamp. The same night Colythorne House, 'an old New Forest mansion', was badly damaged when a can of paraffin was knocked over and caught fire. Three months earlier £25,000 of damage was caused by a fire at Caversham Park near Reading, the second at the property in less than two years. In fact around thirty country houses were either badly damaged or completely destroyed in fires in 1926 alone, with causes ranging from burglars and a painter's blowlamp to smouldering oak lintels and 'an electric iron which evidently had not been disconnected the previous evening'.[29] There were human casualties, too. A cook died when Crowe Hall, the residence of the Mayoress of Bath, went up in flames. (The mayoress's chain of office was saved 'at great personal risk' by a local constable, who found a ladder and climbed through a window to rescue it.[30]) Four people were killed when the ceiling of the saloon at Oulton Park in Cheshire fell in on them as they were working to save furniture and paintings from the flames. A fireman was badly burned at the same time; he died later in hospital. When Reigate Priory, the Surrey home of First Sea Lord Earl Beatty, caught fire at the end of the year, a man sitting on a branch of a tree watching the firefighters broke his leg when the branch snapped.

And 1926 wasn't even a particularly bad year. In 1929, two days after a string of country house fires culminated in a disaster that turned the interior of seventeenth-century Lulworth Castle in Dorset into 'a furnace',[31] there were press calls for insurance companies to step in and advise owners on sensible precautions, chief of which was a proper water supply. 'The water supply available at many of the most valuable and historic mansions', declared one expert, 'is scandalously inadequate, when one considers the interests and the treasures at stake.'[32]

GLANCING THROUGH the newspaper headlines of the 1920s – 'Fire at peer's country mansion', 'Mansion sold piecemeal', 'Wall falls during mansion demolition'[33] – it seems as though big houses were being burned, dismantled and demolished all over the country. But while the loss of some, like Nuthall, was a national disaster, others were not much missed. Few would weep over the disappearance of plodding yellow-brick Victorian piles and plain Georgian blocks which possessed little more in the way of character and artistry than the Stockbroker Mock Tudor suburban villas that replaced them.

Moreover, these lost country houses were only a fraction of the total. A dozen demolitions in Leicestershire ranged from the imposing neoclassical Lindley Hall on the border with Warwickshire to the vast Victorian pile that was Bradgate House, where Edward, Prince of Wales was entertained in the 1880s. But if we include everything from small manors to massive stately homes, ninety-five country houses survive in Leicestershire in the twenty-first century. Lancashire also lost at least a dozen mansions in the 1920s; ten more in the 1930s. But at a rough count, nearly 200 still survive today.

The big agricultural estates whose rents had once provided the lifeblood for many of these houses were less fortunate. So although the Duke of Rutland's Belvoir Castle was one of Leicestershire's survivors, 13,300 acres of the Belvoir estate went for auction in March 1920, including seven entire villages. The duke raised nearly half a million pounds on the sale, together with another £350,000 on 14,500 acres of his Derbyshire estates which were sold two weeks later. But most country houses survived. And if England was changing hands, as the papers frequently declared, it was not necessarily a change for the worse.

CHAPTER TWO

The King's Houses

At noon on a summer's day in 1927 a convoy of Rolls Royces slid out of Windsor Castle. Crowds cheered. Policemen saluted. Men removed their hats in gestures of respect as the cavalcade passed, or hoisted their children high to give them a better view. Women waved handkerchiefs. From one of the leading cars a stout, grey-bearded man in a black morning coat and a silk top hat waved back. He wore a white carnation in his buttonhole.

His Majesty George V, by the Grace of God, of Great Britain, Ireland and the British Dominions beyond the Seas, King, Defender of the Faith, Emperor of India, was going to the races.

Every June the king and queen hosted a house party at Windsor Castle, the sprawling labyrinth of lodgings and halls to the west of London which had been a royal residence since the Norman Conquest. They were there for Royal Ascot Week (which actually only ran for four days, from Tuesday to Friday), one of the centrepieces of the London Season, and they were usually joined by some of their five surviving children: David, Albert, Mary, Henry and George.*

Not all of the family turned up at Windsor every year. In 1922, for example, the Prince of Wales was away on a tour of the Far East, and the king and queen and their guests settled down in the panelled Waterloo Chamber after a day at the races to watch a new film, *With the Prince of Wales Through India and Burma.* In 1923 Bertie was absent because his new bride, Lady Elizabeth Bowes-Lyon, had whooping cough. After 1930, when the Prince of Wales moved to Fort Belvedere in Windsor Great Park, he entertained his own group of friends there during Ascot Week, although he

* King George and Queen Mary's youngest child, Prince John, died after suffering a seizure in 1919, when he was thirteen years old.

George V and Queen Mary at Ascot in 1927, accompanied by Prince Henry and Edward, Prince of Wales.

still came to the Ascot opening day. And in 1929 and again in 1935 George V was himself too ill to attend.

Cousins and other relations were often invited. Princess May Cambridge, niece to Queen Mary and great-granddaughter of Queen Victoria, was at Windsor for the 1927 party. So was her mother, Princess Alice, Countess of Athlone. But the house party wasn't just for family. This particular year King George and Queen Mary entertained three ducal couples, Beaufort, Roxburghe and Portland; and a clutch of other lesser nobles – twenty-four guests in all.

The fleet of motor cars drove through the sunshine, which vanished by the time they reached their first stopping point, Duke's Drive in Windsor Great Park, where everyone disembarked and climbed into seven open landaus. Members of the public gathered to watch the switch, but admission to the spectacle was strictly controlled and by ticket only. The first carriage, containing the king and queen, the Prince of Wales and Prince Henry, was preceded by scarlet-coated outriders and drawn by four greys with postilions dressed in their Ascot livery of white leather breeches, dark blue waistcoats and rows of gilt buttons, a gold-laced black silk hat and a single spur. The other carriages were each drawn by six bays, again with postilions in livery.

When everyone was comfortable the convoy set off through Windsor Park in the grey light until it reached the eastern end of the Ascot course. As soon as the procession came in sight the crowds started cheering. Hats and handkerchiefs were waved from the stands, and a roar came up from the open stretches of heath. *The Times* noted ruefully and without explanation that this year 'the cheering in the Grand Stand and the enclosures seemed a little more subdued, but if the acclamation was decorous it was cordial'.[1]

The royal party usually left for Windsor Castle before the last race. They came back for the Gold Cup, which was run on the Thursday, and most years they put in an appearance on the Wednesday and Friday as well. If it rained, they dispensed with the landaus and arrived in closed cars. And each evening they entertained. Shortly before 8.30, the king and queen and any other members of the family who were dining at the castle would set off toward the Green Drawing Room, one of a suite of reception rooms created for George IV as part of Sir Jeffry Wyatville's remodelling of the castle in 1823–40. At the door they were met by the Master of the Household who bowed and backed into the room, heralding their arrival to the other guests who were arranged in two quarter-circles, men on one side and women on the other. The king, his sons, and members of the royal household wore the Windsor uniform, a tailcoat of dark blue with scarlet collar and cuffs, worn over a single-breasted white waistcoat and plain black trousers. The other men in the party wore black tail-coats and knee breeches. Women were more conventionally dressed in evening gowns and jewels.

Queen Mary moved along one line, shaking hands with the men, while George V did the same with the women. Then whoever had been commanded to escort the queen offered her his arm and led her to the table, where a Guards string band concealed behind a grille in the dining room played 'God Save the King'. The band continued to play throughout the meal, out of sight in a small chamber, wearing their tightly buttoned tunics and, on a warm June evening, drenched in sweat.

Each course was served by liveried footmen in scarlet and pages in blue. The meal lasted no more than an hour, and when it was over the queen would take the women back to the Green Drawing Room, each one curtseying to the king as she left the royal presence. George V would spend twenty minutes with the men over coffee, port and liqueurs and then abruptly stand and lead them out to join the ladies. Punctually at eleven o'clock the company reassembled in its two quadrants, men on one side and women on the other; George and Mary wished them all goodnight, and the royal family left the room. The evening was over.

'Nothing was lacking but gaiety,' recalled the Prince of Wales, who found the abrupt and early ending to these entertainments particularly trying.[2] One night he and his brothers, determined 'to enliven the atmosphere for the younger members of the party', arranged for the Guards band to stay behind in the Green Drawing Room and, after their parents had gone to bed, they returned, rolled back the carpets and held an impromptu dance. It was a failure: the musicians could only manage some outdated foxtrots. 'The ancient walls seemed to exude disapproval,' the prince remembered. 'We never tried it again.'[3]

The episode, emblematic of a familiar gulf between generations, says something more about the world – or rather worlds – in which king, queen and princes moved: the one immensely formal, controlled, ritualised; the other struggling half-heartedly to break free.

George V had a clutch of castles and country houses at his disposal, ranging from Windsor, heavy with history and the accumulated remodellings of nearly nine centuries, to Sandringham, barely four decades old when the king came to the throne in 1910. The main royal residence was of course Buckingham Palace, a place with a troubled architectural history. It had undergone three major transformations since the day in 1762 when Buckingham House, as it then was, was bought by George III as a dower house for Queen Charlotte. The first, and most dramatic, stemmed from a time in 1818 when the Prince Regent, unhappy at the way his existing home of Carlton House stood exposed to public gaze on Pall Mall, decided to remodel Buckingham House. 'I must have a pied-à-terre,' he announced, although his notions of what constituted a pied-à-terre were ambitious. 'The whole expense may probably be kept within £400,000, but it will be safer to reckon upon £450,000.'[4]

Nothing much happened for a while, because George IV, as he became in 1820, focused his passion for architecture in other directions. Another of his pieds-à-terre, John Nash's Brighton Pavilion, was completed in 1821; and Sir Jeffry Wyatville's remodelling of Windsor Castle as a country seat began in 1823. Then in 1825 contracts were finally signed for a massive reworking of Buckingham House, with Nash as architect.

George IV was delighted with his new home. Nash provided private and state apartments with a domed bow room at the centre, and as a grand entrance, a marble arch – *the* Marble Arch – decorated with friezes celebrating British military and naval victories and crowned with Chantrey's statue of the king. He was so delighted, in fact, that halfway through the work he decided that the entire court would move to Buckingham House. Nash pointed out that his scheme had been conceived as a private residence for the king: there was no provision for the various departments of the royal household, the 1,000 or so members of staff. George IV simply told him 'You know nothing about the matter. It will make an excellent palace.'[5]

The excellent palace was still unfinished at his death in 1830, and Nash was dismissed when a select committee discovered he had exceeded the original budget of £252,690 which had been approved by the government, by £360,000. George IV's brother, who succeeded to the throne as William IV, commissioned the plodding architect Edward Blore to finish Buckingham Palace in 1831, after trying unsuccessfully to persuade his ministers that it should become a barracks for the Foot Guards. Then he offered it as a replacement when the Houses of Parliament burned down in 1834. He hated the place, which epitomised all the extravagance that he deplored in his brother, and he never lived there. In the second major remodelling, Blore was called back by Queen Victoria in 1847 to create private accommodation for the royal family in a new east front, which closed off Nash's imposing forecourt and was dismissed by the architectural press as 'little more than an ordinary piece of street architecture'.[6] The Marble Arch was carted off to Cumberland Gate.

Towards the end of her reign Victoria tended to live at Windsor, and Buckingham Palace was rarely used. On her death in 1901 there were suggestions that it should be turned into a museum and picture gallery, with Edward VII and Queen Alexandra moving to Kensington Palace. That plan came to nothing, but Edward VII insisted that before he moved in the building must be redecorated, which it was, with staterooms, vestibules and galleries all painted white with heavy gilding.

In 1911, the year after George V's accession to the throne, the unveiling of the marble and gilt colossus that is Thomas Brock's Victoria Memorial focused attention on the inadequacies of Blore's ordinary piece of street architecture, now acting as a backdrop to the 2,300-ton memorial; and over a three-month period in the summer of 1913 the front of the palace was entirely refaced, without even disturbing the glass in the windows, to designs by the stolid but uninspired architect Sir Aston Webb.*

George V took a keen interest in this third remodelling. The king was personally responsible for the central balcony which has become the most famous stage on which the kings and queens of Great Britain have showed themselves to the world. He insisted to Webb that space was needed 'from time to time on occasions when the King and other members of the Royal Family wish to show themselves to the people'.[7] When the news of the Armistice began to spread on the morning of 11 November 1918, 5,000 people

* The contractors, Leslie & Co., worked round the clock, employing 300 men during the day and 150 at night.

gathered in front of Buckingham Palace, 'the central point of the British Empire'.[8] It was on that balcony that the king appeared to them shortly after eleven o'clock, wearing the uniform of an admiral of the fleet, with Queen Mary beside him, bare-headed and wearing a fur coat. The band in the courtyard played 'God Save the King' and 'Rule Britannia', and everybody sang.

As the Prince and Princess of Wales, George V and Queen Mary had lived round the corner at Sir Christopher Wren's Marlborough House during Edward VII's reign. When they moved into Buckingham Palace in 1910 Queen Mary immediately began to retrieve the Regency character of the interiors. Victorian furniture was discarded, and throughout her husband's twenty-five-year reign she had period upholstery and wall coverings made, and bought good examples of Regency furniture and works of art. In the Green Drawing Room next door to the Throne Room, for example, she found a surviving fragment of green damask dating from 1832 and had fabric of the same pattern woven for new curtains. In 1928 she replaced the threadbare coverings of two sets of gilt chairs made for George IV with silk of the same date as the chairs, which had been found rolled up in a palace storeroom. She designed the canopy *à la polonaise* over the throne dais in the ballroom, and supervised the redecoration of the Balcony Room with chinoiserie.

The royal household operated on a vast, feudal scale, wherever the king happened to be. When he was in residence at Windsor hordes of servants were kept busy. Sir John Fortescue, who retired as librarian and archivist at Windsor in 1926, lovingly detailed their eating arrangements:

> The royal kitchen kept sixty souls busily employed. In the stewards' room – a room contemporaneous with the cloisters of Westminster Abbey and roofed with the like vaulting – there were two dinners of one hundred each for the upper servants. In the servants' hall – a fourteenth-century building with columns and vaulting of that period – there were two dinners of two hundred each for the lower servants.[9]

Some members of the domestic staff stayed put at a particular royal residence. Others, particularly the king's and queen's personal attendants, travelled with them. When Queen Mary paid a visit to the Cavendishes at Holker Hall in Cumbria, she brought with her two dressers, one footman, one page, two chauffeurs, one lady-in-waiting, a maid for the lady-in-waiting, and a detective. Before her arrival, Holker received a list of her requirements, which ranged from having a chair placed outside her bedroom at night for her page to sit on, to having fresh barley water placed in her bedroom at two-hourly intervals during the day and six clean towels to be supplied every day. She brought her own sheets and pillowcases.[10]

Even excluding the hundreds of valets and maids and footmen and cooks and cleaners, there were 205 members of George V's household, and another twenty-two in Queen Mary's. Some had roles which weren't exactly onerous. As Poet Laureate, Robert Bridges was technically a member of the royal household, but was rarely required to perform at court, or even to appear there. Nor was John B. Storey MB often called from his bed to attend the king, even though as 'Honorary Surgeon-Oculist in Ireland', he too was officially a member of the royal household. But grooms-in-waiting were regularly needed. The posts of accountant and storekeeper weren't honorary. Nor was that of postmaster at Buckingham Palace, or head of Household Police.

The inner workings of the royal household were arcane indeed. The operational head, the man in charge of the legions of domestic staff, was the Master of the Household, Sir Derek Keppel. Keppel, who was the second son of the 7th Earl of Albemarle, served the king for most of both their lives. He was appointed equerry or personal attendant to George on the latter's marriage in 1893, and Deputy Master of the Household when his master acceded to the throne in 1910. Two years later he became Master of the Household, and he retained that post until the abdication of George V's son in 1936. It was Keppel who stood beside Edward VIII as his father's coffin was lowered into the vault in St George's Chapel, Windsor; Keppel who as Archbishop Lang intoned 'earth to earth, ashes to ashes', handed the new king a silver bowl containing the symbolic earth for Edward to scatter over it.

In his black frock coat, high collar and waxed white moustaches, Keppel was in effect the general manager of a large hotel, with a staff of around 120 minor officials, clerks, secretaries and menservants, and another eighty female cleaners and maids. This hotel had to feed not only the royal family but also the hundreds of men and women who ate there every day.

The royal chef, who for most of George V's reign was the Frenchman Henri Cedard, sat down in his office after lunch every day to compose the next day's menus, writing them out in a menu book which was sent up for royal approval. Orders for everyday foodstuffs went from the chef's office to the department of the Comptroller of Supply, and the comptroller's staff telephoned out for them. Deliveries were made to the Trade Door in Buckingham Palace Road and taken straight to the kitchens, where a store man noted each item in a ledger that was checked by the deputy comptroller every month. (The comptrollership was a purely political office; the work of the department was carried out by the deputy.) A massive cold store held chickens, beef and lamb, grouse, pheasant and partridge in season. Fruit, vegetables and meats were regularly sent in from the royal gardens and farms at Sandringham, Balmoral and Windsor. Whatever the chef required for the day he had to record on a form which the storekeeper later gave in to the deputy comptroller's office for entering in a ledger, so that in theory every single item of food coming into the palace and being consumed was accounted for. Likewise, wines and champagne brought up from the royal cellars were checked in and out; although it was considered one of the perks of working in the palace that servants could help themselves to an occasional glass.

George V and his queen were careful to maintain a remoteness from the public, from their staff, even from their children. Both believed that the monarchy required it. (George VI, on the other hand, was much more affable, more approachable. At the private dances he gave once a fortnight at Buckingham Palace during the Second World War, he could be seen leading a conga line, followed by Queen Elizabeth, the princesses Elizabeth and Margaret and their guests, out of the Bow Room on the ground floor of the palace and through the maze of corridors, while the dance band played to an empty room until eventually their sovereign reappeared, slightly out of breath.) But that remoteness was, paradoxically, combined with continual exposure. A glance at the court circulars for a single week in May 1927 gives some indication of George V's routine.

On Monday 2 May, the king and queen were driven from Windsor up to Buckingham Palace, arriving in time for lunch. The next morning the king received the prime minister, Stanley Baldwin, the new governor of the Falkland Islands and an official in the Chinese service. Later that day he and Queen Mary, together with their daughter and the ladies and gentlemen of the household-in-waiting, attended a charity screening of a new British war film, *The Flag Lieutenant*, at the Marble Arch Pavilion. On Wednesday they gave lunch to King Manuel and Queen Augusta Victoria of Portugal; and on Thursday to Alexander and Lady Patricia Ramsay, the Duke of Connaught's son-in-law and daughter, before dining at the Marquess of Salisbury's town house in Arlington Street.

On Friday the king gave an audience to the new ambassadors of Italy and Panama, and his own foreign secretary, Austen Chamberlain. The queen went round to Marlborough House to inspect alterations being made there to prepare it as a residence for the Prince of Wales. On Saturday the king was visited by the Duke of Connaught and received senior officers from the army and navy as well as the Earl of Lytton, who was giving up his post as governor of Bengal. (Queen Mary went to the pictures again, this time to a charity matinee of an American melodrama called *The Self Starter*.) When George V and Mary went to church in the private chapel at Buckingham Palace on Sunday morning the fact was published in the newspapers. When they toured the Royal Academy exhibition that afternoon, it was news.

Three weeks later, at the end of May 1927, enormous crowds gathered in The Mall, far more than the usual handfuls of onlookers and tourists who habitually hung around the Victoria Memorial. They were there to catch a glimpse of a living legend. George V was presenting Charles Lindbergh with the Air Force Cross, 'in recognition of the valuable and distinguished service rendered to aviation by his recent flight from New York to Paris'.[11] So great was Lindbergh's fame – the *Spirit of St Louis* had been surrounded on the runway by thousands of cheering people when he landed at Croydon the previous day – that after his twenty minutes with the king and queen he disappeared into an equerry's room to sign autographs. The Duke and Duchess of York's thirteen-month-old daughter, Princess Elizabeth, was brought down by her nurse to see him; he patted her on the cheek.

THERE WAS A PATTERN to the king's annual progress. Windsor for Ascot Week; the Isle of Wight for Cowes Week, where he lived aboard the royal yacht, the *Victoria and Albert*, and went racing in the *Britannia*; Norfolk or the north of England for the Glorious Twelfth of August. Then it was up to Scotland.

Balmoral in Aberdeenshire had been in the royal family since 1852, when Prince Albert bought the estate and commissioned William Smith of Aberdeen to build a rather solid Scots Baronial mansion. (An ability to choose architects with flair was never one of the British royal family's talents.) The king and queen usually spent September there for the annual Gathering of the Braemar Royal Highland Society, a celebration of Scottish traditional culture and sports which is still going strong today.

In 1927, George V went to Balmoral from the Earl of Sefton's Abbeystead estate in Lancashire, where he had been shooting; he was joined later by Queen Mary and the Duke and Duchess of York, with little Princess Elizabeth. Every step of the king's journey was attended by ceremony. At Aberdeen station he was greeted by the Lord Provost of the city, the chief constable and local magistrates; at Ballater, at the end of the line from Aberdeen and the nearest station to Balmoral, he was met by a guard of honour from the King's Guard of the 1st Battalion the Royal Scots, and the Lord Lieutenant of Aberdeenshire.

Queen Mary's journey was no different. She set off from London by train the same day to visit her daughter at Goldsborough Hall in Yorkshire. A special saloon was attached to the Harrogate train, members of the public lined the barriers on either side as the train pulled out of King's Cross, and at Harrogate station there were crowds waiting to cheer as she left by car for Goldsborough. When she arrived at Balmoral five days later, the King's Guard of the 1st Battalion the Royal Scots was there to meet her. So was the Lord Lieutenant of Aberdeenshire.

As at Windsor during Ascot Week, George V hosted a house party and held dinners at Balmoral each night. Twenty thousand people came to the Braemar Gathering itself. George V and Queen Mary arrived in an open carriage with outriders at three o'clock, for a march past by the three clans concerned, the Balmoral Highlanders, the Duff Highlanders and the Invercauld Highlanders. The king and queen missed the first part of the programme, perhaps because it began with a ninety-minute bagpipe competition.

In the midst of so much ritual there occurred an event insignificant in itself, but all the more startling in its banality, its descent from majesty. The Saturday after the Braemar Gathering there was a charity fete in the grounds of Balmoral in aid of the parish hall in the local village of Crathie. For three hours George V stood in the flower tent and acted as auctioneer; hundreds of people filed past to pay him for flowers grown at Balmoral or sent up from Sandringham and Windsor. Sir Derek Keppel acted as cashier. So many people wanted to buy from their king (nearly 5,000 tickets to the fete had been sold at five shillings a head) that when supplies of flowers and Scottish heather began to run low, George asked his attendants to cut down the heather used to decorate the front of his stall, so that he could sell that. Then he began selling off the vases and bowls that had held the flowers. Sir Frederick Ponsonby, Keeper of the Privy Purse, auctioned off a painting of St Paul's Churchyard by Winston Churchill; it made 115 guineas after Sir Frederick pointed out that it was unique, the only picture done by a Chancellor of the Exchequer at the request of a sovereign. The queen and the Duke and Duchess of York sold off a collection of goods donated by various members of the royal family. And behind their stall Princess Elizabeth sat in her pram, playing with a dancing doll.

These descents from Olympus were rare. George V was not a people's king, although by and large, the people adored him. Almost every step he took was public property: when, a few days after the charity fete, he watched a documentary about the First World War naval battles of Coronel and the Falkland Islands, the screening made the national papers. So did his conversation afterwards with the film's director, his surprise that many of the incidents depicted in the film had been shot in the studio; even the fact that he wore the 'conventional evening dress of the Highlander, with kilt and sporran'.[12]

THE ONE PLACE where the king could find a refuge from formality and the cares of state was 'dear old Sandringham, the place I love better than anywhere else in the world'.[13] To George V's children, five of whom were born there, it was simply 'the Big House'. Edward VIII remembered that 'to us "home" always meant Sandringham'.[14] George VI wrote, 'I love the place.'[15]

Sandringham was Edward VII's creation. When he came of age in 1862 his mother and father decided he needed a country home of his own, and one far enough away from London to keep their erring son on the straight and narrow. Lord Palmerston proposed an 8,000-acre shooting estate in Norfolk belonging to his stepson. Prince Albert approved; and although he died before negotiations had begun, Queen Victoria was keen to see her husband's wishes carried out. The country round about was plain and the eighteenth-century stuccoed house at its centre was ugly, but everything was in good order; and the fact that Prince Albert had approved of the scheme was enough to convince his widow that the rather high asking price, £220,000, was worth it. The following year Edward married Princess Alexandra of Denmark, and the couple moved in.

For a time they tinkered with the inadequate accommodation offered by the old house. Two smaller houses were built in the grounds to take the overflow of guests, Park House and Bachelor's Cottage; and a new servants' wing was added to the main building. But it wouldn't do. By 1868 they had four children (with two more to come in the next three years); and they decided to replace the mansion at Sandringham with something fit for purpose.

With that knack which the Victorian royal family had for choosing second-rate architects, Edward went to Albert Jenkins Humbert, who had worked for Prince Albert and who was currently building the Prince Consort's mausoleum at Frogmore. Humbert came up with a design in what Pevsner calls 'a frenetic Jacobean'.[16] That freneticism was compounded by piecemeal additions made by the Norfolk architect Robert Edis – 'a popularizer rather than an innovator', said his kindly biographer – who built on a ballroom in 1883 and a new suite of bedrooms in the early 1890s, also in a florid Jacobethan.[17] The end result was a jumble of turrets and gables and pediments and chimney stacks; and a set of interiors which combined James I, Charles II and Queen Anne in an entirely Victorian way.

But to George V, it was home. At least, the Sandringham estate was – but that's not quite the same thing. After Edward VII died in 1910, his widow Queen Alexandra was reluctant to accept that she no longer had the status of a reigning queen. She was perhaps encouraged in this by her unmarried daughter, Princess Victoria, who lived with her and who didn't like her sister-in-law Queen Mary, describing her as 'deadly dull'.[18] It was seven months before Alexandra moved out of Buckingham Palace to make way for the new king and queen, and she didn't move out of Sandringham House at all.

George V couldn't bring himself to ask his mother to leave. So she shut up her husband's bedroom, keeping everything in it as it had been while he was alive, and stayed put. The king, the queen, their six children, a tutor, a governess, an equerry, a lady-in-waiting and a private secretary all had to cram into the Bachelor's Cottage, renamed York Cottage after Edward VII gave it to George (then Duke of York) on his marriage in 1893. And there they stayed whenever they came to Sandringham, while the Queen Mother and Princess Victoria had the Big House. 'It is my mother's home. My father built it for her,' he would say whenever his exasperated wife suggested they move in.[19]

York Cottage wasn't as small as all that; it had been extended twice since 1893. But it was pokey: a Cambridge vicar who came to preach in 1924 was surprised to see that the drawing room was smaller than his own, while a future Archbishop of Canterbury, Cosmo Lang, was reminded of a visit to a curate and his wife in their home.*

Nor was York Cottage an English Petit Trianon, an exquisite architectural display case filled with elegant baubles. In fact it was downright ugly. Harold Nicolson gave a devastating account of it in his official biography of George V, published in 1952:

> A glum little villa, encompassed by thickets of laurel and rhododendron, shadowed by huge Wellingtonias and separated by an abrupt rim of lawn from a pond, at the edge of which a leaden pelican gazes in dejection upon the water lilies and bamboos . . . The rooms inside, with their fumed oak surrounds, their white overmantels framing oval mirrors, their Doulton tiles and stained-glass fanlights, are indistinguishable from those of any Surbiton or Upper Norwood home.[20]

The situation wasn't ideal. Sir Frederick Ponsonby, who acted as the king's private secretary in the early years of his reign, had to do his work in his bedroom. Most of the servants slept out in neighbouring cottages, because there was no room for them. Sir Charles Cust, one of George V's equerries, said in an unguarded moment that it was absurd that a large house like Sandringham should be inhabited 'by an old lady and her daughter' while York Cottage had to accommodate a married man with a family of six, 'more especially when that man happened to be the King'.[21] Some helpful soul reported Cust's remarks to Princess Victoria, and she

* Visiting clergy were advised to preach for precisely fourteen minutes. Any less, and they risked being accused by the King of being too lazy to prepare a sermon. Any more, and he might say they didn't know when to stop.

swore she would never speak to him again; the king tore him off a strip and told him that who occupied Sandringham was none of his business.

In fact George V could have leased a decent-sized Norfolk country house at any time. There were plenty available, especially after the war. The truth was, a reluctance to upset his elderly, deaf and formidable mother wasn't the only reason he kept the faith at York Cottage. He liked the overcrowded Christmases and the chaotic weekend parties where visiting royalty was boarded out with his mother or in neighbouring houses. He liked his 'glum little villa'.

On 19 November 1925 the 80-year-old Queen Alexandra had a heart attack at the Big House. Her son, who was out shooting on the estate, was sent for immediately, and the royal shooting party dispersed early the next morning after taking leave of the king at York Cottage. He and his wife spent the rest of the day at Sandringham. They were at Alexandra's bedside when she died late that afternoon.

It wasn't until the following spring that the king and queen finally made the move from York Cottage to the main house, and then it was with reluctance. 'Very sad that tonight is the last night we sleep in this dear little house in which we have spent 33 very happy years,' George V confided to his diary at the end of March 1926; and when it came to it even Queen Mary was sorry to leave her 'very cosy and comfortable home'.[22]

Sandringham was neither little nor cosy. A porte cochère, that feature so beloved by the designers of Victorian railway stations and Edwardian hotels, led into an enormous space that was called the saloon, but was really a Jacobethan living hall complete with minstrels' gallery. A long, long corridor ended in the ballroom, also Jacobethan and hung with dark stamped leather. The dining room was panelled and set with a series of tapestries woven from cartoons by Goya and other Spanish artists; the drawing room was all white stucco and mirrors. A full-length portrait of Queen Alexandra presided, and still presides, over its chimney piece.

Queen Mary took to the refurbishment of Sandringham with

the same enthusiasm she had shown at Buckingham Palace. The stamped leather wall hangings came down, to be replaced by wallpaper; glass chandeliers went up, and Georgian furniture moved in while Alexandra's bric-a-brac and stuffed fauna moved out along with Princess Victoria, who went off to live in Buckinghamshire.

The king and queen spent every Christmas and New Year at Sandringham with their children, their children's spouses, their grandchildren and a select assortment of courtiers. Nora Wigram, who came for eleven days at Christmas 1926 with her husband Clive, a royal equerry, found the experience both charming and daunting. Daunting, because she brought with her the three Wigram children, aged thirteen, eleven and six, and she spent most of the stay expecting them to disgrace themselves and her in front of the king. (They didn't.) Charming, because George V and Queen Mary were easy and generous hosts, constantly inquiring after the children's comfort and going out of their way to make the Wigrams feel at home. On their arrival the guests were shown to their rooms by the king and queen, and after they had settled in, George V insisted on the children being brought down to meet him and have some tea.

Christmas Eve afternoon was taken up with the distribution of beef to all the workers on the estate in the coach house, with the entire house party in attendance. Six-year-old Francis Wigram sat on his mother's lap for an hour while men in blue butcher coats handed out the meat. 'His comments had to be restrained at times,' wrote Nora Wigram in her journal of the visit.[23] Christmas morning meant church and, after tea, a gathering in the ballroom for presents. 'I was overcome by the generosity of the King & Queen & these were the things I got,' wrote Nora. 'A Kashmir shawl, a rose bowl, antique tea-caddy of tortoiseshell & ivory, grey leather bag, an evening bag of gold tissue, 2 little enamel boxes and an ashtray.'[24] Bizarrely, six-year-old Francis got a pipe, a tobacco pouch and two ashtrays.

The big celebratory dinner was held on Boxing Day, when there were crackers and paper hats. The queen wore a pope's mitre, the Prince of Wales a penguin's head. Only the king was spared.

Afterwards, everyone decamped to the ballroom again where the Duchess of York and the four princes congregated at one end and sang rude music hall songs (in a low voice, so the king couldn't hear) while the others sat around smoking and chatting. The king turned on a gramophone and played *La Traviata*, the 'Song of the Volga Boatmen' and then, just to make sure his guests were paying attention, the national anthem. Everyone leapt to their feet while he roared with laughter.

It was from Sandringham that George V broadcast his first Christmas message to the empire six years later. Just after 3 p.m. on Christmas Day 1932, he addressed a quarter of the world's population (the ones with access to wireless sets, anyway) from a tiny room under the stairs, empty except for a table and chair and two microphones in cases of Australian walnut. The three-minute speech, which had been written for the occasion by Rudyard Kipling, praised the wireless, 'one of the marvels of modern science', for its ability to bring nations together, before ending with a blessing. 'I speak now from my home and from my heart . . . To all – to each – I wish a happy Christmas. God bless you!'[25]

The rest of the house party, which included the Prince of Wales, the Duke of York with his duchess and the young princesses Elizabeth and Margaret Rose, and the Duke of Gloucester – listened in on a wireless set in another room. When it was done, everyone gathered in the ballroom for the king and queen to hand out gifts from beneath the Christmas tree.

In another sign that Sandringham was embracing modernity, this year the lights on the tree were electric.

CHAPTER THREE

The Old Order Passing?

When William John Arthur Charles James Cavendish-Bentinck was twenty-one years old, his second cousin died. And he inherited a dukedom.

It wasn't unexpected. The 5th Duke of Portland had been an elderly bachelor whose only brother had died without sons nine years earlier. But the mansion that went with the Portland dukedom – along with a vast shooting estate in Scotland, a castle in Northumberland, a house in Grosvenor Square and some very expensive property around Harley Street – did come as something of a shock. The new Duke of Portland didn't know Welbeck Abbey in Nottinghamshire, the family's seat since an ancestor acquired it through a judicious marriage in the eighteenth century, and when he came to take possession he found 'a sombre pile, massive and ugly in many styles'.[1] There were battlements and gables, a square tower and Italianate balustrade roofs, a fan-vaulted Gothic great hall and a rococo drawing room with pagodas and Chinese figures.

There was more. The 6th duke's predecessor had been a recluse with a mania for building, a combination of qualities that showed itself in some curious ways. The 5th duke's projects included the second-largest riding school in the world, connected to the house by a tunnel about 1,000 yards long (the largest was in Moscow). Another skylit tunnel stretching for more than a mile and a half allowed the eccentric duke to ride in his carriage to Worksop railway station unobserved, where the carriage would be lifted onto a flatbed truck so that he could travel to London. Close by the house he excavated tracts of land to create a series of below-ground chambers, the largest of which, 159 feet by sixty-three feet, was intended as a chapel, but was unfinished at his death.

By then the 5th duke had withdrawn to a suite of rooms in the west wing which were painted pink, and devoid of any furniture.

The Duke and Duchess of Beaufort being ceremoniously towed into Badminton by their estate workers after their honeymoon, 1923.

Each room had a lavatory in the corner, and brass letter boxes in the door so that he could exchange messages with his staff.

Once he had got over the shock of coming into his curious inheritance, the 6th duke set to work on the repair and restoration of Welbeck Abbey, helped along by the successful racing stud he established. He had two Derby winners, and the progeny of one horse alone, St Simon, won nearly £250,000 in prize money: a group of almshouses at Welbeck, built with some of the proceeds of racing, were called 'The Winnings'.

Portland turned Welbeck's Gothic Hall into the main sitting room, and a set of Gobelin tapestries found rolled up in tin boxes by the 6th duke's half-sister, Lady Ottoline Morrell, was hung in the drawing room. He turned his cousin's unfinished chapel into a ballroom-cum-picture gallery, and used the rest of the underground suite 'for supper and sitting out during a ball'.[2] Sitting out was enlivened by a collection of stuffed birds and the skins of

St Simon and the two Derby winners, displayed in glass cases on the walls.

Portland was born in 1857, the year of the Indian Mutiny. When he succeeded to the dukedom and began to explore his cousin's subterranean fantasy world at Welbeck, it was Christmas 1879. Disraeli was prime minister, Queen Victoria was spending the holidays at Osborne House and Anglo-Indian troops under General Roberts in Kabul had just repulsed an assault by Afghan forces. Welbeck's golden age began in 1881 when the future Edward VII honoured Portland with a royal visit and crowds cheered as their carriages were escorted from Worksop station by the local yeomanry. It threatened to come to an end with another royal visit, this one drenched in symbolism. In the winter of 1913, Archduke Franz Ferdinand accepted an invitation to a shooting party at Welbeck, in the course of which one of the loaders tripped and accidentally discharged both barrels of the gun he was holding, the shot passing within a few feet of the archduke. 'I have often wondered', wrote Portland rather regretfully, 'whether the Great War might not have been averted, or at least postponed, had the archduke met his death then and not at Sarajevo the following year.'[3]

But Welbeck's golden age didn't die in the mud of the Somme. Having presided over Welbeck Abbey for more than three decades before the First World War, the 6th duke continued there until his death in 1943, adding his voice to those who were prophesying doom for the old order. At a gathering of tenantry to celebrate the coming of age of his younger son in 1921, where the tenants presented the boy with a sporting gun and the estate workers gave him a gold hunter watch, Portland gave a gloomy speech which received national press coverage, predicting that 'if the present high rate of taxation continues, and if the present scale of death duties is maintained, there must be a wholesale closing down of the larger country houses'.[4] Painful though the prospect was, he told his audience, he could foresee a time when his family would have to leave Welbeck and find a new and smaller home elsewhere. He ended by saying that 'I do not wish to cast any shadow upon the happiness of this occasion.'[5] A little late for that, perhaps.

There were cuts in the size of the household; he had to let one of his chauffeurs go in 1932. There were also sales of surplus furniture and duplicate books from the Welbeck library. Outlying parts of his estates went, and even some fine wines, old sherry and Madeira from the Welbeck cellar.

But in plenty of other ways, life for the Portlands continued after the Great War much as it had before it. The shooting parties that had been part of late-Victorian and Edwardian life at Welbeck remained a feature: in the 1934–5 season, when the duke was in his late seventies, 5,148 pheasants were killed on the estate and 3,268 brace of partridge – more partridge than at any time since the duke succeeded to the title. In 1928, somebody at *The Times* thought it worth a paragraph in a national newspaper that 'at Welbeck Abbey yesterday the Duke of Portland presented £5 notes to 60 of his employees who have completed 40 years' service or more'.[6]

Like this distribution of largesse, the celebrations in 1929 to mark the duke's fifty years in the job were Victorian in scale. Welbeck's underground rooms played host to two balls, at each of which around 1,000 guests were present. His tenants presented him with an illuminated address in which they welcomed 'this happy event' and expressed their gratitude that 'Your Grace's relations with us have always been marked by personal interest in our welfare, unfailing encouragement in our work, and unusual kindness in all your dealings with us.'[7]

'We entertain at Welbeck more or less all the year round,' wrote the duke in 1937. 'In the winter there are continual shooting-parties; and during the summer we have parties at Easter and Whitsuntide, and also what was formerly known as our Show Week in August.'[8] This was the tenants' annual agricultural show, when he would entertain as many as 700 to lunch. The prime minister, Stanley Baldwin, came in 1928, addressing an audience of 70,000 at a Conservative Association gala in the park; George V and Queen Mary were entertained at Welbeck the same year; and the Duke and Duchess of York the following year.

In 1934 Portland played host to the England and Australia cricket teams, who were playing a test match at Trent Bridge in

Nottingham. The legendary Australian batsman Donald Bradman visited the duke the same year: he played the piano in the Gothic Hall and told Portland that 'I enjoy playing the piano better than anything in the world.'[9] Leopold III, king of the Belgians, came on a private visit in 1937 with his mother, Elisabeth. It wasn't altogether successful: they both caught colds on the journey and had to stay indoors, prompting a bulletin from Welbeck Abbey of striking banality: 'His Majesty has had a slight cold and is now recovering.'[10]

In the summer of 1923 the Prince of Wales made the first of two visits to Welbeck: at Worksop station, 3,000 flag-waving schoolchildren were there to greet him, singing 'God Bless the Prince of Wales'. When the royal party reached the abbey after a day spent touring the mining towns of north Nottinghamshire, the duke exclaimed, 'Thank goodness that's over!' to which the prince replied, 'It may be over for you, but it's never, ever over for me. Most of my days are like this, and there seems to be no end to it.'[11] He stayed again in 1933, when he landed in the park in his private plane to host a weekend party for an Argentine trade delegation.

Was this really so different to the kind of life lived by the duke in Victorian and Edwardian England? Portland entertained on a vast scale, he shot, he opened his house to royalty and received the grateful thanks of his tenantry. A small army of domestic servants dressed him and fed him and lit fires in his hearth. His gardens and hothouses, opened to the public at a shilling a time in aid of the Queen's Institute of District Nursing – 'the privilege was much appreciated', reported *The Times* – were kept immaculate by another small army of workers.[12] Keepers patrolled his coverts at night to protect his birds from poachers. His duchess was Mistress of the Robes to Queen Alexandra, and devoted herself to good works: she supported local miners and their families, was active in the Royal Society for the Prevention of Cruelty to Animals and was the first and longest-serving president of the Royal Society for the Protection of Birds, a post she held from 1891 until her death in 1954.

Their sons went to Eton; their daughter held a minor position at court in the 1930s. Apart from some technological advances – electric lighting, chauffeurs rather than grooms – how could life at

Welbeck Abbey after the Great War be distinguished from life at Welbeck before it?

This continuity is often neglected in the rush to view the period 1918–39 as one of unmitigated decline for the country house. The 5th Marquess of Bath, another Victorian – he was born in 1862 and inherited Longleat in 1896 – lost his eldest son and his brother on the Western Front. He was forced to sell off 8,600 acres of the Longleat estate between 1919 and 1921. But decline is hardly the word for life at Longleat between the wars. The marquess kept an indoor staff of more than twenty servants – a reduction on Edwardian levels (in 1902 he employed forty-three, including a chef and a groom of the chambers); but not exactly life in bedsit land. On formal occasions his footmen still wore silk stockings, patent-leather pumps and cockade hats. When his surviving son, Henry, came of age in 1926, the year of the General Strike, 1,000 guests sat down to lunch at Longleat – the same number that was invited to a fete to celebrate his own twenty-first birthday in 1883. Music was supplied by the band of the Somerset Light Infantry. The city of Bath and other towns sent addresses of congratulations, and 1,500 local schoolchildren were entertained to tea and fireworks.

This determination to hold state on a Victorian scale went hand in hand with a deep-seated conservatism, a refusal to allow the twentieth century in the house. The 11th Duke of Bedford refused to install central heating at Woburn Abbey in Bedfordshire, so in winter his fifty-odd indoor servants kept seventy or eighty open wood fires burning in the rooms, including the bathrooms. His housemaids all had to be five feet ten inches tall; dinner guests were assigned a personal footman, who stood behind their chair while they ate. When electricity was eventually and grudgingly installed at Woburn, each bedroom was still equipped with a single candle so that house guests could seal their letters with wax, in addition to an electric light. After an elderly guest complained that one candle didn't provide him with enough light, the duke ordered that large enamel plaques must be fitted above the switches with the words 'Electric Light'.

*

In 1918 the Duke of Portland was one of twenty-six non-royal dukes in the various British peerages. There was also one duchess in her own right, the Duchess of Fife, whose father had been given a dukedom on his marriage to the Prince of Wales's daughter in 1889. Between them these dukes owned sixty-five country houses, ranging from monsters like the Duke of Marlborough's Blenheim to the more modest Bestwood Lodge outside Nottingham, built by S. S. Teulon for the Duke of St Albans in 1862–4. There was also an assortment of town houses, shooting boxes, hunting lodges and a substantial bungalow in Alberta, built in 1911 for the Duke of Sutherland when he came to view the farm he owned there. The average age of members of this elite club was fifty-two, so that an 'average' duke would have been born in 1866, when Gladstone's Reform Bill was defeated and London was in the grip of a cholera epidemic. This imaginary Victorian married in 1890 and succeeded to his dukedom as the bells heralded the dawn of the twentieth century. Or to put it more prosaically, in 1899.

Admittedly, these averages conceal some wide variations. Four dukes were unmarried: Bernard Marmaduke Fitzalan-Howard, 16th Duke of Norfolk and Hereditary Earl Marshal of England, because he was only ten years old, the others presumably from choice. Although several dukes were widowers, only one, the 7th Duke of Richmond, had married twice: both wives were dead. The 7th Duke of Grafton was ninety-seven; he had joined the army in 1837, the year Victoria came to the throne, and had been wounded in the Crimean War.

In 1939, when the long weekend between the wars came to a close, eleven of the original twenty-seven dukes in the 1918 list were still alive. The 7th Duke of Grafton was obviously not among them. He died three weeks after the Armistice, and his successors were nowhere near as long-lived: in 1939 the title was held by the 10th duke.

There had been some retrenchment since 1918. The 12th Duke of St Albans, who succeeded his brother to the title in 1934, put Bestwood Lodge on the market four years later and went to live in a house he had inherited in Tipperary. The 11th Duke of Leeds,

Blenheim Palace, Oxfordshire.

who inherited his title in 1927, put his fourteenth-century ancestral seat, Hornby Castle in North Yorkshire, on the market in 1930 along with his 24,000-acre estates and the contents of the house. The sale raised some publicity, partly because it seemed for a time that Hornby would be demolished, but also because of the scale of the sale. Leeds's ducal coronet and his late father's coronation robes were among the items to be knocked down at the auction: the robes 'would be used for amateur theatricals', according to the agent for their anonymous buyer.[13] No one said what the coronet would be used for. The Duke of Leeds decamped to Bordighera, where he basked in the Mediterranean sunshine with his widowed mother and his Serbian wife Irma.

A less august group of country-house owners, consisting of twenty-seven baronets chosen at random from *Debrett's*, shows the same kind of continuities between the Armistice and the outbreak of the Second World War. In 1918, this group had the same average age as the dukes – fifty-two. The oldest, Sir Charles Acland of Killerton in Devon, was seventy-six. Two were teenagers: Sir Edward Reynell Anson, who was serving as a midshipman in the Royal Navy; and Sir Windham Carmichael-Anstruther, who was sixteen and had succeeded his father when he was a year old. Fifteen of the twenty-seven were still going strong in 1939.

This is the merest snapshot. But it demonstrates the pitfalls of periodisation. Many – perhaps even most – country-house owners in the 1920s and 1930s shared the octogenarian Duke of Portland's outlook. They weren't bright young things, or Jazz Age industrialists. They hadn't been through the Great War, although their sons had; they may have served their country in earlier conflicts, in Afghanistan or South Africa or the Sudan. They inhabited the world of England between the wars; but they were not made by it.

LIMITED THOUGH IT IS, the comparison between these two groups of country-house owners, dukes and baronets, at the end of one war and at the beginning of another does suggest one big change in behaviour. In 1918, no duke in any of the British peerages was divorced. By 1939 four of the twenty-seven – Leinster, Manchester, Newcastle and Westminster – had divorced and remarried: twice in Westminster's case, and his third marriage wouldn't last the course. (A fifth duke, the Duke of Richmond, was married to a vicar's daughter, which seems another challenge to traditional aristocratic values until we remember that nobility and gentry had been contracting out-of-class marriages for centuries: a Georgian Earl of Peterborough famously married an opera singer from Fulham, and in 1792 Sir Henry Crewe of Calke Abbey in Derbyshire married a lady's maid called Nanny Hawkins.)

The sample of baronets strengthens the conviction that marriage was no longer an indissoluble union. Three baronets had divorced and remarried by 1939. In addition, Sir George Armytage's wife Aimée had obtained a judicial separation. Sir Adrian Baillie was married to Olive Wilson Filmer, the owner of Leeds Castle, who was twice divorced and would divorce him in 1944. And Sir Henry Havelock-Allan of Blackwell Grange in Co. Durham buried his first wife in 1935, married his second in Vienna in 1936, successfully petitioned for an annulment in 1937 'on the ground of the incapacity of Lady Havelock-Allan', and married his third the same year.[14] His family motto was *Fortiter gerit crucem*, 'He bears the cross bravely'.

Divorce was on the increase after the end of the Great War. The numbers of cases heard at the Probate, Divorce, and Admiralty division (colloquially known as the Court of Wills, Wives and Wrecks) broke four figures for the first time in history in 1918. The total number of divorces in England and Wales went up to 1,654 in 1919, to 3,090 in 1920 and to 3,522 in 1921 – paltry in comparison with today (there were thirteen divorces *an hour* in England and Wales in 2012), but enough to send shivers through Church and state.

The judiciary complained that it was impossible to deal with the influx of cases quickly enough, and argued that the law stipulating that a petitioner could only have his or her divorce case tried before a Judge of the High Court in London, with the witnesses necessary to prove the case being brought from all parts of England, no matter how far from London they lived, needed to give way to a system of regional courts. Arthur Conan Doyle, who in 1920 was the president of the Divorce Law Reform Union, put forward a novel argument in favour of making divorce easier:

> It is not generally appreciated that if the great numbers of both sexes now sterilized by separation were allowed freedom to marry, the results in population would in a very few generations compensate for all the losses in the war, while the happiness and general morality of the community would be greatly increased.[15]

The breakdown of married life was initially put down to the war and the way it had disrupted family life, but the annual divorce rate continued to climb. It reached 4,000 in 1933 and 5,000 in 1936 – ironically enough, the year in which Edward VIII's determination to marry the divorced Wallis Simpson nearly brought down the monarchy.

In the minds of the general public, divorce and remarriage went hand in hand with fast cars, cocaine and jazz. But the ancient families who inhabited the stately homes of England were expected to set an example to their social inferiors; they were supposed to adhere to the respectable bourgeois values established in the previous century, to stand up for God, their country and the sanctity of family life. Their infidelities were their own affair; but when they behaved as though marriage were a social habit rather than a sacrament, the public disapproved, even as they rushed to read the salacious details in their daily papers. The expectation was that 'husbands and wives who could not get on together went their separate ways and in the great houses in which they lived practised a polite observance of the deference each owed the other'.[16]

These words were written by Consuelo Vanderbilt who after eleven years of unhappy marriage to the 9th Duke of Marlborough, had turned her back on polite observance and Blenheim Palace and obtained a legal separation in 1907. Three years later she moved into Crowhurst Place in Surrey, a romantic moated hall house which, as she wrote, 'with its high roof of Horsham stone, its walls half-timbered with silvered oak, its stone chimneys and leaded casements . . . was a dream come true'.[17] She immediately set out to improve on the dream, with the help of an English connoisseur and amateur architect, George Crawley, who had held the lease on Crowhurst before her and whom she probably knew through his work at Westbury House, a neo-Caroline mansion on Long Island which he had just built for the steel magnate John Shaffer Phipps and his British wife Margarita. Together they reinvented the little house (little by Consuelo's standards, anyway), adding tall chimneys, gables, half-timbering and linenfold panelling. Martin Conway, who described the house for *Country Life*, was full of praise for the way in which its battered remains had been 're-endowed with a beauty far greater than was ever theirs in the day of its newness'.[18]

In 1919, having fallen in love with a French airman, Jacques Balsan, Consuelo decided the time had come to divorce Sunny Marlborough. The stigma wasn't as great as it had been before the war (or so she recalled, writing more than three decades later); and Sunny was willing to do the gentlemanly thing, and give her grounds by providing the usual evidence of desertion – a contrived business which usually meant spending a night in a hotel with another woman and making sure that the hotel staff noticed. But they discovered that having undergone a legal separation, Sunny couldn't now be accused of deserting his wife, no matter whom he slept with. So the couple had to undergo another piece of legal fiction and demonstrate that they were reconciled. Sunny moved into Crowhurst for a few weeks: his sister 'kindly shared our solitude', said Consuelo.[19] He then 'deserted' her, leaving behind at Crowhurst a letter which carefully set out, presumably with the help of his lawyers, how the situation now stood:

> We have tried our best to mend the past and start life afresh, but I fear that in the long period of our separation, now upwards of twelve years, we have grown too far apart to live happily together again.
>
> I appreciate all you have tried to do during our reunion, but I am now convinced that it is impossible.[20]

Consuelo wrote back, playing her part with rather more feeling than her estranged husband. 'I wish you had spoken to me instead of writing. It seems a pity now that we ever came together again only for everything to end like this. It is useless to say more.' And again, a few weeks later: 'I am writing to ask you . . . to return to me. If you will do so I can assure you that nothing on my part will be wanting to make you happy.'[21]

The duke replied that it was impossible; and his duchess instituted proceedings – not for divorce, but for the restitution of conjugal rights. Sunny was given fourteen days to comply. Instead, he went to Paris, followed by an English inquiry agent named Reuben Butler. At the Gare du Nord Butler identified the duke to two French private detectives who were waiting. The three men saw him take a room at Le Claridge on the Champs-Élysées, registering under the name of 'Spencer' and adding the words 'et Madame Spencer'. They saw him go into the hotel two days later with an unidentified woman. They took the room next door and kept watch on the corridor all night; and they saw him leave at 8.30 a.m. the next day, followed by the woman at 9.20 a.m. In November 1920 Consuelo was given her divorce. She married her French airman nine months later and lived happily ever after.

LEAVE ASIDE THE RITUALS which demanded dishonesty in a divorce court. Leave aside the sneaking collusion, the enormous costs: the detectives, the endless court hearings, the legal teams. (Sunny and Consuelo were both represented by King's Counsels. Consuelo's was Sir Edward Carson, one of the most distinguished barristers in Britain.) For a couple of the Marlboroughs' status, the worst thing was that this farce was acted out in public. When Consuelo lied in court that she wanted her husband back, tens of thousands of strangers read in their newspapers, under a headline that announced 'Story of a Futile Effort to Live Together', that she did so 'attired in a black silk cloak, fur tipped, and with black toque'.[22] When the court found that Sunny had deserted his wife and committed adultery with an unknown woman (neither of which stories were true), the world discussed the facts of the case at the breakfast table.

All through the 1920s and 1930s the divorce courts saw

frequent appearances by the aristocracy, as dukes divorced their duchesses, countesses sued their earls, and county society had its most intimate secrets aired in public. The Duke of Manchester announced in 1930 that he was off to Cuba to obtain his divorce, since it wasn't forthcoming in England. The Duke of Leinster instituted proceedings against his duchess, a musical comedy actress formerly known as May Etheridge, in 1929, at the same time entertaining on such a lavish scale that his creditors made him bankrupt. With disarming candour he explained to those creditors that 'he was contemplating matrimony with a wealthy widow and entered into those heavy commitments on the strength of possible funds becoming available to him from that source': they didn't.[23] The Earl of Erroll, named as a co-respondent in a 1928 case, was described by the judge as 'a very bad blackguard'. His partner-in-adultery didn't fare much better: she was 'a woman of very low character and a liar', and her husband was well rid of her.[24]

Hugh Grosvenor, 2nd Duke of Westminster, went through two divorces after the war. In 1919 the Divorce Court granted a decree absolute to his first wife, Constance, on the grounds of desertion and misconduct. Some reports let the duke off quite lightly, simply mentioning that the duke and duchess were in the divorce lists (along with three other pairs of peers, incidentally) and, when the divorce was granted, saying merely that the duke 'was said to have stayed at Brighton with another lady'.[25] Others went into much more detail about the behaviour of Bendor – a nickname derived either from the ancient Grosvenor arms, *Azure, a bend or*, or from the name of the racehorse of his grandfather's which won the Epsom Derby soon after the boy's birth. He stayed out all night without explanation, refused to have Constance in the house with him, and went to extraordinary lengths to avoid her. On one occasion before the war she and her sister had travelled to Egypt to join him for a holiday, only for him to leave without seeing her. On another, she joined him at Eaton Hall, the vast and earnest Gothic Revival country house near Chester which Alfred Waterhouse had designed for Bendor's grandfather in the 1870s; the moment she walked in, he walked out, leaving her to entertain the house guests whom he had invited. He had sworn to shut down Eaton Hall and their Grosvenor Square house so that she couldn't live there and, while offering a generous allowance of £11,500 a year if she agreed to a separation, threatened her with the courts if she refused.

The following year the duke married again. His new duchess, Violet Rowley, was herself recently divorced. She was, said the *Manchester Guardian*, 'a very pretty woman . . . extremely fond of sport, especially golf and hunting'.[26] But in 1925 Bendor was in the Court of Wills, Wives and Wrecks once again, accused of adultery with a 'Mrs Crosby'. Violet had taxed him with it, only to be told that he would live just as he liked. He literally threw her out of their town house, and when she climbed back in through a window helped by a friend, Cyril Drummond, Bendor locked them both in the drawing room, telling Drummond, 'Take her. She likes fucking.'[27]

The extent to which the landed classes' moral compass shifted between 1918 and 1939 shouldn't be overestimated. As a corrective to set against the awful Bendor's track record on marriage, picture the 6th Duke of Portland standing up before 1,200 tenants in the underground ballroom at Welbeck in 1930 and celebrating more than forty years of wedded bliss. 'The best thing that ever befell me', he told them, 'was when the lady who is not only the queen of my heart but also the queen of all hearts . . . consented to be my bride.'[28]

End of the Chapter is the final trilogy in John Galsworthy's nine-volume *Forsyte Saga*. Published in 1931–2, shortly before Galsworthy's death, it is a meditation on the life of the landed gentry in an England which questions their role and their values. All three of the novels which make up the trilogy, *Maid in Waiting*, *Flowering Wilderness* and *Over the River*, focus not on the Forsytes but on some rather distant relations, the Cherrells ('for so the name of Charwell is pronounced').[29] General Sir Conway Cherrell and his wife Elizabeth ('by birth the Honourable Elizabeth Frensham') live with their grown-up children, son Hubert and daughters

Dinny and Clare, at Condaford Grange, a small country house which has been in the family since 1217.[30] With parts dating back even earlier than that, Condaford has grown organically as each generation has put its mark on the building. It was once moated; 'but under Queen Anne a restorative Cherrell, convinced of the millennium perhaps, and possibly inconvenienced by insects, had drained off the water'.[31] At the end of the nineteenth century Sir Conway's father, a diplomat, had let the place go a bit; now it was unpretentiously trim without and comfortable within, and Sir Conway was almost too poor to live in it.

The Cherrells live simply. There is no butler at Condaford, no electric light. Dinner is customarily served on a polished chestnut table which gleams in candlelight. Three maids, a groom-chauffeur and two gardeners are all the staff they employ. Yet they struggle to make ends meet, unable to contemplate selling Condaford but equally unable to make it pay. 'What I hate', says Sir Conway's brother Adrian, 'is the thought of Mr Tom Noddy or somebody buying Condaford and using it for week-end cocktail parties.'[32] Sir Conway himself makes small economies, and can't bring himself to make big ones. He dreams of renting. 'But who'd rent it? It wouldn't make a boys' school, or a country club, or an asylum. Those seem the only fates before country houses nowadays.'[33]

The Cherrells weather scandals and crises – big ones, because they are after all characters in a sequence of novels. Hubert kills a man in self-defence during an expedition to Bolivia and faces extradition. Clare's sadistic husband whips her and then divorces her when she leaves him. Dinny has a doomed affair with a poet-explorer who, not believing in any god, converts to Islam to save his life and finds that England won't forgive him.

Dinny herself is twenty-four, thoroughly modern, a product of her time. She believes in the future, but it frightens her. She believes in sex outside marriage, although she doesn't practise what she preaches. She does not believe in a Christian god – Christianity's focus on personal reward seems vulgar to her – but she still goes to the little village church. It is part of her, just as Condaford Grange is part of her.

> Dinny, though the last person in the world to talk of her roots, or to take them seriously in public, had a private faith in the Cherrells, their belongings and their works, which nothing else could shake. Every Condaford beast, bird and tree, even the flowers she was plucking, were a part of her, just as were the simple folk around in their thatched cottages, and the Early-English church, where she attended without belief to speak of, and the grey Condaford dawns which she seldom saw, the moonlit, owl-haunted nights, the long sunlight over the stubble, and the scents and the sounds and the feel of the air. When she was away from home she never said she was homesick, but she was; when she was at home she never said she revelled in it, but she did. If Condaford should pass from the Cherrells, she would not moan, but would feel like a plant pulled up by its roots.[34]

Condaford, like the countless generations of Cherrells who have occupied it and shaped it, is woven into the social fabric of an England which is changing. The newer families in the area do their bit. They support the nearest golf course, they organise tennis and bridge parties. They 'seemed to make country life into a sort of cult.'[35] In contrast, the Cherrells are *part* of country life, unobtrusive, reticent. They are curiosities.

And yet for every Duke of Westminster who ditched his wives when they began to bore him, who didn't give a damn for public opinion, who flaunted his wealth and his mistresses in the casinos of Monte Carlo, there were a hundred Cherrells, clinging on to their ancient homes and hoping against hope that the bank wouldn't foreclose and the dry rot wouldn't spread and the world they knew would last just a little bit longer. They didn't make headlines. But they made England.

CHAPTER FOUR

Reinstatement

For the 31-year-old architect Philip Tilden, the end of the First World War offered a fresh start in a career that had all but ended before it began. In 1914 he had been well on his way to establishing a reputation as a designer in the Arts & Crafts tradition, with a string of small commissions and one big one – the rebuilding of Porth-en-Alls, a romantic vernacular revival house tucked into the cliff at Prussia Cove in Cornwall, which blended modern ferro-concrete construction with traditional granite and oak.

Then came the war, and with it a bout of ill health which kept Tilden out of the army. Work on Porth-en-Alls ground to a halt, never to be restarted. Tilden's practice faded, and he took up farming in Devon. He didn't turn his back completely on architecture, however: a 1916 meeting at the Ritz with Gordon Selfridge led to a commission to design a 450-foot tower for the top of the latter's Oxford Street department store. But that project also came to nothing.

Years later, Tilden recalled how he and his wife heard the church bell ringing out across the Devon moors to announce the Armistice and how, as they walked their land, they resolved to turn their back on 'an interlude of chaotic and incoherent years of agony' and focus instead on the future.[1] 'In the great theatre of the world the lights had vanished, the footlights were on, the curtain lifted, and the play began.'[2]

The first act in Tilden's new post-war career was directed by Sir Martin Conway – art historian, mountaineer, prolific author, politician and first director general of the Imperial War Museum – who as the war ended was in the middle of restoring Allington Castle, a medieval ruin near Maidstone in Kent.

'More ruined castles', wrote Christopher Hussey in 1942, 'have been restored and domesticated in the last thirty years

Philip Tilden.

than probably at any other epoch.'[3] Conway and his wife Katrina were in the vanguard of this rage to domesticate the past. They bought Allington in 1905 after placing an advertisement in *The Times* asking for information on old houses which might be for sale – purely, Conway claimed later, so that it would give them something to do when they were out for a weekend drive in their new Panhard. They motored down to Maidstone one June morning to see the place, and as they approached, both were convinced they had wasted their time. 'The surroundings were abominable,' wrote Conway in 1918. There were neglected farm buildings, a

Allington Castle, Kent: 'Nothing was ever more picturesque, or less fitted for human habitation'.

tar-paving factory 'with all its hideous accessories', fields of nettles and ugly new oast houses. 'But suddenly on turning a corner the thing itself emerged before us – a dream of beauty.'[4]

This dream of beauty was the crumbling, ivy-covered remains of a moated castle put up in the thirteenth century and altered by the Wyatt family in the sixteenth. The floors were propped up with scaffolding poles, the roofs were barely watertight. 'Nothing was ever more picturesque,' said Conway, 'or less fitted for comfortable human habitation.'[5] By 1914, with the help of the architect W. D. Caroë, Conway had cleared away the ivy, the farm buildings and the factory, diverted a right of way that ran by the castle and excavated the partly filled-in moat. The Wyatts' long gallery was reconstructed, and after several rooms had been repaired and made habitable, the Conways sold the lease of their London house to Herbert Hoover and moved in.

Then came the war and a falling-out with Caroë, whom Conway described as having 'a pugnacious disposition'.[6] A month or two before the Armistice Philip Tilden, who knew Conway's daughter Agnes, was invited down to see if he and Allington suited each other. Days later he moved to Kent on a retainer of £2 a week, lodging first in a neighbouring village and eventually in the castle itself. His job was to survey the castle, to continue the long, slow process of restoration and to help Katrina Conway in turning a meadow that sloped down to the moat into an attractive formal garden, with long walk, round lily pool and low lavender hedges of silver-grey.

Tilden frequently found himself at odds with Martin Conway, who couldn't see the point in his wife's garden-making (until it was finished, when he claimed the idea for his own) and whose approach to the reclaiming of Allington was too pragmatic for his architect:

> We set at naught the theories of the so-called antiscrape school [said Conway]. According to them we ought never to have replaced old work by new of the same design. Our renovations and repairs ought to have been obviously modern and of today. My principle was that I must retain every existing old feature, but that I was then free to do what I liked, with a view not to an attempted re-creation of what had disappeared, but to the one controlling purpose of making a beautiful thing of the whole.[7]

Tilden could complain about the way that reinforced concrete ceilings and floors, which Conway insisted on introducing as a fire prevention measure, made the bedrooms into chilly, echoing boxes. He could wince at the steel girders that replaced beams and at how windows had been cut through exterior walls: Conway's response was that 'several generations had made holes in the walls wherever they needed them, and we could do the like'.[8] He could disapprove of Caroë's solution to the problem of damp in the ground-floor rooms, which was to cover a bed of concrete with asphalt and carry it up the walls for a few feet. It made no difference to his client, who wanted warmth, light and comfort. In the meantime the Conways' daughter Agnes toiled away in the British Museum and the Public Record Office to unravel Allington's pedigree, which stretched back to the Norman Conquest. The restoration took more than a quarter of a century to complete; Tilden was still working on it until shortly before Katrina Conway's death in 1933.

'During those first few years after the armistice', he remembered, 'I found that my work lay mostly in the way of mending up things that had become shabby.'[9] Conway reckoned he could take much of the credit. 'The restoration of Allington Castle', he wrote in his memoirs, 'gave a stimulus to other undertakings of like character.'[10] There was a grain of truth in that, but the process of rescuing a castle and turning it into a country home had a distinguished pedigree. In the 1870s the eccentric 3rd Marquess of Bute and his even more eccentric architect, William Burges, virtually rebuilt Castell Coch, a thirteenth-century ruin in the hills outside Cardiff, turning it into a battlemented Arthurian fantasy with working drawbridge and portcullis. In the 1920s Bute's son was still completing the flamboyant reinvention of Cardiff Castle which had been begun by Burges for his father more than half a century before – a riot of exotic medievalism tipping over here and there into downright weirdness, as carved monkeys and painted knights in armour cavort together on walls and ceilings.

On a more modest scale, Edward Hudson, the proprietor of *Country Life*, commissioned his favourite architect Edwin Lutyens to remodel a tumbledown Tudor fortress on Lindisfarne Island in 1902. Lindisfarne Castle was finished ten years later, to mixed reviews: the architectural critic Lawrence Weaver noted with qualified approval that Hudson 'did not demand that wealth of modern devices which some people insist on installing in the most ancient fabrics'; while Lytton Strachey, who stayed at Lindisfarne in the summer of 1918, was scathing: 'very dark, with nowhere to sit, and nothing but stone under, over and round you, which produces a distressing effect . . . No, not a comfortable place, by any means.'[11]

In Conway's corner of England, the exemplar was not Allington but Hever Castle, a fortified and double-moated manor house thirty miles south of London. Hever possessed most of the prerequisites for a successful castle restoration. For one thing, it had the architectural pedigree. Some parts dated back to 1270, while others were from the late fifteenth and early sixteenth centuries, when it belonged to the Boleyn family. Hever was still, as a late-Victorian guidebook put it, 'an excellent specimen of the later castellated mansion'.[12]

For another, it had romantic associations. Anne Boleyn spent her childhood there, and Henry VIII visited her at Hever during their courtship. (Her ghost was said to appear on Christmas Eve and drift mournfully around the grounds.) After Anne's father's death in 1539 the castle came into the possession of the king, who gave it to Anne of Cleves as part of her divorce settlement.

And it had the potential to be a comfortable country home. The Tudor mansion of the Boleyns was still habitable and partly furnished, even though, as an article of 1907 put it, it was being used by 'humble farmers* whose ducks and geese swam in the old moat, whose kitchens were the once proud Hall . . . whose corn and potatoes lay stacked in the chambers that were haunted by so many memories'.[13]

In 1903, two years before the Conways discovered Allington, Hever acquired the final prerequisite, a rich owner. In fact William Waldorf Astor was more than just rich. Born in New York in 1848, he inherited in 1890 a fortune estimated at $100 million, making him one of the wealthiest men in America. But he didn't warm

* These 'humble farmers' were showing Hever to the public in the 1890s, along with what that late-Victorian guidebook described as 'some questionable Tudor relics'. Visitors were allowed to view Anne Boleyn's apartments, which had the date '1584' on the outside (she was executed in 1536); and the room in which Anne of Cleves died in 1557 (she actually died in Chelsea).

to the land of his birth; that same year he decamped with his family to England, declaring that 'America is not a fit place for a gentleman to live.'[14] He bought Cliveden in Buckinghamshire in 1893 and ten years later, having become a naturalised British citizen, he acquired Hever.

Astor and his architect, Frank Pearson, retained the Boleyns' manor house on its original footprint and left the exterior more or less untouched. The interiors, however, were transformed. Everywhere there was panelling in Italian walnut or English oak, brand-new carved work in the style of Grinling Gibbons and chimney pieces of Verona marble. Tapestries and Tudor portraits, bought by Astor to evoke Hever's famous past, hung on the walls; suits of armour guarded the entrance. An entire mock-Tudor village of domestic offices and guest rooms, all designed by Pearson and built by a 750-strong army of workmen, sprang up beyond the moat, an ingenious solution to the problem of providing extra accommodation for visitors and a large staff. 'I could not believe that they had been built a few short months ago,' wrote Astor in 1907, 'they seemed so old and crooked, and possessed such individuality as though they had grown up one by one in various ages, as those old villages did which we sometimes see on our travels, sheltering themselves under the walls of the overlord.'[15]

The picturesque charm of the arrangement is obvious (as are the feudal undertones), although Pearson maintained that the real reason for the village beyond the moat was that Astor, who went in fear of plots against his life, installing a forbidding set of electrically operated gates and keeping a posse of policemen in the grounds to guard against intruders, liked to show his guests off the premises at night and raise the drawbridge behind them.

Casual sightseers were no longer allowed, causing a lot of local resentment; and his obsession with security earned Hever's owner the nickname of William 'Walled-off' Astor. Philip Tilden, looking back after the Second World War, lamented the passing of tumbledown old Hever 'as I first saw it in the 'nineties, with its grey skirts sweeping the waters of the moat, set around with the blue swords of the wild flag . . . it has now become a miniature

Metropolitan Museum of New York'.[16] The castle was somehow un-English, as though Astor had tried just a little too hard, creating a Gilded Age mansion in the heart of the Kent countryside without exhibiting that *noblesse oblige* which would have made the gilt more palatable.

'Walled-off' Astor died in 1919. In the sixteen years between his purchase of Hever and his death, what Philip Tilden called 'a veritable infection of reinstatement' had begun to sweep through the Home Counties. Tilden himself was working on Allington for the Conways. Down on the Kent coast, Henry Beecham bought the medieval Lympne Castle, perched on a spectacular site high above Romney Marsh with views across the Channel to France, from Frank Tennant, who had rescued the castle and commissioned a gentle and sensitive Arts and Crafts restoration from Sir Robert Lorimer, 'the Scottish Lutyens'.*

A few miles to the west, Bodiam Castle was being rescued by George Nathaniel Curzon, 1st Earl Curzon, 5th Baron Scarsdale, 9th Baronet and, from 1921, Marquess Curzon of Kedleston, with a pedigree stretching back to the Conquest, and a seat, Kedleston Hall in Derbyshire, that the family had occupied in its various forms for almost as long.† Curzon had already bought one castle: in 1911, when it was rumoured that the fifteenth-century Tattershall in Lincolnshire was to be sold to an American syndicate which planned to tear it down and ship it across the Atlantic, he stepped in to save it for the nation: such buildings, he said, 'speak to us of the valour and strength of our ancestors'.[17] Four chimney pieces

* Lindisfarne and Lympne both changed hands as a result of the War. Hudson, who had no children of his own, intended to leave Lindisfarne to Billy Congreve, the young son of his friend General Sir Walter Congreve; but Billy was killed in France in 1916, and Hudson sold the place five years later. The Tennants' son Mark was also killed in 1916; they put Lympne on the market the following year.

† The lines of doggerel written against the famously aloof Curzon when he was a student at Balliol followed him for the rest of his life:

> My name is George Nathaniel Curzon,
> I am a most superior person.
> My cheek is pink, my hair is sleek,
> I dine at Blenheim once a week.

were discovered in packing cases at Tilbury Docks and returned by Curzon to Tattershall in a triumphal procession of wagons decorated with the Union Jack.

Curzon first saw Bodiam, a romantic fourteenth-century ruin on the border between Kent and Sussex, in about 1905. (With his characteristic cheery egotism, Sir Martin Conway claimed that it was a visit to Allington which spurred Curzon to restore both Tattershall and Bodiam.) Enchanted with a building which, he said, 'transports us at a bound to the days when the third Edward was fighting his foreign wars or the hunchback Richard was casting his nefarious die for the throne', he tried to buy it, but the owner, the 1st Lord Ashcombe, refused to sell.[18] He didn't give up, and in 1917 Ashcombe's son agreed to the sale. Two years later William Weir, an architect who had made his reputation as a restorer of historic buildings and who had worked for Curzon on the repair of Tattershall, began a careful programme of restoration. The moat and basement area were excavated, trees and ivy were cleared away and the stonework was repaired.

At this point Curzon parted company with his neighbouring castle-owners. He briefly entertained the notion of moving into Bodiam, but rejected the idea, perhaps because with his father's death in 1916, Kedleston Hall, 'the glory of Derbyshire', was now his, along with its stunning Adam furnishings. He was also renting the late-Elizabethan Montacute House in Somerset. He didn't need a castle to live in. So, in a barbed response to his neighbours' veritable infection of reinstatement, he refrained, he said, 'from what might have easily degenerated into an archaeological crime' and left Bodiam roofless and ruinous.[19] Philip Tilden was in complete agreement, praising the fact that no attempt had been made to reconstruct the interior of the castle. 'It still remains now a permanent and austerely satisfying ruin,' he wrote. 'There is nothing to criticise.'[20]

Yet although there were other, grander precedents for the castle habit which swept through south-east England in the 1910s and 1920s, Sir Martin Conway's Allington did play its part. In 1911, the Unionist MP Claude Lowther came to lunch at Allington. 'We

Herstmonceux Castle, East Sussex, in 1935.

discussed restoration all afternoon,' Conway noted in his diary.[21] Lowther had just bought Herstmonceux Castle in Sussex, a magnificent redbrick mansion of the fifteenth century thirty miles to the south of Allington. It had lain in ruins since 1777, when its then owner decided it was too costly to repair and pulled down a large part of it, leaving only the shell of its walls and towers.

Lowther was an eccentric character – he greeted weekend guests wearing a formal courtier's uniform of black knee breeches, black silk stockings and buckled shoes, and kept a pet ram who was allowed to roam round the house at will among the tapestries and antique furniture which he bought for Herstmonceux. 'He cared nothing about archaeology or historical correctness,' commented Conway without a hint of criticism; and as they worked away throughout the 1910s and 1920s Lowther and his architect Cecil

Perkins paid scant attention to the past, sweeping away courtyards, widening the moat and lowering its banks to improve the view, building a new great hall on a different site and introducing features that ranged from an old wall reputed to have once formed part of Hastings Castle to a great staircase that came from Theobalds, the prodigy house built by Lord Burghley in the sixteenth century. The result, to quote Conway again, 'is one of the most beautiful sights in England'.[22]

Down on the Kent coast, thirty miles south-east of Allington, yet another castle was being rehabilitated. On Wednesday afternoons tourists could climb to the ramparts of Saltwood Castle to enjoy the striking views across the Channel to France, while guides regaled them with stories of how at dawn on 29 December 1170 four of Henry II's knights left Saltwood for Canterbury Cathedral, where they murdered Archbishop Thomas Becket. Fragments of that twelfth-century castle survived, along with a later castellated gatehouse, although in 1580 the castle was badly damaged in an earthquake which considerably diminished its attraction as a residence. It remained a romantic ruin until the 1880s, when the Deedes family converted the gatehouse into a home and moved in.

The expense of maintaining Saltwood and the discomfort of living in it eventually proved too much for them. 'Water ran down the walls, there was no electricity or gas, and fires had to be lit in every room just to keep the damp at bay,' wrote the journalist William Deedes, who spent part of his childhood there.[23] In 1926 Saltwood was sold to Reginald Lawson, whose family owned the *Daily Telegraph* and whose Texan wife Iva had a passion for castles.

But one castle wasn't enough for the Lawsons. When Claude Lowther died in 1929 Herstmonceux was put on the market. Lowther's restoration of the house was far from complete, and his great hall still lacked a roof: nonetheless Iva Lawson persuaded her husband to buy it. The couple's plans came to a sudden end one day in December 1930, when Reginald failed to return to Saltwood in time for afternoon tea and a search revealed his body lying in nearby woods with a gunshot wound to the head and a discharged shotgun lying beside him. The coroner brought in a verdict of death

Workers rebuilding the central courtyard of the Gloriette at Leeds Castle, Kent.

the new castle in 1822. Rateau gutted it and created an entirely new bedroom suite, a set of guest bedrooms and a set of reception rooms. The chapel was converted into a panelled writing room, with a radiogram which piped music around the castle. The great chamber built by Edward I and used by Henry VIII was converted into an evening saloon, although the way Rateau treated it – introducing carved oak beams and a massive sixteenth-century stone chimney piece – suggested a Tudor great hall. By way of contrast, Olive's dressing room was elegantly neo-Georgian, while her onyx-lined bathroom was pure art deco.

Most of the ironmongery, the linenfold panelling and the oak beams were brand new, straight from Rateau's workshop. And it was good. A few years after it was installed, a timber-framed stair tower was mistaken by *Country Life*'s Christopher Hussey, who certainly knew his stuff, for a Regency copy of an original feature; and the staircase itself was presided over by a battered crusader, sword and shield in hand, who perches on the newel post with a lion at his feet and pretends to be the real thing. But in a manner entirely typical of the period, Rateau and his clients combined the new work with genuinely old pieces. Some chimney pieces came from different parts of the castle; others were imported from France, imparting a faint air of Fontainebleau. Antique furniture was also bought in: seventeenth- and eighteenth-century tables and beds and cabinets from France, Spain and England, nineteenth-century candelabra. The most impressive introduction was that of the panelled parlour from Thorpe Hall in Cambridgeshire, which was built in 1653–6 for Cromwell's Lord Chief Justice, Oliver St John; it was bought in 1928 from the firm of White Allom and installed in the castle's main drawing room.

Leeds Castle was a hive of activity in the late 1920s, with local labourers mixing with contractors from London and Bath and specialist craftsmen from France and Italy. Mains electricity and water were brought in. A new bridge was built across the lake to take a light railway, which moved materials to the site and took away the unwanted rubble. The works office was on floating pontoons. The main contractor was the London firm of

Leeds Castle in 1936. 'I had heard of such wonders,' wrote E. V. Lucas, 'but only in the realms of grand opera and fantasy'.

Keeble & Sons, whose men lodged in the neighbourhood during the week, travelling down to Maidstone by train on a Southern Railways coach marked 'Leeds Castle only'. The Wilson Filmers spent the week in London, coming down at weekends to inspect the work, sometimes with Olive's two young daughters from her first marriage.

Work went quickly, so that by 1928, only a year after the sale of Leeds Castle went through, the Gloriette was sufficiently finished for Arthur and Olive to entertain there; Rateau was one of their first guests. Zebras and llamas were introduced into the park, along with twenty-four flamingos who spent a few months enjoying the lake before flying away.

Architect Owen Little died in 1931. So did the Wilson Filmers' marriage. They divorced; Arthur moved to Yorkshire; and Olive, the Lady of the Lake, kept her fairy stronghold in Kent. Her third husband, whom she married the same year, was a Scottish baronet, Sir Adrian Baillie. They had a son, whom they christened Gawaine – an appropriate name for the heir to a fantasy castle.

At the other end of the scale from a vast moated castle like Leeds was the manor house, late medieval perhaps, or Elizabethan or Jacobean. Most likely all three, with some Georgian panelling thrown in for good measure, and a Victorian addition it would have been better off without. These smaller country houses were more numerous than their bigger brethren and more affordable. They attracted a different class of saviour.

The Rev. Frederic Meyrick-Jones is a perfect example. Cultured, sporting, with antiquarian tastes and a strong social conscience, Meyrick-Jones exemplified muscular Christianity in the early twentieth century. After Marlborough, where he didn't distinguish himself academically, he went up to Cambridge, where he got his cricket blue in 1888. He went on to play first-class cricket for Kent and Hampshire. He became a legendary squash amateur and an ordained priest in the Church of England. For eight years from 1899 he ran a mission in Notting Hill, where he gained a distinguished reputation as a billiards player, and that 'by the exacting standards of a working men's club', according to *The Times*.[29]

In 1908 Meyrick-Jones, now married with children, leased Home Place in Norfolk, a masterpiece of the Arts and Crafts movement designed by Edward Schultz Prior. He filled it with antiques and ran it as an establishment for difficult boys for whom a spell in a public school was out of the question.* 'Although he never again resumed a cure of souls ecclesiastically,' recalled a friend, 'he never

* Home Place, also known as Voewood and Kelling Place, was built for another clergyman, Rev. Percy Lloyd. Shortly after it was finished a sanatorium opened next door and Mrs Lloyd, concerned about contracting tuberculosis from her neighbours, insisted that her husband let the house.

ceased to inculcate, more by example than precept, a real standard of Christian life on all who enjoyed his friendship.'[30]

Soon after the end of the First World War Meyrick-Jones and his wife moved to the West Country and decided to restore Woodlands Manor, a medieval manor house at Mere in Wiltshire. Woodlands had been in the Meyrick family since the late eighteenth century. It was reckoned to be 'one of the quaintest old world dwellings in Wiltshire'.[31] However, it was let to a local farmer and in a poor state: floors were rotten, walls were bulging and some elaborate geometrical plasterwork which had been introduced in Elizabethan times was disintegrating. The tenant used the fourteenth-century chapel as a cheese store.

In 1920 Meyrick-Jones and his wife began what he called 'the restoration of this small, very old home by two amateurs'.[32] The chapel was no longer needed for a cheese store – cheese production on local farms had petered out during the war – so the farmer, whose lease would in any case be up in April 1921, allowed the couple to tear out the shelves which lined the room and remove a modern stove which filled an Elizabethan fireplace. They replaced an iron tie-rod which was preventing the walls from bulging outward with a carved sixteenth-century beam. They repaired the ceiling and replastered the walls, and they introduced small panes of seventeenth-century glass into the windows.

A blocked doorway which had originally given out onto an external stair was reopened, fitted with an old studded door and turned into a little balcony, with an Elizabethan balustrade they had acquired years before in Worcester, and some medieval tiles with the arms of Richard, Duke of Cornwall that came from a priory in neighbouring Somerset. Over the chimney piece they fixed a large carved angel bought in Cambridge. 'If we happened to have among our gatherings some fine carved bit of grey oak,' wrote Meyrick-Jones in his 1924 account of the restoration, 'it was not always easy to refrain from inserting it somewhere!'[33]

And Meyrick-Jones did have quite a collection of 'gatherings'. There were tapestries, pewter and ironwork, Caroline tables and early Georgian walnut, oak bedsteads and fragments of medieval painted rood screens. He also acquired architectural fragments and salvage, mainly in the West Country. 'Whenever possible, old doors – especially studded ones – were collected from any possible source,' he wrote. 'Also windows, hinges, latches of the sixteenth and seventeenth centuries, "durns" or door-frames, "Crown" glass and anything else "early", domestic and likely to be of use – the older the better.'[34]

The patient tenant-farmer, a Mr Day, allowed Meyrick-Jones's builder to get to work on the chamber below the cheese-store chapel, which was currently fitted out as a kitchen. The range was ripped out; a cupboard with doors of linenfold panelling was removed to reveal another blocked doorway, and Meyrick-Jones installed a Henry VIII oak frame and an early studded door, more of his gatherings.

In April 1921, having lost his cheese store and his kitchen, Mr Day finally vacated the premises. That same evening Meyrick-Jones personally took a sledgehammer to the walls, and over the summer his small army of labourers and masons worked to remove the later introductions which had turned Woodlands' two-storey-high great hall into an assemblage of bedrooms and reception rooms:

> The glory of housebreaking, of letting in more light, started. Partitions were ruthlessly knocked to pieces – good firewood! The floorboards of the bedrooms above were torn up. This floor sliced the height of the hall in two. The ceiling of these bedrooms which hid the roof was torn down. The nineteenth-century staircase . . . which jutted out into the hall was taken down – to be used again elsewhere.[35]

With advice from the ubiquitous Philip Tilden, the clergyman reinstated the minstrel gallery overlooking the hall, making use of three bedroom doors which turned out to be the original linenfold panels of the gallery screen.

By 1924 the Meyrick-Joneses had moved into Woodlands, filling it with their eclectic collection of English furniture and recycled historic fittings. There were some casualties among the manor house's own fittings: in 1929, for instance, one of its best

Elizabethan chimney pieces found its way to the Wilson Filmers' Leeds Castle, reputedly sold to fund the continuing restoration of the house.

By the end of the Second World War the couple, now quite elderly, moved to another historic house, this time at Shaftesbury in Dorset; and because they had no room, or because they had no money, Frederic sold off some of their gatherings, including five seventeenth- and eighteenth-century oak bedsteads, one of which was a four-poster with tester dating from the 1630s. He offered the lot for £185.

IT WASN'T ONLY MUSCULAR CLERGYMEN like Frederic Meyrick-Jones who rescued smaller country houses and turned them into shrines at which to pursue the cult of the antique. Within a twenty-mile radius of Woodlands, Meyrick-Jones had two excellent examples to inspire him. One was Lytes Cary in Somerset, the remains of a medieval manor house which had been lovingly restored from 1907 onwards by Sir Walter Jenner, son of the famous Victorian physician. The other was the exquisite Westwood Manor near Bradford on Avon in Wiltshire, a lovely mixture of late medieval and Jacobean which, after spending much of the nineteenth century as a farmhouse and apple store, was bought in 1911 by the diplomat Edgar Lister, who according to James Lees-Milne, a frequent visitor to Westood, 'cordially disliked and despised' the present and 'positively immersed himself quite contentedly in the past'.[36]

Like the Meyrick-Joneses at Woodlands Manor, both Jenner and Lister made free use of fittings and furnishings from different periods – to create an ambience, a romantic evocation of the past with no attempt at authenticity or at establishing a period. That isn't a criticism: they weren't making museums.

But the obsession with the past could be carried to extraordinary lengths. All over England, old stone tiles were removed from ancient barns and cottages and recycled, along with the moss on them and gave a patina of authenticity to the roofs they covered

The architect Sir Albert Richardson at home.

– roofs which were carefully repaired so that they sagged in the right places. Chipped and broken bricks were no longer discarded: instead, they were put to one side until some eager antiquarian came along to turn them into new walls, laying them crookedly, of course, and making sure there was no uniformity of colour. Warped and weatherworn old timbers were placed in prominent positions; clean, smooth-cut wood was only used where it couldn't be seen. Every detail of these 'restorations', inside and out, had to be old. More important, it had to *look* old.

Country Life, in an article of 1924 describing Basil Ionides' restoration for himself of Howbridge Hall, a small Elizabethan country house at Witham in Essex, noted with admiration that nothing new had been used, right down to the door handles and hinges, the finger plates and the tiles in the grates. Ionides, later to dispense with the antique dramatically in his art-deco work at Claridge's and the silver and gold interior of the Savoy Theatre, wouldn't have an electric or pneumatic bell system to summon the

from chemical manufacturing, that of his successor at Lympne Castle, Henry Beecham, from patent medicines. Claude Lowther was the son of a naval officer – although admittedly he was the grandson of a peer, since his father was the illegitimate son of the 2nd Earl of Lonsdale and an opera singer. Olive Wilson Filmer was half-American, Iva Lawson wholly so.

The old order was doomed, complained the Duke of Marlborough in 1919 in a reference to Tennyson's 'The old order changeth, yielding place to new'. Death duties were killing it. What new order would replace it, he asked? 'Are these historic houses, the abiding memorials of events which live in the hearts of Englishmen, to be converted into museums, bare relics of a dead past?'[42]

Martin Conway had the answer. 'If the old order changes,' he wrote, 'it is not to give permanent place to barbarism and civil night, but to some other equally great manifestation of that divine power which . . . always pours forth something new.'[43]

CHAPTER FIVE

A New Culture

Sir Philip Sassoon, who was one of the greatest country-house connoisseurs of the twentieth century, had a vast fortune and a distinguished pedigree. His family had been bankers to the caliphs of Baghdad for 1,000 years. His great-grandfather moved from Persia to Bombay in the nineteenth century, establishing a trading empire so powerful that it was said 'silver and gold, silks, gums and spices, opium and cotton, wool and wheat – whatever moves over sea or land feels the hand or bears the mark of Sassoon & Co'.[1] His grandfather's philanthropy earned him a baronetcy, and his father Sir Edward married a Rothschild, Aline. The Prince of Wales, later Edward VII, named his yacht after her.

Sir Edward Sassoon died in 1912, three years after his wife. He left behind an eighteen-year-old daughter, Sybil, and Philip, who was twenty-three. He also left his enormous Park Lane mansion,

Sir Philip Sassoon.

built in the 1890s for the Randlord Barney Barnato; and an even more enormous fortune. Sir Edward's estate was valued at over £750,000.

'Elephants in different attitudes': José Maria Sert's curious allegorical mural at Port Lympne.

Within a year of her father's death Sybil married George Cholmondeley, Lord Rocksavage, who was heir to the Marquessate of Cholmondeley and vast estates in Norfolk and Cheshire, including the Palladian masterpiece Houghton Hall. She received a quarter of the Sassoon fortune; the rest went to Philip, now Sir Philip Sassoon, Bt, to be held in trust until his thirtieth birthday. In the meantime he had to make do with an annual allowance of £12,000, well over a million pounds in today's money. When the Rocksavages set off to India on their six-month honeymoon in November 1913, Sir Philip sent them a white Rolls-Royce as a wedding present to get around in while they were there.

Sir Philip inherited the parliamentary constituency of Hythe in Kent, where his father had sat as Liberal Unionist MP. (His rival for the seat was Sir Arthur Colefax, decorator Sibyl Colefax's husband, who was said to be so boring that he could have dug the Channel Tunnel.) He was to be Hythe's Conservative MP for the rest of his life, successfully fighting seven general elections. And rather than choosing to occupy Shorncliffe Lodge, the Regency-Gothic villa in Sandgate which his father had used as a base in the constituency, Sir Philip bought a 270-acre site overlooking Romney Marsh, with a view across to the Channel and the lights of France. He commissioned Herbert Baker to build him a weekend retreat, to be called Belcaire. It was 'on the lip of the world', he used to say, and so peaceful that 'one can hear the dogs bark in Beauvais'.[2]

Belcaire was a pleasant enough house of red brick, with the kind of Dutch gables that recalled Baker's twenty years as an architect in South Africa. It was barely finished in 1914 when Sassoon went out to France, spending most of the war as private secretary to Douglas Haig, commander-in-chief of the British armies. Even in a foreign country and in the middle of a world war, the young man (he was twenty-five when war broke out) continued to direct work on the gardens at Belcaire, and managed to commission a striking series of allegorical murals for his new drawing room from

a Catalan artist, José Maria Sert. In gold and sepia and black, they depicted France being harried by German eagles while her allies, in the form of naked children, came to her aid with cannon spouting flames and a pair of huge elephants reared up unaccountably to perch on the mantelpiece.

The prime minister, Herbert Asquith, who dropped in to see Belcaire in 1915 while its owner was away, was appalled at walls 'of highly burnished mustard-gold, on which are frescoes of a darker shade, representing elephants in different attitudes'; his fellow tourists, Lady Desborough and Sir John Simon, the Attorney General, couldn't find words to describe 'their horror and disgust'.[3] Sassoon, when he came home on leave, was more measured; but even he couldn't disguise his shock at what Sert had done. He was only half joking when he called the murals 'monstrous', and told his friend Sir Louis Mallet they had made the drawing room so dark 'that you have to whip out a pocket torch at midday or you're as good as lost'.[4] Disappointed or not, after the war he still commissioned Sert to decorate the enormous ballroom at his Park Lane mansion with an even more fantastic concoction, this time in blue and silver, showing camels and more elephants making their way past temples and across desert wastes.

Sassoon held on to his Hythe seat in the khaki election of December 1918 with a majority of 5,382 over the Labour candidate. (Rumours that his cousin Siegfried might stand against him proved unfounded.) Having come into his inheritance that same month, he decided to extend and remodel Belcaire and to rename it Port Lympne, a reference to the ancient Roman Portus Lemanis which stood close by before Romney Marsh was drained. Herbert Baker was busy working with Lutyens on the government complex at New Delhi, and Sir Philip brought in Philip Tilden to replace him.

One suspects that artistic direction remained with the client. Certainly Tilden never had created, and never would create again, anything as satisfyingly theatrical as the country house which took shape over the next couple of years. Glyn Philpot decorated the dining room with a frieze of white bullocks and naked black Egyptians against a chocolate-brown ground; the walls were

Glyn Philpot's Egyptian frieze in the dining room at Port Lympne.

panelled with lapis lazuli, 'a living wall of moving colour' beneath a ceiling of opalescent pink. The dining chairs and table were gilded. (Legend has it that Philip called Philpot back in 1936 at short notice to add loincloths and skirts to the naked figures in preparation for a visit by Queen Mary.) Paintings by Sargent, William Nicholson and Steer hung on the walls.

The Wrenaissance woodwork in Philip's small library was silver tinged with gilt; in the drawing room, reached through sliding bronze doors, Tilden set off the elephantine Sert murals by covering the walls in a dramatic black and gold faux marble, created for the purpose in a workshop at the back of Marylebone station. He also hit on the clever idea of lightening the darkness by matching the real windows with *trompe l'oeil* versions of black and oyster-coloured mirror-glass in gilded lead cames. Halfway up the main staircase there was a large plate-glass window which, at the press of a switch, slid soundlessly up into the wall to give access to an enclosed Alhambra-like patio built over the domestic offices, where seven fountains played around a central well-head. 'At night,' said *Country Life*, 'the stars are always visible from this enchanted garden and golden lights flood the arcades with mysterious radiance.'[5]

Rex Whistler's Tent Room at Port Lympne: somewhere, just out of reach, a story lurks.

Unable to bear the Sert elephants, even with the marble composition and the mirrors, Sir Philip eventually had them painted over in a range of creams, brilliant whites and off-whites; but he compensated for their absence in grand style, commissioning the young Rex Whistler to decorate his billiard room in 1931. Sassoon was a trustee of the Tate Gallery, where Whistler had come to prominence in 1927 with his mural of *The Expedition in Pursuit of Rare Meats* for the restaurant there. Whistler transformed the Port Lympne billiard room into a Tent Room, its ceiling a huge painted *trompe l'oeil* canvas awning, perhaps in reference to the house's main function as a summer home for Sassoon. Around the walls the young artist created a strange riverside landscape, populated with real and imaginary figures: their mutual friend Gerald Berners, as a small boy; the proprietor of Whistler's favourite Soho restaurant, La Tour Eiffel; a mysterious woman in mourning leaning against an urn marked 'In Memoriam'. James Gibbs's St Martin-in-the-Fields is prominent in this urban riverscape, towering behind the Palladian Bridge from Wilton. Berners' own country house, Faringdon, can be seen in the distance; so can a group of black-robed priests, and a well-dressed woman in an eighteenth-century carriage. As so often with Whistler's murals, one has the impression that somewhere, just out of reach, a story lurks, a linking narrative that would make everything clear, if only we could find it.

The sense of theatre that pervades the interiors spilled out into the fifteen acres of gardens. Sassoon masterminded the planting, with advice from the garden designer Norah Lindsay. Behind the house, Tilden cut a steep stone stairway into the cliff, with classical pavilions and fountains. On the terrace below, where Baker had marked out a site for a swimming pool before the war, he created one of the most dramatic bathing pools in England, flanked by raised quadrant pools and balustraded steps and fountains, the whole seeming to float above the marsh, with spectacular views

The terrace at Port Lympne: Sassoon used to say it 'stood on the lip of the world'.

to the Channel and the thin line of the Pas de Calais coast on the horizon.*

Tilden believed Port Lympne was Sassoon's response to the war, a challenge, a declaration that 'a new culture had risen up from the sick-bed of the old, with new aspirations . . . [a] mind tuned to a new burst of imagination'.[6] Other reactions ranged from astonishment to sneers. The unnamed *Country Life* correspondent who reviewed the house in 1923 was ecstatic: 'An example of the artistic power and ability of its own generation . . . The splendid success of Sir Philip's bold experiment should be a great encouragement to all who have faith in the future of British art and architecture . . . The rooms at Port Lympne are a compact fairy palace in which one walks, wide-eyed, as though on air.'[7] The house enchanted him. Honor Channon, on the other hand, said it reminded her of a Spanish brothel.[8] Her husband Chips, the American-born British politician, was mesmerised by its oddness, describing it as 'a triumph of beautiful bad taste and Babylonian luxury, with terrace and flowery gardens, and jade green pools and swimming baths and rooms done up in silver and blue and orange'.[9] Max Beerbohm called it an 'extraordinary elaboration of Persian fantasy, controlled by Etonian good taste'.[10]

Port Lympne was the antithesis of both the carefully constructed historicism of Allington Castle and the romantic myth of rural England that men like Buchan reached out to grasp after the war. It was the archetype of the outsider's country house, a stage on which its owner could act out the role of English baronet and, more importantly, could direct the characters who flocked to take advantage of his lavish hospitality at Port Lympne, from Winston Churchill and Lloyd George to Lawrence of Arabia and Charlie Chaplin, all willing players in his extraordinary fantasy.

Sassoon shimmers through almost every memoir of the period.

* The bathing pool didn't float quite well enough: when Tilden filled it with water, it showed signs of sliding down the hill and had to be reduced in size.

He never married – indeed, had no obvious sexual inclination in any direction, in spite of persistent rumours that he was homosexual. His was the kind of life that attracted legends: in 1930s Folkestone, for instance, it was whispered that he was attended by black eunuchs, and that he bought his shirts at Marks & Spencer. The one story was about as likely as the other. His Jewishness and his Indian blood were constantly referred to by those who knew him, not often in the ugly way Virginia Woolf had with words (she called him 'an underbred Whitechapel Jew'), but in the coded, casual racism of the day.[11] He was 'exotic', 'oriental'. 'A strange, lonely, un-English little figure,' wrote Harold Nicolson.[12] Robert Boothby, who knew him as well as any man, said that he was 'not part of England, and whatever gods he worshipped were not our gods'.[13] Interestingly, Sybil Sassoon's marriage into the ranks of the English nobility meant that none of this sense of otherness clung to her at all.

Chips Channon, who as an American was a fellow outsider, was intrigued, unsure, admiring of Port Lympne's owner, calling him at various times 'this strangest of sinister men' and 'one of the most exciting, tantalizing personalities of the age'.[14] When Sassoon died at the age of only fifty in June 1939, from complications following a bout of influenza, Channon wrote a measured obituary in his diary, praising his wit and his amiability; noting his hunger to be in the society of the great – 'royalties haunted his house always, and he was loyal to them as he was to no-one else' – and judging, rightly, that while Sassoon's political career was less than glittering, his taste and his passion for the arts were his great achievements. 'What he really loved were jewelled elephants and contrasting colours – the bizarre and the beautiful.'[15]

Sassoon was also capable of restraint at times, especially when, alongside the jewelled elephants and contrasting colours, he sought to add to his collection that most ephemeral of art-objects, Englishness. Port Lympne wasn't his only country house: on the death of his father in 1912 he had inherited the leasehold of Trent Park in Hertfordshire, an enormous Victorian house built of mauve bricks which stood in 500 acres on the southern edge of Enfield Chase. Modernised in the 1890s, Trent Park boasted thirty bedrooms, a large lake, Japanese water gardens and tennis courts, and a tower 'of peculiarly hideous appearance'.[16] It was only forty-five minutes from London by car ('thirteen miles from the Bank of England'), and every conceivable modern comfort was installed: electric light, lift, telephones and central heating. There were also 'ten furnished rooms for visiting chauffeurs'.[17]

For ten years Sassoon was unsure exactly what to do with Trent. There was Port Lympne to play with, 25 Park Lane to fill with eighteenth-century treasures. Trent was advertised to let fully furnished in 1916, while he was in France; some of the furniture was sold off in 1919.

There was a second, larger sale of furniture in 1924, when Sassoon disposed of eighteenth-century French pieces, Sèvres and Ming porcelain, Beauvais tapestries and a collection of seventeenth- and eighteenth-century English chairs and tables. There was so much interest in this sale that a motor coach was laid on to meet trains at New Barnet station and bring them the three miles to the house on viewing and sale days.

Disposals of contents like this were usually auguries of doom, precursors to the break-up of an estate and the dismantling of its mansion or its transfer to institutional use. Not so at Trent Park. With Port Lympne more or less complete, Sassoon had bought the freehold of Trent in 1923. Around the same time he acquired brick, stone and internal fittings from William Kent's recently demolished Devonshire House in Piccadilly, 'ducal, demure, secure in its estate', as his cousin Siegfried wrote in his 'Monody on the Demolition of Devonshire House'.[18] Having made a half-hearted attempt to soften the worst Victorian excesses of Trent, in 1925 he gave up and embarked on a wholesale remodelling.

The result, as Christopher Hussey reported in 1931, was a great country house in the pure English tradition, with none of the Palladian tricks or self-conscious period features which marked out so many other examples of the period. Everyone has assumed that Philip Tilden acted as Sassoon's architect at Trent Park, although Tilden – not normally slow to take credit – failed to mention the

The drawing room at Trent Park, Hertfordshire, in 1931.

fact (or even the house) in his memoirs, and Hussey spoke as if Sassoon himself were responsible. There is another name in the frame, a Lieutenant Colonel Reginald Cooper, a shadowy figure who designed the orangery in 1923 and who restored a number of small country houses for his own use in the 1920s and 1930s. But whoever was responsible for the new Trent Park, they did a beautiful job of reinventing it. The peculiarly hideous tower came down; Kent's rose-red Devonshire House bricks were used to reface the exterior, punctuated with stone window surrounds, string-courses and cornice from the same source. Inside the house, Sassoon installed an oak staircase with spiral balusters from Devonshire House, and panelled the main reception rooms and painted them soft blues, greys or yellows. There were no elephants, no Moorish patios. Rex Whistler was brought in again, but this time his work was confined to overmantel panels with classical trophies (and a

Rex Whistler, Trent Park with Philip and Sybil, *1934.*

lovely painting of the house with Sassoon and his cousin Hannah Gubbay, who often acted as his hostess, made while the artist was staying at Trent in May 1934). The furniture was good quality, but the kind of quality that might have been accumulated over the years by a family who had lived at Trent since the early eighteenth century.

If Trent were another stage, the subject of the play was English landed life, with Sassoon in the leading role. 'Sir Philip has produced a building at once dignified and unpretentious, practical yet civilized,' wrote Hussey. It 'can be regarded as an ideal example of English domestic architecture unalloyed by fashion or fantasy'.[19]

But the fantasy kept on breaking through, even at Trent. Sassoon was powered by a desire not to impress, exactly, but to please; and that, coupled with his immense wealth and an impetuous nature, had startling consequences. Rex Whistler suggested one day in 1933 that some of the statuary in the gardens might look well with gilded highlights: the next time he visited, an enormous lead gladiator had a gleaming golden sword and a shield that looked like a gold dish cover. 'I must say he has gone further with the idea than I should have dared!' Whistler wrote to a friend.[20]

The gilded statues gave rise to all sorts of stories about Trent. The drainpipes were golden; the antlers of the stags in the park were golden, because their owner liked the way they glittered in the sunshine. On one occasion Sassoon was supposed to have had the Union Jack lowered from its flagpole on the roof, because he felt its colours clashed with the sunset.

These stories may have been true: one never knows with Sir Philip Sassoon. It *was* true, for instance, that he kept scarlet ibis and pink flamingos on the lake at Trent, and that he made a point of personally feeding his small flock of king, rock-hopper and black-footed penguins whenever he was there. It *was* true that when the Duke and Duchess of Kent honeymooned at Trent Park in 1934, Sassoon bought three monuments of eighteenth-century dukes of Kent at the Wrest Park sale and had them set up to make the newly-weds feel at home; and that he had his flower beds planted overnight. Robert Boothby spoke of an occasion when he arrived at Trent late one night, ahead of the rest of the house party. Early the next morning he was woken by the sound of cartwheels on the drive. 'I got up and went out in my dressing gown to find six horse-drawn carts coming up the avenue, laden with flowers from Covent Garden in full bloom. An army of gardeners [there were eighteen] was waiting to plant them out in borders which had been carefully prepared. By the time the [other] guests began to arrive for lunch, they were all in.'[21]

PHILIP TILDEN'S NAME crops up in these pages so frequently that a reader could be forgiven for thinking there were no other country-house architects at work in the 1920s and 1930s. Far from it: scores of new country houses were built between the wars as architects and clients groped towards a new definition of the country house, one which took account of changing requirements, changing social structures, and a world in which the past was no longer the only style manual.

The uncertainty which characterised post-war architecture in Britain meant that no one style dominated the field in new country-house building. Old stagers who had carved out careers for themselves as builders of Wrenaissance mansions before the war continued to design in much the same vein after it, although inevitably, that side of their practices tended to decline as more and more country houses came onto the market. And the Arts and Crafts movement continued to appeal to those who liked to bury themselves in rural romance.

The greatest Arts and Crafts country house of the 1920s, Rodmarton Manor in Gloucestershire, was designed and started before the war, but not completed until 1929. Claud Biddulph had been given the 550-acre Rodmarton estate by his father in 1894, when he was eighteen. There was no mansion to go with it, but Claud preferred a career in the City to life as a country squire until 1906, when he and his new wife Margaret decided to make a home for themselves in Gloucestershire. They commissioned Ernest Barnsley to come up with designs for what Claud called their 'cottage in the country' – half-jokingly, because for all its quiet charm and its studied references to the farms and manor houses of the Cotswolds, Rodmarton is a substantial country house.

Barnsley, who had moved to the Cotswolds from London with his brother Sidney and Ernest Gimson in the 1890s to rediscover and reinvigorate traditional crafts, produced his first designs for Rodmarton in 1909, and shortly afterwards work began on the kitchen court and domestic offices in the east wing and progressed slowly westwards. Although the shell was roofed by about 1912 and the Biddulphs were able to move in in 1915, the house wasn't finished until 1929, three years after Barnsley's death, when his son-in-law Norman Jewson completed the chapel in the west wing. The long gestation period was due entirely to Barnsley's insistence on traditional working practices. No contractor was employed, something which by the early twentieth century was most unusual

Rodmarton Manor, Gloucestershire: an educational enterprise, a quiet attempt to change the world.

for such a large project. All the stone and slate was quarried nearby and brought to the site by wagon, to be worked by local masons. Timber for beams and rafters was cut and seasoned on the estate; Barnsley wouldn't allow planks to be shaped with a circular saw – that smacked of an industrial process, and came between the workman and his materials. So a sawpit was constructed on site, and two men slaved away sawing every single one with a two-handed saw. Metalwork was made by the local blacksmith; the Rodmarton foreman acted as clerk of works.

The emphasis on local involvement continued inside the house, with furniture made by estate joiners and designed by Ernest Barnsley, his brother Sidney and the cabinetmaker Peter Waals. The workmen also produced oak panelling from drawings by the designer Alfred Powell, whose wife Louise contributed pottery and the decoration of a piano designed by Waals. Both the Powells were regular visitors to the house, as was the Labour politician Ramsay MacDonald. The main hall was often given over to craft classes in canework, needlework and woodwork for the villagers, presided over by Margaret Biddulph.

There was a serious point to all this. Rodmarton was an educational enterprise, a quiet attempt to change the world. If traditional crafts were dying out they must be revived; and their revival depended not on city-bred reformers like Barnsley and the Biddulphs, but on people like the Biddulphs' estate workers, and on the women who lived in the surrounding villages. Give them the skills and the confidence to make beautiful things, and they would pass their knowledge on to others.

This was the sort of radical social adventure which the Arts and Crafts movement had always dreamed about. It was rare to see it made real; but other architects, motivated less by a desire to change the world than by the picturesque possibilities of the vernacular, continued to work in the same tradition well after the war. Oswald Milne, who was articled to Sir Arthur Blomfield at the end of the 1890s and worked for a couple of years in Lutyens' office, was one such, continuing after the Armistice the vaguely Arts and Crafts country-house practice he had established in 1904, when he first set up on his own. In 1919 he went into partnership with Paul Phipps, whom he knew from Lutyens' office, and produced a series of pleasant but hardly inspiring country houses, of which the most interesting – as much because of the site and the clients as because of Milne's treatment of the project – was Coleton Fishacre on the south Devon coast.

The site of Coleton Fishacre is dramatic, a narrow combe which descends to a little cove. It is best appreciated from the sea, which is how Milne's clients, Rupert and Lady Dorothy D'Oyly Carte, first came upon it, while they were yachting between Brixham and Dartmouth in 1923. D'Oyly Carte's father was the impresario Richard D'Oyly Carte, whose exclusive business arrangement with Gilbert and Sullivan had led to the formation of the famous opera company and the building of both the Savoy Theatre and the Savoy Hotel, all of which Rupert now managed.

Coleton Fishacre was a weekend retreat for husband and wife and their two teenage children. It is old fashioned for the 1920s, unadventurous: Milne took rather too much to heart Philip Webb's dictum that 'I never begin to be satisfied until my work looks commonplace.' Nevertheless, the walls of shale stone (quarried on the estate in best Arts and Crafts fashion), the unpainted oak window frames, the steep roofs of Delabole stone slates, do give a sense of tranquillity, of a house which is not too quaint and not too modern.

And the weekend retreat became a residence, a country house rather than a seaside holiday home. It was big enough to accommodate an indoor staff of four – butler, housekeeper, housemaid and cook – as well as a chauffeur and six gardeners. Soon after the house was finished Lady Dorothy came to live there permanently, while her husband lived in London and motored down on Friday evenings. They spent their time yachting – Rupert had a cutter named *Content* – and gardening. By the 1930s the gardens at Coleton were well enough established to be opened to the public in aid of the Queen's Institute of District Nursing. The family swam in the sea or in a concrete tidal pool they had built down in the cove, and entertained friends from the world of the arts. There were bridge parties and concerts, everything, as it turned out, except happiness. The D'Oyly Cartes' son Michael was killed in a motoring accident in 1932 and their marriage didn't long survive his death: they separated in 1936 and Rupert divorced Lady Dorothy on the grounds of her adultery five years later.

In their different ways Rodmarton and Coleton Fishacre suggest that the post-war country-house tradition was backward-looking, locked into a quiet and self-effacing love affair with the past. And in the hands of some architects, it was. There were too many thatched mansions, the twentieth-century equivalent of the Regency *cottage ornée*, with catslide roofs and leaded lattice windows, turning their back on the brave new world of the future while their owners listened to the latest news of financial disaster on the markets and the march of terror across Europe on wirelesses that were disguised in distressed oak 'antique' cabinets, and powered by generators hidden away in half-timbered Stockbroker Tudor garages.

But there were also the modernists. A scattering of Modern Movement country houses sprang up between the wars, their gleaming white walls, flat roofs and horizontal bands of glass meeting with a public response that was always amazed, often downright hostile. Local councils were reluctant to grant planning permission for these experiments, while the older generation of architects condemned the style as inappropriate, foreign, out of step with tradition. In 1934 Sir Reginald Blomfield, whose pre-war practice had turned out numbers of conservative Wrenaissance mansions, launched a savage attack on what he called 'Modernismus', condemning houses that looked like oblong boxes on posts, covered in birthday-cake icing, with interiors like operating theatres. 'What is the particular advantage of a flat roof?' asked *Country Life* in 1930, immediately providing the answer to its own question. 'There isn't any.'[22] A couple of years later it announced that 'houses of this type . . . can never fit into the English landscape in the same way as buildings constructed of local materials and in traditional styles'.[23] Ironically, this was exactly the kind of criticism that two centuries earlier had been levelled at Palladianism, now the most revered of country-house styles.

There was something dangerously un-English about both modernism and its supporters. Many of the leading modernist architects working in England were, or at least *sounded,* suspiciously foreign – Eric Mendelssohn, Walter Gropius, Ernö Goldfinger, Serge Chermayeff, Berthold Lubetkin. Many were Jewish; most were left wing and pro-Soviet. And there was no doubting the fact that modernist buildings looked unusual, especially when they reared up out of the rural landscape. One of the first big modernist houses to appear in Britain was Crowsteps, near Newbury in Berkshire, designed by Thomas S. Tait of the Scottish firm of Sir John Burnet and Partners. In 1927 Tait had begun work on Silver End, a modernist settlement for workers at the factory of Francis Crittall, whose firm manufactured the metal window frames which seemed to grace every modern building of the period. The housing, flat-roofed with triangular oriel windows and rendered walls, included terraces of three-bedroomed 'cottages', each with sitting room, living room and scullery; four-bedroom detached houses, presumably intended for senior members of the Crittall staff; and the grandest house in the village, Le Château, sleek and elegant, the horizontal lines of its roofs and balconies emphasised by steel casement windows (by Crittall, of course) without vertical glazing bars.

Tait's client at Crowsteps, Dr Alan Simmons, had been inspired by Silver End. The white ziggurat that Tait gave him, more a villa in its own grounds that a country house (it stands in glorious isolation in early photographs, but it actually formed part of a leafy new suburb on the edge of town), was equally uncompromising. 'This house not only invites criticism,' wrote the architectural writer Randall Phillips, 'it challenges it.'[24] A stepped series of boxes with sundecks and balconies looked out onto a long concrete-lined pool. The cement render that encased the entire house was mixed with a little ochre to give a cream finish. Inside the doors were single panels, the dining table, specially designed for the house, was coated in black cellulose paint, 'proof against marking by hot plates and dishes', and the staircase had solid walls in place of balusters, with a vermilion handrail. The maids, whose bedrooms were at the top of the house, had a sitting room of their own next to the kitchen, which in turn was next door to the dining room, a piece of practical planning which by the 1920s was becoming common in new houses, even the biggest and grandest.

It is hard today to recapture some of the astonishment that greeted a house like Crowsteps. There was more. If anyone wants an illustration of just how thoroughly un-English the new architecture could be in the interwar years, High and Over is it. Even today, more than eighty years after it was finished, its hard white angles and blind, staring windows startle the eye. This is exciting, we think; it is architecture at its most provocative. But it is not what a country house is supposed to look like. Not an *English* country house, at any rate.

The client for whom High and Over was designed was as

English as they come, and a man, moreover, who cared more than most about historical precedent. Essex-born Bernard Ashmole (1894–1988) was thirty-five years old when he decided to build himself a new house at Amersham, deep in the heart of commuter-belt Buckinghamshire. He was married with a young family, and had just been appointed professor of classical archaeology at University College London.

Ashmole, who had established a reputation as an expert on numismatics and classical sculpture, took up the chair at UCL in 1929, shortly after returning from a three-year stint as director of the British School in Rome. It was while he was there that he first met his architect, the brilliant young New Zealander Amyas Connell. Connell had served his articles in an architect's office in Wellington before working his passage to England as a stoker on the SS *Karamarin* in 1923, in company with his friend and fellow student, Basil Ward. Further studies at UCL led to his winning the Rome Scholarship in architecture in 1926, which is how he came to meet Bernard Ashmole.

Ashmole's decision to choose Connell as the architect for his new house was quite courageous. The younger man had built nothing of any substance, his views were extremely progressive, and the designs he *had* produced were heavily influenced by Le Corbusier, whose work provoked reactions ranging from rage and horror to blank incomprehension among the British architectural establishment.

One of the most intriguing things about High and Over is its plan. As its name implies, the house stands high on a hill overlooking the Misbourne Valley. It is built in the shape of a Y, with three more or less equal arms radiating out at 120-degree angles from a hexagonal hall. Stark, flat-roofed and clad in cement-rendered brick over a frame of reinforced concrete, it is carefully asymmetrical, in spite of its broadly symmetrical plan. The fenestration varies from one wing to another; an angular oriel projects out over Ashmole's library in the south wing, and a low single-storey extension containing domestic offices unbalances the north-east wing, which houses the dining room and kitchen. Most striking of all is the pair of flat

High and Over in Buckinghamshire, designed by Amyas Connell in 1929.

concrete hoods or canopies supported on columns which hover above the south and north-west blocks like giant aeroplane wings: in spite of the obvious associations with the machine age, they were intended primarily to provide shade and support for the Ashmole children's hammocks. The rest of the roof was taken up with an airy (and suitably remote) hexagonal day nursery, a night nursery and nurse's bedroom. A lift brought meals up from the kitchen on the ground floor.

The three faces of the hexagon which don't connect to the sitting room, dining room and library were still made to do some work. One took the chrome-plated steel front door; the second opened onto a terrace which led to the gardens; and the third was filled with a polygonal glass staircase which, on the rare occasions when the sun shone in Amersham, would let sunlight flood into the hall and the landing above. Four main bedrooms led off this landing: the master bedroom and dressing room were in the south wing, over the library, and included a built-in shower – quite a novelty in 1931.

The hall itself formed the most elegant interior in the whole house. In the centre of a black marble floor inlaid with pieces of glass Connell sank a glass basin, with a fountain which could shoot a stream of water as high as the first-floor gallery. This lit up at night. The sets of doors to the dining room, library and sitting room – all capable of being folded back to create a single large space for entertaining – were made of steel and glass, with the inside surfaces of the glass sprayed with translucent patterns of cellulose. The main rooms had lighting concealed behind glass panels set into the ceilings, and decoration varied from plain orange walls in the dining room to chrome and jade-green cellulose in the sitting room, which also had a built-in wireless. 'English towns and cities and our countryside cannot assimilate this new architecture,' declared Sir Reginald Blomfield. It was too cosmopolitan, and 'as an Englishman and proud of his country, I detest and despise cosmopolitanism'.[25]

*

MODERNIST COUNTRY HOUSES were something of an anomaly. Their owners had to grapple with the fact that not only did their new rural retreats flout the principles of architectural authority, but they ran counter to the English country house's most powerful attraction, its ability to evoke stability, continuity, sanctuary, a still point at the centre of a maelstrom of cultural and social change.

Sometimes those owners couldn't reconcile the tension between the shock of the new and the pull of the past. That, ultimately, was what happened at Joldwynds in Surrey, arguably the greatest modernist country house of them all. Joldwynds came with all the trimmings: twelve bedrooms, six bathrooms, five sitting rooms, domestic offices, garage and stables with three flats, a swimming pool, a hard tennis court and twenty acres of woodland to explore in the unlikely event that the fifteen acres of beautiful gardens lost their charm. The polished white mansion was 'the striking country house of the future', to borrow a phrase from the agent's particulars.[26]

Its architect, one of the most intriguing country-house architects of the period, was Oliver Hill, whose work immediately after the war tended to be either romantically thatched and picturesque, or formal and neo-Georgian in the mould of Richard Norman Shaw, Reginald Blomfield and Sir Edwin Lutyens. (Lutyens was actually a friend and neighbour of his parents.) After a visit in 1925 to the Paris Exposition Internationale des Arts Décoratifs et Industriels Modernes, Hill's work began to show affinities with modernism, although never to the exclusion of traditional styles. It seemed as if he were eager to experiment, but lacked the opportunity – and the necessary supportive client.

He found him in 1930, when a prosperous barrister, Wilfred Greene, and his wife Nancy commissioned a weekend retreat at Holmbury St Mary, about ten miles south-east of Guildford in Surrey. There was already a Victorian mansion on the site, a rather splendid thing surrounded by parkland, with gables and outrageously tall chimney stacks. It had been built by Philip Webb in 1873. But it was too big, too impractical and too

was £50,000 for the house, and another £10,000 for the grounds; a huge sum, but then Drewe wanted a huge house. A castle, in fact, which would commemorate (and publicise) his centuries-old connections with the area. 'I do wish he didn't want a castle,' Lutyens wrote to his wife, 'but just a delicious lovable house with plenty of good large rooms in it.'[4]

In the event, only half of Lutyens' original scheme for Castle Drogo, a splayed U-plan with a central great hall, was built, and even then the budget was trebled, partly as a result of Drewe's decision that Lutyens' cavity walls should give way to more authentic solid granite.

The war brought the building work to a halt. Materials were scarce, and Drewe actively encouraged the workforce to enlist. (He refused to employ any single men at Castle Drogo, for example, maintaining that they should all be fighting.) In 1917 his eldest son Adrian was killed at Ypres; Drewe's daughter recalled that 'the joy very much went out of life as far as my father and mother were concerned, and things were very much quieter'.[5] But work resumed in 1919 and Castle Drogo was ready for the Drewes to move into by 1927.

And it *is* a castle, complete with battlements and towers, a heraldic Drewe lion above the front door and a 644 lb working portcullis behind it. But Drogo is more than a toy fort built on the shifting sands of an outmoded historicism. Whatever Lutyens' private desires for the maintenance of a social and architectural status quo which was already beginning to fragment around him, he achieved a new, raw and very modern elementalism, defining the very essence of a castle, stripping it of its externals, and then reinterpreting it to suit the needs of a wealthy family in the twentieth century. Drogo is a dramatic and ambiguous tour de force, which simultaneously conjures up and repudiates the past. Its composition and materials establish links with the medieval, while at the same time rejecting the hazy, idealised romanticism of the late nineteenth century in favour of a wholly contemporary conception which is every bit as cold and hard-edged as the granite blocks from which it is built.

The library at Castle Drogo, photographed for Country Life *in 1945.*

Inside, there are surprises everywhere. Wide passages punctuated by shallow saucer domes disappear round unexpected corners, or fade into the distance – and quite a distance it can be, since the kitchens are some fifty yards away from the dining room. Walls rear up like cliffs as the floor suddenly falls away in long flights of steps. Vaults and arches intersect like medieval undercrofts, while above the main staircase, which revolves around an apparently solid core but in fact conceals a complete servants' stair within it, the ceiling alters at each turn, changing from coffered vault to dome to arches to oak beams, but remains at its original height, so that by the time one reaches the bottom the distance from floor to ceiling is a towering twenty-seven feet.

The more you get to know Drogo, the more you come to realise the extent of Lutyens' achievement. The almost unnatural precision of the masonry, the perfect regularity of the vaults and arches and domes, the great windows breaking through the walls and flooding the rooms inside with light, all remind us that it is a wholly twentieth-century conception. At the same time, the restrained treatment, the absence of ornament, the grim granite of the interiors, demonstrate that this is no Scotch-baronial exercise in historicism. The house is neither a 'real' castle nor a sham folly: Lutyens managed to create a building that was modern, while still conveying that sense of timeless solidity which Julius Drewe needed to validate his ancestry.

LUTYENS WAS INVOLVED IN 200 projects between 1919 and his death in 1944, but only half a dozen or so were country houses. There was Drogo, conceived in Edwardian England, stripped down and simplified for a post-war world. There was a startling and austere extension which he made to Penheale Manor in Cornwall in the early 1920s – itself an indirect consequence of the war, in that the owner, Captain Norman Colville, MC, had been gassed and bought the house after being advised by his doctors to move south from Scotland for his health. And there were several remodellings of older buildings, such as the work he carried out in 1928 at Plumpton Place in Sussex, a romantic timber-framed manor house that he repaired and enlarged for his old patron Edward Hudson.

Lutyens only built two entirely new country houses after the war, both in collaboration with other architects and for very different clients. Yet at a time when the country house was meant to be in crisis, they were among the largest he had ever designed.

The first, Gledstone Hall, was for a cotton lord so self-made that his career borders on caricature. Amos Nelson was born into a working-class family in Lancashire in 1860. He went to work at the age of eight and by the time he was twenty-one he had saved enough from his meagre earnings to set up in business as a small-scale cotton manufacturer in partnership with his father, a weaver. He sold that business in 1946 for £3.7 million, one of the biggest ever mill transactions.

In 1919 Nelson bought the 9,000-acre Gledstone Hall estate in Yorkshire, which had at its core a classical country house of the 1770s, said to have been designed by Carr of York. He commissioned a local architect, Richard Jaques, to modernise the house and then, as the scale of the task grew, persuaded Jaques that it would be a good idea to enlist the help of a more experienced country-house architect. Lutyens worked up a design aboard the SS *Caledonia* in December 1920 en route to India, after finding himself in the unenviable position of having his client as a fellow passenger. 'I have to work to keep his interest to a pitch higher than the toss of waves,' he wrote to his wife. 'But Lord! how I sweated in that little red hot room at the top of the ship.'[6]

He sweated in vain. Nelson decided that the cost of remodelling was going to be prohibitive. But he still wanted a country house which would reflect both his status and his political aspirations: he was knighted in January 1922, and stood unsuccessfully for Parliament as a Conservative in the November election of that year. So between 1922 and 1926 the old Gledstone Hall was replaced by a new house on a new site, designed by Lutyens but with Jaques giving a helping hand. (The old hall remained in limbo for a couple of years before being demolished in 1928. The stable block survived, and has since been turned into a house.)

A more eminent collaborator was Gertrude Jekyll, who provided a mail-order planting scheme without visiting. Gledstone was the last time that Jekyll and Lutyens worked together in a partnership that stretched all the way back to 1889 when the 20-year-old architect was beginning to work out his Surrey vernacular style and 'Aunt Bumps', as he called her, was already well known for the apparently artless artistry of her garden designs. The garden at Gledstone is architectural, formal, perfect; more Lutyens than Jekyll, with a long narrow canal stretching out from the south front of the house to emphasise the north–south axis and beyond it, a stone-edged circular lily pool.

The house is more problematic. Lutyens opted to give visitors the kind of grandly eclectic introduction they might have expected from a cotton lord's un-ancestral pile in the nineteenth century: a rigidly symmetrical neo-Palladian mansion with steep, rather French roofs, flanking pavilions and an enormous Ionic porte cochère, the only portico Lutyens ever built in England. This entrance front, half chateau, half house of parade, conceals the fact that Gledstone is smaller than it seems, and in its planning at least, more modern. There are only seven bedrooms, for one thing. The kitchen was placed almost next door to the dining room – no long processions of lukewarm food – and while the kitchen, servants' hall and other domestic offices filled one wing, its companion was false, not much more than a screen wall hiding a little courtyard and garaging for Sir Amos's cars.

The interior was simple and only one room deep with a cross-corridor running east to west. There was a low-ceilinged central entrance hall, a dining room, a drawing room and a big games room with a billiard table, all looking out over the south-facing garden. A morning room and library were tucked into the angles formed by the two wings. Lutyens made a great thing of the black and white marble flooring. The hall had a typical Palladian chequerboard floor; the main staircase, alternating black and white steps which were, as Pevsner commented, 'handsome to look at and neck-breaking to walk on'.[7] In a nod to the Jazz Age, the ground-floor corridor was given a striking pattern of swirling black and white, culminating in a cluster of marble teardrops.

Despite touches like this, there is something a little humourless about Gledstone, which has none of the wit, none of the sense of playing with a genre which characterises Castle Drogo. But Nelson was happy with the result. A series of photographs of the house taken for *Country Life* in 1935 show the rooms peppered with good-ish antiques and reproduction furniture, a refectory table in the entrance hall, a small mahogany dining table and a circular rug in the dining room. Several of the Georgian chimney pieces from the

The second Lady Nelson poses on the staircase at Gledstone Hall, Yorkshire, in 1935.

old house found their way into the new one. And judging by the number of times she appeared in the photo shoot, posing on the staircase, sitting on sofas, talking to the nurse who held her baby, Nelson was just as proud of his new wife. The first Lady Nelson, to whom he was married for fifty-two years, had died in 1931 and within six months he had found and married her successor, who promptly gave him his seventh child in his seventies.

Lutyens' last great country house was Middleton Park, near Bicester, for the 25-year-old 9th Earl of Jersey. Completed in 1938 (and given statutory protection as a building of exceptional interest only thirteen years later, which must be some kind of record) it was another collaboration, this time with the architect's son Robert.

For a long time, the two Lutyens men had endured a difficult relationship. In 1920 the teenage Robert left Cambridge and eloped with a research chemist called Eva Lubryjinska, who was seven years his senior, painted her fingernails and was a Polish Jew. They were married in Edinburgh, and the anti-Semitic Lutyens found it hard to forgive his son.* The fact that the marriage turned out to be unhappy didn't help their relationship: being proved wrong does little to make an erring son forgive his disapproving father. In the 1920s Robert made a living as a journalist (he was a leader-writer on the *Daily Mail*) and then as an interior designer before going into architectural practice in 1933 without any formal training. He produced interiors for several members of the board of Marks & Spencer and their relatives, and as a result he was involved in the design of a string of Marks & Spencer stores in the 1930s.

Their client at Middleton Park succeeded to the Jersey earldom in 1923 when he was only thirteen years old, and he also married young. 'Grandy' (the Earl of Jersey was also Viscount Grandison of Limerick in the Irish peerage) was twenty-one and his wife, Patricia Richards, was eighteen when they married in January 1932. They had three country houses. Their main home was Middleton Park, then an impressive Georgian mansion with a domed central block and two wings linked to it by curving colonnades. There was also Osterley Park in Middlesex, an Elizabethan house remodelled by Robert Adam in the 1760s and opened to the public by the earl in 1939. And they owned Baglan House in Glamorgan, another Georgian house where the family spent a couple of weeks each summer.

Like many others, Jersey appeared to be feeling the financial pinch in the Depression years. In 1933 the head gardener at Middleton Park was dismissed 'owing to curtailment of expenses';[8] and the following year Hampton & Sons held a nine-day sale at Middleton, attracting buyers from all over the

*Eva was the niece of Chaim Weizmann, later the first president of Israel.

country. Jersey sold off thousands of items: a set of twenty-four Chippendale mahogany chairs; Adam side tables and George I giltwood torchères; a pair of Indian ivory armchairs (which alone fetched a considerable 280 guineas); and the contents of the guest bedrooms – all forty-four of them. The family library, including rare works on costume and travel, first editions by Charles Dickens and an 800-volume set of parliamentary debates, went under the hammer. So did a mixed bag of pictures and drawings. The highest price for a painting was ninety-four guineas, paid for a portrait of the 5th earl's sister, Lady Sarah Bayly, by a nineteenth-century president of the Royal Academy, Sir Martin Shee.

The Countess of Jersey's bathroom at Middleton Park, Oxfordshire. Lady Jersey had 'no idea of what an Englishman's house should be' said Lutyens.

Rather than heralding the break-up of the Middleton Park estate and a flight to Monte Carlo or Happy Valley, the sale helped to finance a new beginning of a different sort. In 1935 the old house was demolished and work began on a brand-new mansion. Jersey initially consulted Robert Lutyens, but Edward Hudson advised him to bring Lutyens senior in as well. The partnership cemented an uneasy rapprochement between father and son, with Robert later explaining generously that it was far from being a union of equals. Writing of himself in the third person, he acknowledged that his role was to mediate between 'disparate generations', and that 'his chief desire . . . was to stand sufficiently close to his father to be able to watch him actually at work. The work that mattered was all the father's.'[9]

Middleton Park is big, and meant for entertaining. The north-facing eleven-bay entrance facade is 120 feet long, and behind it lie rooms of a scale and number which wouldn't be out of place in a country house built a century earlier. Tall windows with shutters, and a row of flat-topped dormers in the hipped roof, contrive to give the house a faintly French air, contradicting Robert Lutyens' opinion that with Middleton Park his father achieved a 'quintessential Englishness'.[10]

The interiors, all arches and vaults and filled with the kind of playful, stripped-down geometries which showed that Lutyens was still at the top of his game as he approached his seventies,

were carefully zoned. On the west there was a traditional male complex of interconnecting study, smoking room and library. A huge drawing room filled the centre of the south front, with a dining room finishing off the sequence of ground-floor reception rooms. Above there were eight principal bedrooms, each equipped with its own en suite bathroom. A substantial service wing was supplemented by four detached lodges for visiting valets, maids and chauffeurs. In lieu of stables there was garaging for nine cars.

In January 1937, with Middleton Park still unfinished, the Earl and Countess of Jersey divorced, and six months later Grandy married an American film star.* Virginia Cherrill is best known today for two roles: one as the blind flower-girl in Charlie Chaplin's 1931 classic *City Lights*; and the other as Cary Grant's first wife. She left Grant after seven months of marriage.

Edwin Lutyens didn't like her. He called her 'a common little woman without brain [who had] no idea of what an Englishman's house should be'.[11] Robert also found her difficult, complaining that she insisted on having a cocktail bar and other Hollywood features included at Middleton Park. However, it was probably Virginia who was responsible for one of the house's finest interiors: her bathroom, which was rightly described by *Country Life* in 1946 as 'a notable instance of the between-wars cult of the tub'.[12] With walls of pink onyx and white marble, taps of gilt bronze and a shower enclosed in mirror-glass, it was a magnificent piece of English deco. One suspects this was an instance where Robert stepped in between those disparate generations and took a hand in its design.

The earl and his Hollywood countess weren't destined to enjoy Middleton Park. They spent only two nights there before war broke out. Then Grandy went off to join the army. Virginia went off with a Polish airman. The couple divorced in 1946 and the same year the earl sold Middleton Park to an industrialist, A. C. J. Wall.

Lutyens died of lung cancer on New Year's Day 1944, eulogised

* Grandy's first countess also remarried that summer. By the end of their lives, they had amassed seven spouses between them.

as England's greatest architect since Wren, the inventor of the modern English country house, and the best-known British architect in the world. But among all the praise was the occasional acknowledgement that he had outlived his time. 'He appears as the last great exponent of the architecture of an age that had passed,' observed one obituarist.[13] And in truth, the grandiose classicism of Gledstone and Middleton already seemed to belong to another age when they were still brand new. Most of those who chose to build themselves a country house between the wars might like the *idea* of marbled halls and Ionic porticos: but when it came down to it, convenience and practicality meant more to them than grandeur.

CHAPTER SEVEN

Making Plans

Vita Sackville-West's writing room at Sissinghurst, still kept as it was in the 1930s.

'TODAY WE SHOULD NOT tolerate basement kitchens or long corridors between the culinary department and the dining-room', wrote P. A. Barron, author of *The House Desirable: A Handbook for Those who Wish to Acquire Homes That Charm.*[1]

The balancing act which so many owners of older country houses had to perform was to live in a congenial 'muddle of museum carpets [and] ruined castles'[2] – Harold Nicolson's description of life at Sissinghurst – and yet still have mod cons and home comforts. The older the house, the harder that was. By the 1920s light, sun and air were prized in a way that medieval and Tudor forebears would have found incomprehensible. So were bathrooms.

One agent of change was the fast-moving property market. Families who had lived content for generations with all the inconveniences of inadequate or labour-intensive heating, lighting and plumbing, gave place to less tolerant new owners, 'people for the most part keen and alive to the priceless heritage of architectural beauty which these houses represent, but conscious also that the defects . . . shall be remedied'.[3] It is easy to imagine a Duke of Rutland or a Duke of Bedford being prepared to put up with candles and oil lamps at Belvoir or Woburn; much less easy to think of a Sir Philip Sassoon or a Lady Baillie doing so at Port Lympne or Leeds Castle. Even the dedicated restorers demanded a degree of comfort. At Allington, Sir Martin Conway was clear from the start that while he set out to preserve every old feature of the castle, he wouldn't scruple to insert new doors, windows, staircases and the like wherever they were needed, or 'to make the place into a thoroughly warm, dry, light, and comfortably fitted home'.[4]

Change was in the air. In 1929, when *The House Desirable* was published, it seemed ridiculous to put the kitchens in a basement or even in a separate building, as the Tudors had done; or to adopt a favourite Victorian scheme of linking them to the dining room by a deliberately circuitous route that kept cooking smells out of the main house. The modern country house was planned for modern living.

But for people blessed with a sprawling old mansion that had been built in the days when servants were cheap and convenience not a consideration, the options were limited. An owner could demolish his or her house and start again, as Amos Nelson did at Gledstone; or as Wilfred and Nancy Greene did with Philip Webb's Joldwynds. Or they could remove the inconvenient bits. The paint was scarcely dry on the high-Victorian Tyntesfield, near Bristol, before the Gibbs family, who had just built it, began to dismantle it. An immense domed conservatory that had been inspired by the Crystal Palace went in 1917, falling prey to storm damage, wartime labour shortages and changing horticultural fashions; and in 1935 the splendid Gothic clock tower which loomed over the entrance porch was dismantled after it was found to have dry rot, and the roofline was adjusted accordingly.

Less radical, less expensive, and therefore more popular, was a tendency to tinker and make do, changing or blurring the historic function of a room. A billiard table or bookcases might be installed in a seventeenth-century long gallery or a Tudor great chamber. (Books do furnish a room.) An enfilade might become a corridor; partition walls and false ceilings could make huge bedchambers more manageable, and also provide opportunities for introducing a bathroom or two.

One of the trickiest problems for the owner of an ancient ancestral pile was how best to use the great hall. This cavernous space might be medieval and open to the rafters, with a screens passage at one end and a dais at the other; it might have a grand carved staircase, marble floors and an Adam ceiling. But no stately home with any pretension to the name was without one.

Yet what was it *for*, exactly? The medieval hall had been a place where the lord presided over gatherings of the entire household, seated beneath a canopy of state – an act that even the most theatrically inclined antiquarian would find rather hard to pull off in the twentieth century. Over the centuries the great hall had evolved into a quasi-public entrance space, a waiting area for servants, until the introduction of effective bell-pull systems in the early nineteenth century consigned those waiting servants to the netherworld behind the green baize door. Victorians who looked wistfully on a mythical Merrye Englande peopled by benevolent landowners and grateful tenants sought to keep something of the communal function of the great hall, holding tenants' dinners here and summoning village children to receive their oranges at Christmas in front of a blazing Yule log. The old halls presented, as Pugin put it, 'a standing illustration of good old English hospitality'.[5] The prolific Victorian architect George Gilbert Scott agreed. 'The residence of a great landed proprietor should never be without [one],' he declared in 1857. 'Its disuse was accompanied by the decay of that ancient hospitality which is impossible without it.'[6]

By and large, the twentieth century was of the same mind as Pugin and Scott. Some few country-house owners partitioned their great halls, perhaps horizontally to give an extra bedroom floor, or – less commonly – vertically, to create reception rooms of manageable proportions. But in the 1930s it was still common to see old armour, antlers and ancient weapons decorating the walls of a baronial great hall, interspersed in that more well-travelled age with the occasional head of an ibis or a rhinoceros, with a tiger-skin rug spread out beside the hearth. A lick of paint might brighten things up: the Marquess of Lothian, who moved back into Blickling Hall in 1932 after years of letting his Norfolk estate, removed the stained glass from his great hall, a remarkable mixture of Jacobean and Georgian Gothic, took down most of the portraits and painted it white. The English hall was become 'the centre of great memories of a proud past', Hermann Muthesius told German readers of his *Das Englische Haus* in 1911.[7]

The twentieth century also understood that there was an easy answer to the question of what to do with the great hall – live in it.

It was their parents and grandparents who made the discovery. The gender-based zoning of the Victorian country house – drawing room and boudoir for the women, library, smoking room and billiards room for the men – meant that here and there families and guests began to use the hall as neutral territory. An organ or a grand piano might be installed – there was plenty of space, after all – and from here it was a short step to adding chairs and sofas where guests could listen to the music. In the 1930s Sir Charles Trevelyan often held dances, charades and other party games in the top-lit hall at Wallington, although the acoustics were so bad that house parties usually decamped to the drawing room for recitals.

'Halls of this sort always house a grand piano for music-making and sometimes a billiard-table,' Muthesius reported. 'The hall tends to become the comfortable all-purpose room of the house, in which each member of the family can follow his favourite pursuit and spend his time as he likes.'[8] It was precisely this flexibility, this absence of a defined function which appealed: in smaller country houses the lounge hall, as it became known in the 1920s, might even contain a dining table, returning it to its medieval roots. With high-backed sofas, writing tables and that must-have Arts and Crafts feature, an inglenook, the hall was another reception room, to the consternation of the architectural critic Harry Goodhard-Rendel, who complained about the curious fashion of sitting 'not in one's sitting rooms but in the hall outside them . . . with a stream of housemaids issuing with slop-pails from the bedrooms after breakfast in full view'.[9]

As far as other requirements for the modern country house were concerned, there was general agreement that size mattered; rather less agreement on what constituted the *right* size. In 1919 it was possible to announce that the big country house was a thing of the past and still to suggest that for a man of moderate means, the bare minimum accommodation must consist of three or four sitting rooms and ten bedrooms, with day and night nurseries for young children and servants' quarters to match. Sixteen years later the Conservative politician Sir Samuel Hoare sold his family seat, Sidestrand Hall in Norfolk, and twenty acres of gardens, complaining that it had all the inconveniences of a big house and 'none of the spaciousness that is so essential to country life'.[10] He and his wife would rather have 'a Petit Trianon in the middle of my woods and far away from the roads and noises of the modern world';[11] and in 1938 they commissioned John Seely and Paul Paget to design for them a pretty single-storey villa in the remaining grounds of Sidestrand, a shooting box which they planned to use in the summer.

The heart of Templewood, as it was called, was a central saloon about forty feet by thirty feet. 'It is a single big room that is needed in a small country house, and not the network of *cabinets particuliers* that Victorian England seemed to prefer,' said Hoare.[12] The saloon opened onto a south-facing loggia, with all the other rooms grouped around it. To the west there was a small entrance hall, cloakroom and WC, with maid's rooms and a guest bedroom. The east range consisted of separate bedrooms for Sir Samuel and his wife, Lady Maude; a small dining room; and in the north-east corner a kitchen, joined to the dining room by an increasingly popular feature, a servery. And the rest of the north side was filled with pantry, wine cellar, broom and linen cupboards and a servants' hall. The house was equipped with four bathrooms, for Sir Samuel, Lady Maude, their guests and the servants. If critics complained that Templewood was too small, said Sir Samuel, 'my answer is that no house can nowadays be too small'.[13] In any case, there was also a large garage block with more accommodation for staff and extra guests.

There was only one possible architectural style for this villa. During the Great War, when Sir Samuel headed a British intelligence mission in Rome, he took the opportunity to travel up to Vicenza to explore the architecture of Palladio. Ever since then he had worshipped him 'as the great master of the art of country life'. After Nuthall Temple, Nottinghamshire's own Villa Rotunda, was stripped and demolished in 1929, Hoare bought the portico, the ironwork for balustrading, swags, sphinxes to guard the drive and other pieces of stonework. Herbert Baker's demolition of Sir John Soane's Bank of England in the late 1920s provided Ionic columns for the loggia and the entrance facade. Seely and Paget did the rest.

The trend in new country houses was all towards compactness and convenience. Monsters like Middleton Park were rare. So were brand-new houses that functioned as their forebears had before

1914, as the headquarters of great agricultural estates. The large-scale country house was giving way to a more manageable house in the country, still with extensive gardens, perhaps, but without the let estate that was the norm at the beginning of the century. Homes with a smaller footprint were cheaper to heat, required fewer staff (and that meant lower wage bills and lower food bills) and they were generally easier to manage. Natural light was important, even for those who jibbed at the optimism of a liner-style sun deck on the roof: tall windows and well-lit bedrooms and corridors were the order of the day. 'Our first thoughts today', declared an anonymous *Country Life* critic in 1937, discussing what shape the contemporary country house should take, 'are of the amenities and technique of living – how a house shall be planned, not only to make the most of the site, of light and air and the view, but also to be efficient and economical in running.'[14]

The hall still had a part to play. It should be 'not too large as to be wasteful', said another *Country Life* writer, Randall Phillips, 'but yet sufficiently ample to give a generous welcome to the visitor and to serve as a household rendezvous'.[15] In practice this meant almost anything. Rhowniar, an Oswald Milne house overlooking the Aberdovey golf links and the sea, had a long outer hall which was in effect a ground-floor corridor; opening off it Milne created an 'inner hall' which was commended in the 1920s because it was 'comfortably furnished and it serves the purposes of a sitting-room'.[16]

At Ashcombe Tower on the south Devon coast, built in 1933–6 by Brian O'Rorke for the local MP, Major Ralph Rayner, the great hall was simply renamed. O'Rorke, who is best known for his modernist designs for the liners of the Orient Steam Navigation Company, produced a house which was all Arts and Crafts on the outside and Modern Movement on the inside, and tied the knot between past and present with a central great hall, forty feet by twenty-two feet and entered at one end, which he called simply 'the Big Room'. Concealed lighting and low sofas, rugs and curtains by Marion Dorn and an electric clock over the fireplace set the contemporary tone; but those contemporaries were quick to note the similarities between the position and function of the Big Room and its counterpart in a Tudor mansion. The introduction and reinvention of such a traditional space was, said one, 'natural today when we have abandoned many of the formalities that we have inherited from the eighteenth century'.[17]

Ashcombe incorporated typical 1930s flourishes: built-in bedroom furniture, flush walnut panelling, a cocktail bar tucked away beneath a half-landing, a newel post capped with a chromium-plated ball finial. But it was basically an Elizabethan H-plan, adapted to twentieth-century use. A morning room and study occupied most of one upright of the H, a dining room the other, with kitchens and domestic offices leading off it; and the cross-bar was the Big Room.

One shouldn't carry the comparison too far. Attached to the house was a purpose-built squash court with shower and changing rooms, one of half a dozen that appeared in Devon country houses in the 1920s and 1930s. (The court at Hazelwood House, Loddiswell, was made out of one half of a disused Congregational chapel next to the entrance drive; the other half, formerly a Sunday school, was converted into a billiard room.) At a country-house party in Scotland in the 1920s, a young Lady Marjorie Murray found herself playing squash, a game she'd never played in her life, with a very good-looking young man who turned out to be the reigning British squash champion. 'He weathered the resulting scene with great patience and kindness,' she remembered decades later.[18]

The first floor of Ashcombe Tower was filled with guest rooms; with the Rayners' bedroom suite, which came with built-in wardrobes and a blue and pink bathroom; and at the opposite end of the house from their bedroom, with a pair of day and night nurseries for their children. There were five servants' rooms in the attics along with a playroom for the children and another bathroom. Outbuildings included a garage for four cars, complete with petrol pumps.

In one other respect Ashcombe Tower was also entirely of its day: and that was in its relationship with the outdoors. The dining room had huge double French windows which opened onto

White walls, cherry-red chair coverings and fabrics, and furniture in ash burr in the dining room at Ashcombe Tower, Devon.

a south-facing loggia where the family could breakfast, with views out to sea; and just beside it, in the angle formed by the dining room and the service wing, O'Rorke supplied a swimming pool.

It sometimes feels as if the post-Armistice generation invented fresh air. In California, theorists like the naturopath Dr Philip Lovell, author of *Diet for Health by Natural Methods*, advocated fruit, vegetables and plenty of sunshine as a recipe for the good life, while Swiss clinics pioneered heliotherapy as a treatment for tuberculosis. In Germany, Hans Suren's *Der Mensch und die Sonne* went through sixty-seven editions between its publication in 1924 and its appearance in an English translation as *Man and Sunlight* three years later.* Suren turned sun worship into a religion, and he played the part of high priest with a messianic zeal. 'Greetings to you, you who are sun lovers,' he wrote in his introduction. 'You bear ardent longings in your hearts! Longings after warm sunshine, blue skies, light and nature; after victorious strength, spiritual loftiness and childlike faith.'[19] In England the architect Oliver Hill, who combined interests in nudism, adolescent girls and photography in a way that doesn't sit comfortably with twenty-first-century sensibilities, predicted that 'a maximum of sunlight and such facilities for recreation and exercise, dancing, swimming, and squash, will be large factors to be provided for in the modern house'.[20]

Sun worship had some curious impacts on the country house and its architecture. The most advanced modernist houses came supplied with big balconies and rooftop sun decks: the aeroplane-wing canopies that hover over the flat roof of Amyas Connell's High and Over are one of the more extreme examples. A few houses, and not only those built by modernists, were provided with sleeping porches, an import from the more reliable climate of California. The Biddulphs' bedroom at Rodmarton Manor, which was about as un-modernist a country house as one could imagine, was equipped with one.

Landfall, an Oliver Hill house of 1938–9 set amongst pines overlooking Poole Harbour in Dorset, is a sun-worshipper's house like no other of the period. The main living areas – a big staircase hall and an even bigger sitting room – quite literally opened onto a south-facing terrace, in that they were equipped with plate-glass screens in cedar frames running on tracks which could be rolled back. On the floor above, the principal bedrooms, also south-facing, gave onto a continuing balcony, while above them Hill created a glazed sunroom and roof terrace. As if all these opportunities for open-air living weren't enough, an external spiral stair of concrete

* One of the more plausible reasons for the phenomenal success of *Der Mensch und die Sonne* was the fact that it contained copious illustrations of semi-naked men and women.

Sliding south windows open on to the terrace in the living room of Oliver Hill's Landfall in Dorset, 1938–9.

linked the terrace with the balcony. Landfall caught the *zeitgeist* in other ways: Marion Dorn rugs, fitted furniture, a cocktail cabinet-cum-radiogram, and a projector 'lodged under the stairs [and] throwing through two apertures in the wall on to a screen in front of the windows'.[21]

Then there were the swimming pools. They were a rare but not unknown feature of the late-Victorian and Edwardian country-house landscape, when they tended to be called 'bathing pools', and were tucked discreetly out of sight in woodland or inside a temple in the park. There were always ornamental lakes, of course; but they were often visible from the house, which made them inappropriate for swimming or bathing. After the First World War, purpose-built swimming pools began to appear in increasing numbers. By the 1920s, two pre-war Lutyens houses had them: Marsh Court in Hampshire; and neo-Georgian Wittersham House

Technology in action: the boiler room at Charters in Berkshire, built for the industrialist Frank Parkinson in 1938.

scattered about the house, or if the battery charge dropped, then the smaller plant started automatically. If the castle required more power, the larger plant kicked in and the smaller one shut down; and on those rare occasions when even that wasn't enough, both plants operated simultaneously, generating 23.5 kW.

'As is usual with a large country house,' went an enthusiastic review of Kimbolton's system in 1939, 'electricity takes its full share of those domestic services which it can do so well.' Water was pumped round the castle's central heating system, which was presumably oil- or coal-fired; a small workshop was fitted with a powered lathe and a saw bench; and 'in the kitchen a small electric cooker has been installed for occasional use and a large refrigerator is operated electrically'.[26]

With a smaller house, and especially one which was close enough for a direct connection to the mains, it was possible to be even more ambitious. The Manor House at West Wick near Marlborough, a lovely five-bay ex-farmhouse with a Georgian facade and thirteenth-century innards, was connected to the mains and made all-electric in 1938. A combination of electric fires and low-temperature convection heaters did away with the need for a central heating system that would involve cutting through the structure of the house, and also got rid of 'that chilly feeling which is generally present in winter in a spacious house of this type'.[27] Light fittings in the reception rooms were either central electroliers or candle-type wall sconces; concealed lighting was used in the bedrooms; and four water heaters were installed, including a hundred-gallon heater for the main bathrooms upstairs and a more modest thirty-gallon heater for servants' bedrooms and the kitchen.

Getting an electrical supply was only one half of the story. Not for nothing did an advertisement for a firm specialising in the installation of electrical equipment for country houses claim that its system 'can be carried out without damage to the fabric of the buildings or to the decorations'.[28] An owner also had to have the building wired – easy enough in the case of a new house, or a major restoration, but not a task to be undertaken lightly if it involved chasing out rococo plasterwork or cutting a channel through a baroque mural. The guides at Stanford Hall in Leicestershire used to tell the story of how in the 1920s Lord and Lady Braye were baffled by the prospect of having to run cables through their long ballroom without wrecking its delicate eighteenth-century stuccowork. Then someone had a bright idea: they prised up a floorboard at one end and dropped a dead rabbit into the void; then they prised up a floorboard at the other end and unleashed a ferret, with a string tied to his collar. When the ferret had managed to negotiate the joists and reach the rabbit, the string was used to pull through a cable and hey presto! the problem was solved.

ONE UNUSUAL BY-PRODUCT of the general availability of electricity was the floodlighting of country houses. In 1931 the International Illumination Congress was held in Britain to mark the centenary of Michael Faraday's discovery of electromagnetic induction, the principle behind the electric generator and transformer. As part of the celebrations, the organising committee arranged for the floodlighting of an eclectic array of landmarks and monuments across the country, from Edinburgh Castle to the facade of the municipal baths in Stoke Newington and the new art deco Carreras cigarette factory in Camden Town, where 300 powerful electric lamps gave two-colour effects with four colour changes each minute. In all, fourteen London boroughs and fifty-four towns and cities took part in the scheme, along with hundreds of castles, cathedrals and churches.

In central London, hundreds of thousands of people turned out on the first night to see the capital 'touched by a magic wand', as a journalist from the *Illustrated London News* put it.[29] Throughout September, army searchlights illuminated St Paul's Cathedral and the steeples of Wren's City churches. St James's Park was transformed (by gaslight rather than electricity) into 'a nocturnal fairyland'.[30] The Tower of London, Tower Bridge, Big Ben, Nelson's Column and the National Gallery were all floodlit. The Houses of Parliament, said *The Times*, was 'the colour of old

'Flood-lighting will surely do great things in days to come', said The Times *in 1935.*

ivory, built into the gentle darkness'. Westminster Abbey 'wore a more mysterious look, as though all of it had vanished except the hollow, white, enclosing walls'.[31] Buckingham Palace, moon-coloured and lit by 250 electric floodlights, was the most beautiful sight of the evening. From the top of the 273-foot campanile of Westminster Cathedral, the public could look out on the pockets of bright light which flared across the city, an eerie dress rehearsal for the Blitz ten years later.

A few disapproving voices were raised. Complaints about the cost were silenced by an announcement that everyone – the manufacturers of the equipment, the contractors who installed them and the electricians who maintained them – had given their services for free. The *British Journal of Ophthalmology* huffily dismissed some of the illumination as 'merely a glare', before grudgingly admitting that 'occasionally, it rendered visible architectural features which are not ordinarily observed'.[32] The

Sibyl Colefax's showroom in Bruton Street.

in Britain; the prominent politician Lord Stanley and his wife Portia, who had once been touted as a bride for Edward. Tom Lamont, chair of the board of J. P. Morgan, and Robert Vansittart, the Foreign Office official who was exasperating everyone with his dark prophecies of a coming war with Germany, were there with their wives; so was the Polish pianist Artur Rubinstein.

As the evening wore on, other guests arrived: Winston Churchill and Noël Coward; Gerald Berners, forgiven for his P. of W. joke, and the society beauty Lady Diana Cooper, who was just about to go cruising down the Dalmatian coast with Edward and Wallis. Rubinstein played Chopin after dinner, which bored the king so that he stood up to take his leave; then Noël Coward sang 'Mad Dogs and Englishmen', which persuaded him to stay. It was a triumph, Harold Nicolson (who was there) reported to Vita (who was not). 'I was glad for Sibyl's sake, since I fear it is her last party in that charming house and never has it looked so lovely.'[4]

Sibyl Colefax's entertaining had a purpose. As well as being a society hostess, she was one of London's most successful decorators, a dealer in chintzes and wallpapers, in 'the most charming and carefully designed modern furniture', as her business card declared; in 'antique furniture, glass, china, with a special feature of Regency pieces'. Customers who visited Sibyl Colefax Ltd, her shop at 24 Bruton Street in fashionable Mayfair, were told that 'Everything here is different.'[5] And as Nicolson's comment revealed, the Bruton Street premises weren't her only showroom. She was adept at displaying her talents at Argyll House. 'From the moment that one arrived in the small panelled hall and savoured the aroma of dried rosemary burnt on a saucer,' said Cecil Beaton, 'one knew one had arrived in a completely different atmosphere.'[6] Argyll House was decorated with 'all the restraint of an eighteenth-century intellectual', he thought, although he reckoned that Sibyl never managed to achieve the same relaxed restraint in her work for clients. And those clients were the people she mixed with, artists and actors and noblemen. They were the friends who came to dinner.

The blurring of social and commercial boundaries between decorator and client was used ruthlessly by the decorator. Soon after the dinner for Edward VIII and Mrs Simpson, Sibyl was lobbying Wallis, who was a good friend, to use her influence with the king on her behalf. 'As far as I know', Wallis wrote back, kindly but firmly, 'neither Buckingham Palace nor the Fort [Fort Belvedere, the king's country house in Windsor Great Park] are having anything done in the way of "face lifting".'[7] In Charles Allom's case, the division between tradesman and social equal was even more blurred. Allom was knighted in 1913, had a country house of his own – Westbury Court in Gloucestershire – and sailed regularly with George V. Allom's ability to mix business with social life did a good deal to raise the status of the decorator between the wars. Of course that meant that when it came to the delicate matter of presenting his bill, there was occasionally some awkwardness. When he was working on William Randolph Hearst's St Donat's Castle in the 1930s, he supplied hundreds of items while politely leaving the matter of his buying commission up to his client: ten years later Hearst still owed White Allom £222,000 – the equivalent of tens of millions of pounds today – and the decorator had to sue to get his money.

The big difference between a professional architect-furnisher like Sir Charles Allom and society decorators like Sibyl Colefax was training. Most Mayfair decorators didn't have any, relying instead on their experience of remodelling their own homes and for inspiration on visiting the homes of their friends, on browsing antique shops and auctions, and on the high-quality halftone illustrations, particularly of historic interiors, which had been coming onto the market for the past decade or so. In 1909 Francis Lenygon allowed his name to appear on the title page of *The Decoration and Furniture of English Mansions during the Seventeenth and Eighteenth Centuries*; and five years later on two volumes for Batsford on historic interiors, *Decoration in England from 1660 to 1770* and *Furniture in England from 1660 to 1770*, although all were in fact ghostwritten by the furniture historian Margaret Jourdain. A. D. F. Hamlin, professor of architectural history at Columbia, produced a two-volume *History of Ornament* (1916, 1923) expressly commending it to 'teachers and students of architecture and decorative design, and to designers generally'.[8] Then there were the magazines: *Vogue* to find out what period was in fashion; *Country Life* to understand why.

It was the business of actually decorating one's own home that set so many Society decorators on the path to their own little showroom off Grosvenor Square. Sibyl Colefax's interest dated back to 1912, when she and her husband took a long lease on Old Buckhurst, the remains of a mansion built by the Sackvilles in the early sixteenth century. Little was left except a gatehouse, an oast house and some nondescript stables; but 'the place was full of magic', remembered Sibyl, and their architect, Cecil Brewer (best known today for his designs with partner Arnold Smith for the National Museum of Wales in Cardiff) managed to maintain that magic while turning the tumbledown country house into a comfortable modern home. Sibyl bought up oak furniture from England and the Low Countries 'which in time and in character complete the picture', said an approving H. Avray Tipping when Old Buckhurst was written up in *Country Life* in 1919.[9] Two years later, their finances looking a little rocky, the Colefaxes sold the lease on Old Buckhurst and moved out of the town house they also occupied at Onslow Square in South Kensington and consolidated their fortunes by moving to Argyll House, which was within easy reach of central London and at the same time functioned as what its architect Giacomo Leoni had called 'a small country house'.[10]

By 1930 Sir Arthur Colefax's practice at the Bar was shrinking, a result of his increasing deafness, and Sibyl began to think of interior decoration as a way of propping up the Colefax fortunes. She first began to 'help' her friends, and quickly found that they liked her ideas and were prepared to pay for them. She worked for a time for another London decorator, Dolly Mann, and then took up an offer from the antique dealers Stair & Andrew to open a first-floor showroom at their Bruton Street premises, in return for sharing her contacts with them. 'I do hope the shop is doing well,' wrote one of her friends in September 1930. It was: on Christmas Eve 1931 she told Harold Nicolson over lunch at Boulestin's in Covent Garden that she had made £2,000 that year.

Sir John Lavery's painting of Syrie Maugham and Sibyl Colefax on the staircase at Sibyl's home, Argyll House, in the 1920s. The pair were rivals and next-door neighbours.

Time hasn't been kind to Sibyl's interiors. Only one is known to have survived from these years: the pink-and-white bedroom she created for the Marchioness of Anglesey at Plas Newydd in Wales. There are also photographs of work she did for Evelyn Waugh's brother Alec at Edrington, a Queen Anne rectory in Hampshire. She was recommended by Evelyn, who told his brother, 'you'll be saved the kind of mistakes that are made by decorators who are not used to dealing with persons of quality, and she's very businesslike'.[11] In fact she wasn't. She was always late for appointments, and the Waughs were bewildered by the way she filled their house with pieces of furniture which she wrongly thought might fit, and annoyed to find that the curtains in their library looked odd. It was because they had been hung inside out.

Interior decoration was an intense and competitive business. At the height of her success in the late 1920s and early 1930s that other great doyenne of society decorators, Syrie Maugham, who was saluted by *Vogue* 'for teaching us to use white in our houses . . . and for being one of the few lady decorators who kept her head during the modernistic deluge by consistently combining old and new',[12] spent six months of the year in England and six in America. She had warehouses and workshops in a four-storey factory building in Chelsea, a stone's throw from the Embankment. Altogether Syrie Ltd employed more than twenty people, as well as contracting out work and buying in antiques, papers and other items. Textiles and wallpapers were imported from France. Syrie bought used furniture from a shop just off Marylebone Road, and replicas of seventeenth-century pieces from a firm in High Wycombe. She used a north London firm to make her curtains and pelmets from textiles bought in France. She rarely designed items herself. Like Sibyl Colefax, her skills lay in combining things to create a look – and in promoting herself. She cultivated Wallis Simpson, never quite achieving the same intimacy as Sibyl, but profiting in other ways. She sold furniture to Mrs Simpson and decorated several rooms at the Prince of Wales's Fort Belvedere, reckoned by contemporaries to be some of her best work.

*

PIERO MALACRIDA DE SAINT-AUGUST was the epitome of the society decorator, a figure who would have been invented if he hadn't already existed. He was artistic, aristocratic and Italian, with an equally aristocratic British wife, Louisa, who played the part of bright young thing to perfection. He was an ex-cavalry officer. She was an aviator, a racing driver, a poet and playwright and theatre designer. Her portrait, by Flora Lion or in miniature by Alfred Praga, hung in the Royal Academy; gossip columnists took care to mention her in their columns, where she was always 'the beautiful Marchesa Malacrida', always 'the loveliest figure in the room'.[13]

This golden couple was seen in the right places. When the Court Circular mentioned a musical party in Portland Place, they were there, chatting to the Duchess of Rutland and the Egyptian chargé d'affaires. Another night they might be at a reception at the Polish Embassy, or a Belgrave Square fund-raiser for the League of Nations, or a charity garden fete in aid of a children's hospital. It seemed that whenever there was a masked ball or a society wedding or a fashionable Mayfair at-home in the late 1920s and early 1930s, the Marchese and Marchesa Malacrida were on the invitation list.

Like other semi-professional decorators of the period, Malacrida was a master of social connection and self-publicity. In an article on 'Modern Tendencies in Decoration' which he wrote for *Vogue* in 1928, he set out his stall, half-smiling, tolerant, urbane. Applauding the new, more intelligent interest that people were taking in their homes after the 'colouristic blunders' of their Victorian and Edwardian forebears, he nevertheless lamented that taste seemed locked in the past. All that seemed on offer were

> The cottagey-inglenooky-pickled-oak school; the walnutty-Queen-Annish, real or false, but chiefly false; a few sporadic cases of Adam and Regency, decorous mahogany being tolerated if believed to be extremely good; a few endemic cases of Victorian-papier-mâché-dogs-in-the-hearth-glass-shaded-flowers for the aspidistra section of the community; and then, above all, triumphant and unchallenged, the Hollywood-Italo-Spanish.[14]

At least these looks were safe, he said, and both client and designer pretty much knew what the end result would be. Things weren't so simple for decorators like him, who cast the past aside and worked in the modern manner. Materials weren't obtainable in the right colours; furniture had to be specially made; every 'dreary little detail', from the door handles to the tassels on the end of a blind cord, had to be designed from scratch. Plumbers and plasterers and carpenters and electricians informed you that 'they have worked for twenty years for Sir Blankety Blank and that pipes or switches or what-nots as you want them are simply not done'. And always in the background was the client, wanting to know exactly what you were going to do to their dining room or bathroom – 'a very difficult and embarrassing question this, because, at that stage of things, one often has only very hazy ideas about the finished article one is going to turn out'.[15]

There is something endearing about the bewildered, self-deprecating tone that Malacrida adopts here, especially his honesty in admitting, as he does, that his pleasure at completing an interior is always marred by the knowledge that in ten or twenty years' time someone is going to walk in and say, 'Isn't it pathetic? The poor fellow thought he was doing something new.'[16] But there is nothing self-deprecating about the photographs that accompany Malacrida's essay. They all show his recent work at 20 Portman Square for the immensely rich industrialist Samuel Courtauld, perhaps the greatest collector of French Impressionism in the country. Courtauld had taken over the lease at Portman Square the previous year and begun a careful restoration of the Adam staterooms. His wife, however, clearly wanted something modern. Malacrida provided it, in the form of a large studio-boudoir at the top of the house, with wall lights by Oliver Messel and a *trompe l'oeil* blind by the painter and set-designer John Armstrong, showing nude figures cavorting on tightropes and clambering up ladders into open windows. A bathroom had enormous fish-scale panels on the lower walls, beneath a ceiling in which more figures by Armstrong danced and juggled and worshipped the sun.

Malacrida's career as a designer is mysterious, the narrative fragmented. He indulged in a little property speculation on his own account, buying flats in smart London addresses, remodelling them and selling them on. But most of his work seems to have been undertaken for White Allom & Co. Between 1926 and 1929 the Malacridas lived in and decorated an eighteenth-century house in Upper Brook Street, Mayfair. As so often happened with the decorators of the period, none of this work has survived, but according to the *Survey of London* the marchese created 'an exotic ambience with a strong Italianate flavour', painting the ceiling of the main staircase* as 'the underside of an arboreal bower'.[17] Around the same time he did some unspecified work for Nancy Cunard, who lived nearby in Grosvenor Square.

In 1929 the Malacridas moved to Grosvenor Street, just off the Square, and their apartment featured in another *Vogue* article that November. The anonymous writer was intrigued by a set of interiors which were relentlessly modern, without a hint of Sibyl Colefax's muted neo-Georgian pastels or Syrie Ltd's off-whites and painted Spanish wood carvings. Instead there were steel furniture and black glass in the marchese's bedroom, built-in furniture and shelving – and a bar with washable white walls, so that the Malacridas and their friends could draw pictures on them with coloured crayons and then wipe them clean and start again. 'The idea is typical of the modern restlessness of spirit,' said *Vogue*, 'and the execution is also typical of the times, as it encourages a more or less artistic self-expression.'[18]

It must have been through his links with Samuel Courtauld that the marchese obtained his only country-house commission, and the work for which he is best known today. In 1933 Samuel's brother Stephen Courtauld acquired a Crown lease on Eltham Palace, six miles from Westminster on the outskirts of London. Eltham had once been the residence of kings: a vast, moated complex of lodgings and courts where Edward IV celebrated Christmas with

* A photograph of this staircase in 1926 survives, showing lanterns perched on tasselled posts, painted plaster figures in robes perched in alcoves, and the arboreal bower. It all looks very odd.

2,000 guests and retainers, where Cardinal Wolsey took his oath as Lord Chancellor of England and Henry VIII walked in the *allées* and arbours with Catherine of Aragon. But it had never recovered from being stripped by Oliver Cromwell in the 1650s. Now only the medieval Great Hall was left, and there were plans to surround it with a housing estate.

Stephen Courtauld was happy to restore the hall, but he didn't want to live in a medieval ruin. He and his wife Ginie decided to attach a modern house to the remains of the palace. Their architects, John Seely and Paul Paget, produced a splayed U-plan, with the old hall as one arm, the new house as the other, and a triangular entrance hall in the angle formed by the two wings. It was only partly successful: Seely and Paget opted for a slightly old-fashioned exterior based on Wren's work at Hampton Court, all red brick with stone dressings; and although the Courtaulds were pleased, critical opinion was not favourable. 'An admirably designed but unfortunately sited cigarette factory,' was the verdict of historian G. M. Young.[19] Sir Herbert Baker, Lutyens' partner at New Delhi and the first architect of Port Lympne, spent a pleasant day picnicking with Seely and Paget in the garden and then went away and announced that 'Romance has gone from Eltham.'[20] 'Very unusual' was as far as Christopher Hussey was prepared to go in *Country Life*.[21]

The interiors were a different matter. Stephen Courtauld was reserved and deeply introspective. His half-Hungarian, half-Italian wife Ginie, was not. She was a marchesa herself, on account of a previous marriage to an Italian nobleman, and had a pet ring-tailed lemur which she bought in Harrods and a snake tattoo above her right ankle. No doubt both the Courtaulds were responsible for the fact that Eltham was a very modern mansion, with electric fires, gas central heating, internal telephones, a loudspeaker system to relay the sound of gramophone records around the house, and a centralised vacuum-cleaner system in the basement. But one suspects that the vitality of the interiors owed most to Ginie.

The triangular entrance hall, a startling introduction to the house, was the work of the Swedish designer Rolf Engströmer,

The entrance hall of Eltham Palace (1933–6), created by Rolf Engströmer with marquetry panels by Jerk Werkmäster.

who also produced the blackbean and walnut furniture which stood on a circular rug commissioned from Marion Dorn, whose bold, geometrically patterned carpets and textiles could be found in fashionable London interiors from the famous White Room in Syrie Maugham's Chelsea house to the lobby of Claridge's. But the two most spectacular features of the hall are the shallow glass dome which lights it; and the blackbean veneer which lines it, with marquetry panels by Engströmer's fellow countryman, Jerk Werkmäster, depicting buildings in Italy and Scandinavia. The room is guarded by two larger-than-life marquetry figures, also by Werkmäster – a Roman soldier and a horned Viking bearing a halberd, who flank the glazed entrance doors.

Seely and Paget decorated the guest bedrooms, fitting them out with built-in liner-style laminated furniture. But if one had to identify an *ensemblier* who defined the Eltham look, it was Malacrida. Paget resented his arrival, later claiming ill-naturedly that the commission came because of Sir Charles Allom, 'who sailed a yacht in Cowes week and was very much received by royalty'; and explaining that 'Mrs Courtauld . . . was of Italian–Rumanian extraction' and was thus friendly with the marchese. Whatever the reason – and the connection with Samuel Courtauld seems the most likely – Malacrida was given the task of designing the drawing room, the dining room, the library and Ginie's bedroom suite.

He had hardly begun to think about the commission when tragedy struck. At the end of September 1934 he and his wife went down for the weekend to a cottage they had borrowed in the Chilterns, just north of Henley-on-Thames. He went back to Grosvenor Street on Monday morning, leaving Louisa to follow on in their car later in the week.

On Wednesday morning the marchesa was driving along the Henley–London road with their pet spaniel in the passenger seat when for no apparent reason she swerved and braked hard. The car skidded through a hedge and rolled down a forty-foot embankment. The marchesa broke her neck. The jury returned a verdict of 'Accidental Death'. Louisa was thirty-eight. Stephen and Ginie Courtauld came to the funeral.

Malacrida went abroad for a month. He sold off his library, and published *Finale*, a collection of his wife's letters to him. 'Under their brilliant and witty surface is hidden a beautiful love-story,' wrote a reviewer in the *Observer*.[22] And then he disappeared. No more mentions in *Vogue* or the Court Circular. No more appearances at receptions and charity balls. Nothing, really, to earn him more than a footnote in history.*

Except for Eltham Palace. The drawing room, which like Malacrida's other Eltham interiors was executed by White Allom & Co. to his designs, was comfortable rather than exciting, with antique rugs, cream walls and painted faux ceiling timbers,

* Malacrida died in 1980.

although it looked rather like the triumphant and unchallenged Hollywood-Italo-Spanish interiors he had dismissed in the 1920s. But it was specifically designed to show some of Stephen Courtauld's collection of Italian pictures and furniture, so perhaps he can be forgiven.

The dining room was all Malacrida – black marble and ebonised woods inlaid with bold geometrical patterns, concealed beam lighting to show off Stephen's landscapes by Turner and Crome, and most remarkable of all, a ceiling of shining aluminium leaf. 'Not really quite our taste,' recalled Paget, still smarting from having the interior decoration of Eltham taken away and given to Malacrida. 'It had a silver ceiling.'[23]

On the first floor was Ginie's suite, 'the outstanding decorative achievement', according to an admiring Christopher Hussey.[24] The marchese lined Ginie's oval bedroom with pale pinkish maple and weathered sycamore veneer, punctuated with pilasters, like

Ginie Courtauld's bedroom at Eltham Palace, designed by Piero Malacrida.

some shrine to an ancient goddess. The walls were inlaid with exquisite marquetry in patterns which led Hussey to strive so hard for definition that he invented an entirely new style – 'modern Swedish rococo'. Curved doorways opened onto the landing and into the goddess's inner sanctum, a bathroom lined with onyx and gold mosaic, its bath set back in a golden recess and presided over by a marble Psyche. Even in an era which excelled in the creation of beautiful bathrooms, an era in which *Vogue* declared that bathrooms looked more expensive than any other room in the house, Ginie's bathroom – her entire suite, in fact – stood out as a redefinition of country-house style: modern without falling into the easy vocabulary of the *moderne* or the stark white austerity of modernism; opulent without vulgarity; making use of traditional materials but refusing to bow down to tradition. It makes one wish that more of Marchese Malacrida's interior designs had survived.

'We would have done something much better,' said Paget.[25]

CHAPTER NINE

The New Georgians

MALACRIDA'S TASTE, urban and urbane, helped to make Eltham Palace the outstanding example of high deco country-house design. But its sleek lines were a step too far for most owners, as they were for Seely and Paget. The pull of the past was just too great to resist: not a scholarly, 'authentic' reconstruction of the past, but a more lyrical evocation of a world that had been lost – if indeed it had ever existed at all.

The most influential country-house decorators of the interwar years, then, were not marchesas with flair or society matrons with an eye for modernity, but an unlikely young American couple with a taste for the English eighteenth century.

Ronald Tree and Nancy Field were twenty-one when they met aboard the Cunard liner *Mauretania*, bound for England on the return leg of its first transatlantic voyage since returning to private service after the war. Nancy, already a widow, was on her way to spend Christmas 1918 with her aunt and namesake, Nancy Astor, at the latter's Buckinghamshire country house, Cliveden. Her husband, Henry Field, the grandson of a Chicago department-store magnate, had died the previous year after only five months of marriage. Ronnie, who was Henry's cousin, had known Nancy for some time.

Their shipboard romance outlasted the voyage. Eighteen months later they were married at the Wren church of St James's Piccadilly. The bride, who was an orphan as well as a widow, was given away by her uncle, Viscount Astor.

Ronnie Tree had been raised in Warwickshire, initially in Ashorne Hill, a big Jacobethan mansion built in the 1890s; then in one of the farmhouses on the estate, after his father was forced to rent out the main house when his mother, who had the family money, ran off with a young naval officer (who was to become Earl Beatty, First Sea Lord). Shortly before Ronald and Nancy's wedding, Ronald sold Ashorne Hill and the young couple spent the first years of their married life in America, where the groom pursued a career in journalism and his bride remodelled Mirador, an antebellum family home in Virginia, with help from a family friend, the architect William Adams Delano, who turned Mirador into one of Virginia's most handsome Georgian Revival country houses.

Fox hunting was one of Ronnie's passions, a legacy of his adolescence spent in England. Each winter the Trees crossed the Atlantic to ride to hounds with the Quorn and the Cottesmore, and in 1926 they upped sticks and came to live permanently in England, partly so that Ronnie could pursue a political career – he had been told that his English accent precluded anything of the sort in America – but also because he had been invited to become joint master of the prestigious Pytchley Hunt, which met in some of the finest hunting country in England, along the border between Northamptonshire and Leicestershire.

For a time, the Trees rented Cottesbrooke Hall, a beautiful redbrick Queen Anne house in the heart of Pytchley country, and supposed to be the model for Jane Austen's Mansfield Park. But Cottesbrooke was on the market, so in 1927 they took a lease on Kelmarsh Hall, three miles away.

Northamptonshire is one of those not-quite-in-the-Cotswolds counties that have been overlooked by topographers and seekers after the picturesque. Dismissed by travellers in the eighteenth century as 'disagreeable . . . [all] wide pastures, and hopeless views' and known mainly in the twentieth for its fox hunting and its boot and shoe factories, it has always been somewhere to pass through on the way to something more exciting, unless one was interested in boots or shoes or chasing foxes.[1]

Yet Northamptonshire's country houses rank with the best. There are rambling Elizabethan beauties like Deene Park and the ruined Kirby Hall; baroque splendour at Boughton and Hawksmoor's Easton Neston; gentle classicism in Lamport Hall and Cottesbrooke. And for reticent, quiet beauty, Kelmarsh is hard to beat. Designed by James Gibbs and built *c.*1728–32, it is a two-

COUNTRY LIFE

The entrance hall at Kelmarsh Hall, Northamptonshire, photographed in 1933. An equestrian portrait by Alfred Munnings of Ronnie Tree as Master of the Pytchley Hunt hangs over the chimneypiece.

storeyed, redbrick house of seven bays, the centre, which contains the hall and saloon, breaking out very gently under a triangular pediment. There are low pavilions to either side. When the Trees moved in on a ten-year repairing lease, the place was run-down and disfigured with various Victorian accretions. Its owner, Claude Lancaster, was two years younger than them and happy enough to let his tenants tidy it up while he pursued his family interests in coal and iron in Nottinghamshire.

The remodelling of Kelmarsh – and it was more of a gentle facelift than a wholesale reinvention – was a collaboration between the Trees and a stable of artists and craftspeople. The architect Paul Phipps, who had worked in Lutyens' office and was married to Nancy Astor's sister Nora, was put in charge of the modernisation work and it was he who installed modern heating, plumbing and electric light. William Adams Delano, who had remodelled Mirador for Nancy Tree, designed the library panelling. A painter called Mr Kick advised on colour schemes, and for help with textiles the Trees went to Elden Ltd on Duke Street, one of Mayfair's best-known firms of interior decorators.

The proprietrix of Elden Ltd, Ethel Bethell, was a 'genius in the arrangement of old damask, brocades and painted or embroidered stuffs';[2] and she as much as the Trees and their craftsmen was responsible for the Kelmarsh look. She provided the brocade curtains in the hall, and a set of more elaborate swagged silk curtains in blue-grey for the saloon. She also supplied a complete dressing room, created for a decorators' exhibition at Olympia in 1927 and bought in its entirety; and decorated Nancy Tree's bedroom, which had walls hung with white silk and curtains to match and a specially made bed hung with white damask trimmed with silver lamé. Old gilt mirrors and gilt finials to the bed created an effect which Nancy called 'ice with a glint of gold'.[3]

Elsewhere there was Chinese hand-painted eighteenth-century wallpaper acquired from a house in Norfolk, Aubusson carpets and Chippendale dining chairs, Italian painted furniture. The colours were generally pale and the overall effect was comfortable without clutter, restrained and in keeping with the spirit of the place. It spoke of a sophisticated and complex relationship with the past rather than slavish imitation. Above all, the Trees' Kelmarsh was quietly elegant.

Nancy loved Kelmarsh. In 1948, after the failure of her marriage to Ronald Tree, she took as her third husband Claude Lancaster, and her friends were convinced that her emotional attachment was to Kelmarsh rather than its owner – an impression confirmed when this marriage also failed after only three years, and Lancaster was forced to cut off the electricity to Kelmarsh before Nancy would leave.*

But that was later. In 1933 Ronnie Tree came into his inheritance and, having taken out British citizenship, he was elected to Parliament as Conservative MP for Harborough in Leicestershire. That June the Trees were out driving in Oxfordshire with Claude Lancaster's uncle, Crawley de Crespigny, when they came upon Ditchley Park, another Gibbs house, but much larger and grander than Kelmarsh, with about thirty bedrooms and dressing rooms and seven reception rooms. They talked their way in to see it, ignoring the objections of an ancient butler in a red wig who protested that his master, the 17th Viscount Dillon, had just died.

Dillon had been a well-known antiquary, the first curator of the Tower of London armouries and chair of the National Portrait Gallery. His nephew inherited the title, but not the antiquarian interests, and he was in the process of dispersing Dillon's collections. What the interlopers saw, Ronnie recalled later, was 'an unforgettable picture of magnificence and accumulated junk . . . a Sleeping Beauty waiting to be called back to life'.[4] A week or two later the 18th viscount put the Ditchley Park estate of 3,500 acres onto the market, together with its 'stately mansion rich in historical associations'.[5]

Ronnie bought it.

Like Kelmarsh, the refurbishing of Ditchley was a collaborative effort. Ronnie bought the grand pieces of furniture that he felt

* Claude was a regular guest of the Trees in the 1930s. Ronald Tree's daughter by his second marriage later suggested he was Nancy's long-time lover and that this was the real reason why the Trees' marriage failed.

a stately home required, and the good paintings, while his wife was responsible for the overall look, the choice of fabrics and the arrangement of the furniture. They made a great team, and long after their divorce their son Michael recalled that 'my parents, from a decorating point of view, were a marvellous pair'.[6] And there were other members of that team. Paul Phipps supervised the building work again, and again he installed decent lighting and bathrooms. (When the Trees took possession of Ditchley there were no bathrooms at all, and they had to grope their way to their bedroom by the light of acetylene lamps.) Ethel Bethell had died in 1932, and Elden Ltd was now being run by the Dutch decorator Herman Schrijver. The Trees didn't use him, perhaps considering him too modern, too flamboyant in his use of colour. Instead they bought chintzes and furnishings from a range of other London decorators.

They also employed the French interior designer Stéphane Boudin, director (and later president) of the prestigious Paris firm of Maison Jansen. After parting from her husband, Olive Wilson Filmer – or Lady Baillie as she now was – used Boudin to create a series of interiors at Leeds Castle which blended English and French eighteenth-century themes; and in 1935 the *ensemblier* designed an astonishing rococo dining room for Chips Channon's Belgrave Square house, based on the Hall of Mirrors in the Amalienburg near Munich. ('It will shimmer in blue and silver,' wrote Channon in his diary. 'It will shock and perhaps stagger London. And will cost us over £6,000.'[7]) The project for which Boudin is best remembered today was still a long way in the future – his redecoration of the White House for the Kennedys in 1961–3.

Ronnie and Nancy Tree weren't in the market for Bavarian rococo. They bought Ditchley Park at a time when the so-called New Georgian Age was flourishing in all its restrained elegance, even as George V, who had given his name to it, was nearing the end of his life. There had been a burst of enthusiasm for New Georgianism when the king came to the throne in 1910: Harrods opened a Georgian Restaurant in 1911, and later a Georgian Salon. Harold Monro and Edward Marsh published the first of their five

The white drawing room at Ditchley Park, Oxfordshire, in 1934.

anthologies of *Georgian Poetry* in 1912. Thomas Hardy talked of living 'in neo-Georgian days'.[8] Fashion commentators talked of the modern woman as a 'Neo-Georgian [with] a boyish smile which matches her two-piece suit'.[9] As the reign wore on and modernist literature, art and architecture fragmented and mystified, the gentler and more conservative New Georgians found themselves looking more and more to the Old Georgians for solace, and for inspiration.

An indication of the long eighteenth century's popularity can be seen in the story of Sir Philip Sassoon's Royal Northern Hospital exhibitions. In 1928, Sassoon began to host a series of annual exhibitions in his Park Lane mansion in aid of the Royal Northern, where he was on the board. The first, an eclectic display of 'Early English Needlework and Furniture' which included the veil worn by Mary Queen of Scots at her execution and William

that the life of the house in this particular incarnation stretched back two centuries rather than a year or so. Little wonder that other new owners of old country houses should try to achieve the same effect.

Because in 1944 Ronald would buy Nancy Sibyl Colefax's share in the firm of Colefax & Fowler (Sibyl took on the young designer John Fowler as a partner in 1938), and because she would go on, as Nancy Lancaster, to a glittering post-war career as an interior decorator, the temptation is to give Nancy most of the credit for Ditchley. In his autobiography, Ronald Tree makes no mention at all of Stéphane Boudin, whose idea it was to bleach some of the fabrics. Sibyl Colefax and Syrie Maugham were involved in some way, even if only as suppliers. But Ronald preferred to attribute good ideas, such as the discovery and reinstatement of a streaked ochre and orange beneath eight layers of paint in the little hall, to his wife; or to use the vague and inclusive 'we'. 'We' emptied the entrance hall and painted it a light green; 'we' demolished a wall between two small libraries to create a fifty-foot space which eventually became the principal sitting room.

THE GREAT MAYFAIR DECORATORS were such accomplished self-publicists that it seems as if they completely dominated the 1920s and 1930s, as they vied with each other for the lucrative privilege of creating a new drawing room for David and Wallis, a new bedroom suite for this earl or that plutocrat. They didn't. Look around an English country house today, and you will see how pervasive was the taste of discerning amateurs Ronald and Nancy Tree.

But what about the legions of new brides and new chatelaines ordering willow-green silk damask from Waring & Gillow, finding fine old furniture in the corners of a saloon or long gallery? Their tastes in interior decoration, still surviving in hundreds of country houses around England, were gleaned from weekends at the homes of friends and neighbours and copies of *Vogue* or *Country Life*. Their contributions have passed almost unnoticed by historians of the decorative arts. But if any one group typified the country-house interior between the wars, it was them.

These less adventurous country-house owners, unashamedly wanting the 'so-called good taste' dismissed by the experts as walls panelled with pine stripped from old discarded Georgian houses, all limed to greyness, might go to the department-store ateliers. Maples, Harrods and Waring & Gillow all ran perfectly competent decorating operations.[19] The vast majority of owners, however, spurned the off-the-shelf drawing room or boudoir, and at the same time rejected the expense of engaging a firm like White Allom or Syrie Ltd. Instead, they did it themselves – perhaps not with the flair and judgement of Nancy and Ronnie Tree, but with enthusiasm.

When Loelia Ponsonby became the Duke of Westminster's third duchess in 1930 at the age of twenty-eight and moved into the vast Victorian pile that was Eaton Hall in Cheshire, she found a housekeeper in black bombazine with a bunch of keys chained to her waist who acted like Mrs Danvers in *Rebecca*; a pack of inbred dachshunds who were not house-trained; and suits of armour on the grand staircase which were padded with pink leather that protruded obscenely between greave and cuisse. Her husband also kept a cartload of Himalayan monkeys on an ornamental island in the lake, and a Brazilian capybara (a kind of giant guinea pig and the largest rodent in the world) who ran loose in the gardens.

Bendor's two previous marriages had not been happy. None of his relationships were happy. Loelia, who was twenty-three years younger than her autocratic husband, came from a well-connected but poor background: although her father was keeper of the privy purse to George V with apartments in St James's Palace and a medieval moated manor house in Surrey, she was used to making her own underclothes and at one point in her youth had to be taken out of school because her parents couldn't pay the fees. She was keen to put her own stamp on the private wing at Eaton, and Bendor, who could never be accused of numbering excessive thrift among his many faults, encouraged her to order anything she liked, and to bring in pieces from the main staterooms of the house.

She didn't go to a Malacrida or a Sibyl or a Syrie. She didn't order up interiors from Maples or distressed damasks from Harrods. Instead she did it herself. Her bedroom was panelled and painted a pale fawn. There was an embroidered Queen Anne bedspread on the bed, green velvet bed curtains and pale pink sheets of crêpe de Chine decorated in satin appliqué. She had a big dressing room of her own – Bendor slept in his own room, in a bed hung with blue taffeta which clashed with the blue walls – and a connecting bathroom with a bath of fawn-coloured marble which spouted water through a lion's mouth.

> My sitting-room was [she recalled] the most successful of all the rooms I decorated. On the walls loose, willow-green silk-damask hung in gentle folds above the pine skirting board. At one end a French armorial tapestry just fitted above a green velvet sofa. The carpet was a bronze-toned Aubusson, and the same colours were picked up in a painted leather screen, the greens and red-browns complementing each other perfectly. Between the windows was a magnificent pair of Chinoiserie lacquer cupboards and in the bay there was a Carlton House writing-table, with a semi-circle of little drawers surmounted by a gilt gallery. A Waterford glass chandelier glittered overhead, and the final touch was [an] enchanting Hogarth which we hung above the mantelpiece.[20]

Eaton Hall was scarcely sixty years old, and a monument to Victorian Gothic Revivalism to boot. That didn't stop Loelia reaching for the long eighteenth century. She was a New Georgian.

CHAPTER TEN

The Princess Bride and her Brothers

All of George V's children acquired country houses of their own between the wars, although some managed it sooner than others. And for all except the Prince of Wales, marriage was the catalyst.

Mary was the first. In 1922, when she was twenty-four, the Princess Royal married Henry, Viscount Lascelles, the 40-year-old son and heir of the Earl of Harewood. 'I dread the idea of losing her,' wrote the king, 'but thank God she will live in England.'[1] The newly-weds' London home was the Palladian Chesterfield House in South Audley Street, reckoned to have one of the finest marble staircases in London, and one of the last surviving great mansions in the capital. But the Harewood estates were concentrated in Yorkshire, and besides the principal seat of Harewood House near Leeds, then still occupied by the princess's elderly father-in-law, the family owned Goldsborough Hall, a Jacobean house ten miles to the north-east and variously used as a dower house, a shooting box and a convenient country home for the married heir-in-waiting.

Goldsborough had been let since the 1890s, but the long-time tenant, a Mrs Lamb, obligingly vacated it for the couple, even giving the princess a brace of peacocks as a house-warming present. They moved in at the end of the year.

Goldsborough Hall was an attractive gabled pile of red brick on the main street of the little village that shared its name. It was big, with twenty-two bedrooms, four oak-panelled reception rooms and a striking oak staircase of the early seventeeth century which wound right up through the house. After an initial surge of publicity when the village was swamped with sightseers from Leeds and Mary refused to set foot outside for fear of being mobbed, she settled into the congenial life of a twentieth-century

Princess Mary with her eldest son at Goldsborough Hall, Yorkshire, in about 1923.

noblewoman – a life which offered the privileges of being royal without the responsibilities. She hadn't enjoyed her official public duties before her marriage, and now she slipped into the role of chatelaine, revelling in the relative independence it gave her. 'She would have occupied a throne with distinction,' wrote the anonymous author of a fawning 1929 biography, 'but to be queen of her own household has more truly satisfied her ambitions.'[2]

The same biography, which claimed to be 'published with the approval of her royal highness', gave a gushing account of a typical day for the princess at Goldsborough. It began with a visit to the nursery – the Lascelles had a son less than a year after their marriage, and a second the following year – followed by breakfast with her husband. The rest of her morning was spent dealing with an avalanche of correspondence: begging letters, requests for advice or a job or a reference, invitations to open a fete or become a patron of something. Her lady-in-waiting usually sifted through all the letters first, 'but every letter, unless of a wholly trivial nature, is brought to her notice'.[3] After this, menus would be brought up for her approval, followed by a stroll in the gardens and then a quiet lunch. Afternoons were spent either paying calls or receiving visitors with her husband. If Lascelles was away, she sometimes went over to see her in-laws at Harewood. 'The evenings were spent with books or music. The Princess is an excellent musician, with a taste for modern composers.'[4]

It wasn't an arduous life. Nor was it a fair picture. In spite of her reluctance to play a big part in public life, Mary's royal rank and her position as the wife of Lord Lascelles meant that she was obliged to do rather more than inspect menus and play the latest composition by Elgar or Edward German. The newspapers of the 1920s show her giving out the annual prizes to nursing staff at Leeds General Infirmary one week and representing the Benevolent and Orphan Fund at a union conference the next; opening an exhibition of disabled soldiers' embroidery at Norfolk House and being guest of honour at a matinee in aid of the Waifs and Strays Society.

The Lascelles moved to Harewood House in 1930 after the death of the viscount's father. Goldsborough was let furnished; Chesterfield House was sold. 'The reason . . . it is assumed, is the need for economy, owing to the new increases in taxation,' commented the press.[5] The couple was not as well known at Harewood as one might have expected: when they opened the gardens to the public for charity shortly before they moved in, they arrived at the gate in their car to be asked for an admission charge of a shilling each and another shilling for parking.

Harewood was by far the most architecturally distinguished of all the houses occupied by George V's offspring. Designed in 1758 by John Carr of York, it had interiors by Robert Adam and his stable of craftsmen, a landscape by Capability Brown, and nineteenth-century alterations made by Sir Charles Barry while he was taking a break from building the Houses of Parliament. But by 1930 it was coming to seem a little old-fashioned: there were only two bathrooms, for example. The earl and Princess Mary brought in the elderly Sir Herbert Baker, then in the middle of replacing Sir John Soane's Bank of England, an act described by Pevsner as 'the worst individual loss suffered by London architecture in the first half of the 20th century'.[6] Baker's work at Harewood was harder to take exception to: he modernised the private apartments and installed twenty new bathrooms, along with central heating and two lifts, one for staff and the other for guests. A nursery for the two boys was put in on the top floor of the east wing, and most of the main rooms were redecorated, under Princess Mary's personal supervision. Blue was the dominant colour, according to press reports at the time.

Harewood was meant for entertaining, on a scale which hadn't been usual at Goldsborough. Every August Queen Mary spent ten days with her daughter on her way to Balmoral, as she had in the past; but now there was a stream of shooting parties, and Christmas parties, and parties for the races at Wetherby or York. Everything was planned with meticulous care. Before a big dinner, the butler, Slade, prepared a plan of the silver or gold to be used for the table decoration, and the head gardener, Hall, did the same with the flowers. The earl and princess went down to the plate room to approve Slade's scheme, and before they went up to dress for dinner they came into Sir Charles Barry's spectacular State Dining Room to inspect the table. They kept an indoor staff of twenty-seven throughout the 1930s, but even that wasn't enough to cope with some of the dinners, so that extra servants had to be drafted in from the surrounding villages. With thirty or forty sitting down to eat, Slade superintended three service tables and nine serving.

Prince George and Princess Marina, The Duke and Duchess of Kent, around the time of their marriage in 1934.

While Mary was settling down to motherhood and the life of an aristocratic landowner's wife, Prince George, the youngest of the Princess Royal's four brothers, showed no signs of settling down to anything. George spent most of the 1920s in the navy or in the arms of one of his many lovers, both male and female. At various times his name was linked romantically with Noël Coward, the art historian Anthony Blunt and the musical actress Jessie Matthews. His most notorious relationship was with Kiki Preston, an American socialite and ex-cabaret performer known as 'the girl with the silver syringe' because of her fondness for cocaine and morphine; a fondness which George came to share. In his memoirs, the Duke of Windsor recalled his brother as being 'somewhat Bohemian by inclination', glossing discreetly over the fact that in the late 1920s he was charged with supervising George's rehab, and that on at least one occasion he had to step in to save George from an unpleasant blackmail attempt which centred on some letters the prince had written to a young man in Paris.[7]

In 1934 Prince George was married to Princess Marina, third and youngest daughter of Prince Nicholas of Greece. (It was at their wedding in Westminster Abbey that George's niece, the eight-year-old Princess Elizabeth, first met her husband-to-be: Prince Philip was Marina's cousin.) The following year George's aunt, Princess Victoria, died at The Coppins, the country house in Buckinghamshire she had bought when she was ejected from Sandringham on Queen Alexandra's death in 1925. The Coppins was an undistinguished two-storeyed house in 132 acres, with four reception rooms, a large music room and fourteen bedrooms. Built in the middle of the nineteenth century by a successful theatre manager named John Mitchell, it was all gables and high chimneys. It looked vaguely like York Cottage on the Sandringham estate, in fact. There was also a model farm, with a pedigree herd and other livestock. And in her will Princess Victoria left it to George.

The newly-weds, now the Duke and Duchess of Kent (the king had conferred the title on his youngest boy shortly before their

wedding), spent the spring of 1936 renovating The Coppins inside and out. An important part of the work was the construction of a big nursery overlooking the gardens: they already had a son, Prince Edward, and the duchess was expecting a second child. Princess Alexandra was born on Christmas Day 1936. They supervised the work themselves, and often drove down from London to inspect progress, as did other members of the family. Queen Mary motored over from Windsor to see the house in April 1936, bringing Queen Victoria's granddaughter, Princess Alice.

'The district will expect much from [the Duke and Duchess],' predicted one press report when the legacy was first announced, 'as the Princess Victoria had been Lady Bountiful there.'[8] By the time they moved in on 6 June 1936, to the cheers of local villagers assembled at the gate, The Coppins had been provided with six bathrooms, mains electricity and water, central heating and modern drainage. The ground-floor reception rooms were fitted out in an easy neo-Georgian style, and – one of the most talked-about improvements – they looked out onto modern flower gardens and lawns which had taken the place of a dark and unkempt mass of laurel, yew and holly.

For the next few years Coppins (the Kents dropped the definite article) was often in the news. The duke and duchess celebrated their son's second birthday there, with a tea party and a two-tier birthday cake with pink icing created by the royal confectioner at Buckingham Palace. Respectful visitors were photographed trooping across the lawns and resisting the temptation to press their noses against the windows when the gardens were opened in aid of the Queen's Institute of District Nursing. The duchess caused a stir when she popped over to Slough one Saturday and bought a kite and a rubber quoit-ring at Woolworth's. 'She had nearly completed her shopping before she was recognised,' reported a breathless *Manchester Guardian*, going on to say that she also visited the haberdashery and food counters.[9]

To the twenty-first-century reader, cynically accustomed to the manipulation of the media by everyone from royals and senior politicians to Z-list celebrities, stories like these smack of a

The Duke and Duchess of York pose on the steps of Polesden Lacey during their honeymoon in 1923.

The fact that Princess Mary married a country house, Prince George was left one and Prince Henry bought one with a legacy, might suggest that their father didn't have much in the way of spare country property to bestow on his children. Quite the reverse. Besides the various lodges and cottages on the Sandringham estate, which were George V's personal property, there were literally hundreds of rural homes managed by the Commissioners of Woods, Forests and Land Revenues, who morphed in 1924 into the Commissioners of Crown Lands. Most of this property was let, or occupied by current and past members of the royal household. The eighteenth-century Thatched House Lodge in Richmond Park, for example, became the home of Sir Louis Greig in 1932, after he resigned as the Duke of York's equerry. Bagshot Park, a vast and ugly mansion built in 1877, was occupied by Queen Victoria's son, Prince Arthur, Duke of Connaught, from its completion until his death in 1942.

At Queen Mary's suggestion, the Yorks set up home at White Lodge, an early Palladian house in Richmond Park built as a hunting lodge for George II in 1727–9. The queen had happy memories of the place – she and George V had started their married life there, and the Prince of Wales had been born there in 1894. And it was beautiful: designed by Roger Morris and, like his Marble Hill House in Twickenham, a model of early Palladianism, elegant and compact. (Although not too compact: there were sixteen or seventeen best bedrooms.)

But the Yorks didn't like it. The central heating was woefully inadequate, the electric lighting was dangerously unpredictable, the drains were suspect and the only downstairs lavatory was in a secretary's office. Literally. The setting was too public for their taste: Sir Frederick Ponsonby passed on their complaints to the Office of Works, pointing out that 'Richmond Park has been brought very near London by charabancs and motor cars', so that at weekends the crowds of sightseers were so great that the duke and duchess hardly dared step outside.[17] Even on weekdays there was always a knot of people gathered at their gate. And the cost of keeping up the lodge was prohibitive: £11,000 a year, according to the duke, and 'the greater part of their income is spent in paying for quite unnecessary servants'.[18] They couldn't go on living there, and they wanted a house in London instead.

Sir Lionel Earle, who as permanent secretary to the Office of Works was responsible for finding them somewhere else to live, was sceptical. He refused to believe that White Lodge cost so much to run, and suspected that its distance from town was the real reason for the Yorks' unhappiness. 'They are both passionately fond of dancing, and naturally wish to come to London practically every day for this purpose.'[19]

It was four years before that wish was granted, when a lease on White Lodge was granted to Lord Lee of Fareham and in return the Yorks moved to 145 Piccadilly, once the London home of the marquesses of Northampton. Both before and after their move the duke, who was an enthusiastic huntsman, rented country houses in the Midlands for the hunting season, which implies that perhaps

White Lodge was both too far from London and not far enough. In the first winter of their marriage he took Guilsborough Hall in Northamptonshire, an exotic mixture of architectural styles. The exterior was long, low and castellated; there was an Italian roof garden, a neoclassical music room and a Moorish bathroom with marble walls and something called 'an electric light bath'. The main attraction for the Yorks was that it boasted good stables and was only a couple of miles from the kennels of the Pytchley hounds, and there were four days' hunting a week to be had.

Guilsborough went up for sale in 1925. In the winters of 1928–9 and 1929–30 the Yorks took the eighteen-bedroomed Naseby Hall, also in the heart of Pytchley country, and rather less exotic. Then in July 1931, Major Frederick Featherstonhaugh, the manager of the king's racing stables, died at the Royal Lodge, his residence in Windsor Great Park. The Royal Lodge was in the gift of the sovereign, and George V offered it to Bertie and Elizabeth.

Originally a *cottage ornée* designed as a refuge for the Prince Regent by John Nash, and extended by Sir Jeffry Wyatville, the Royal Lodge (and it was *the* Royal Lodge, 'by which name it has been known ever since George IV built it', as the king was quick to point out to Bertie when he inadvertently referred to it simply as 'Royal Lodge') was virtually demolished by Queen Adelaide in the 1830s, except for Wyatville's saloon, which was later partitioned into five separate rooms.[20] It was subsequently rebuilt as a big, rather bland block, with a whiff of the hotel or convalescent home about it.

But the duke and duchess were delighted. 'It will suit us admirably,' Bertie told his father; and they set to work to turn it into a home for them and their two daughters, Princess Elizabeth, born in 1926 at the Mayfair home of the duchess's father, the Earl of Strathmore; and Margaret Rose, born at Glamis Castle in August 1930. The Yorks removed the partition walls to restore the Wyatville saloon to its original, magnificent proportions, forty-eight feet long and twenty feet high. They extended their private accommodation and redecorated the house throughout. The duke's bedroom was simple and austere; his wife's was a more opulent grey-blue, with blue silk trimmed with lemon-yellow for the bed and white applewood furniture.

The Yorks moved into the Royal Lodge in the early summer of 1932, and from the start they were happy there, motoring down from 145 Piccadilly at weekends, staying for longer periods when they could. The duke took Princess Elizabeth out riding on her pony, and he and his wife became enthusiastic gardeners. Even after Bertie's income was cut along with his brothers' by their father, who set an example to his people in the Depression by lopping £50,000 off the Civil List, he stayed cheerful. He had to give up hunting and sell his six horses, but at least he had the Royal Lodge, his wife and his daughters.

LIKE HIS BROTHER BERTIE, the Prince of Wales rented a series of furnished country houses in the late 1920s, usually for a few months at a time. His requirements were simple. A rural retreat had to be reasonably private, it had to be fitted with modern conveniences and, most important of all, it must be within easy reach of a golf course.

The prince's favourite golf links at Sunningdale in Berkshire offered plenty of suitable property, and by an odd coincidence, he rented three houses in a row designed by the same all-but-forgotten architect, Walter Sand. The first was Middleton House, a stone's throw from the golf club, which he took for several summers in the late 1920s. When the lease on Middleton ran out in September 1929 he decided to stay on in the neighbourhood, taking a two-month lease on Craigmyle, built in 1903 in a mixed Tudor, all half-timbering and gables on the outside and a cheery mixture of oak rafters and Adamesque decoration within.

Then for the last two months of 1929 the prince moved to Little Court, a neo-Georgian house overlooking the links which Sand had built the previous year for an old soldier, Brigadier General Basil Buckley. *Country Life* immediately rushed out an article on Little Court, 'a temporary residence of HRH the Prince of Wales', which showed an attractive house whose newness had been tempered by the extensive use of old materials.[21] The roof was made of old tiles; the bricks came from a demolished eighteenth-century house in Twickenham, and Sand recycled all sorts of architectural details. The door to the garden came from a Georgian house in the Strand; an unusual triple Palladian window overlooking the rose garden, curved in plan, from the West Country; and the oak staircase, Queen Anne or very early Georgian, from a manor house in Norfolk. *Country Life* approved. 'Mr Sand has shown in this house how comfortable 18th-century dispositions can be and how easily they can be brought into line with present-day requirements.'[22]

Comfortable or not, the Prince of Wales had no intention of prolonging his stay into the New Year. He had already found a country house that he was going to call his own. Earlier in 1929 a shuffling of sinecures meant that Fort Belvedere in Windsor Great Park had fallen vacant. Like the Royal Lodge, the fort was in George V's gift, and in the summer the prince went to his father and asked to live in it. 'What could you possibly want that queer old place for?' asked the king. 'Those damn week-ends, I suppose.' But then he smiled and relented. 'Well, if you want it you can have it.'[23]

Fort Belvedere was a queer old place, with a queer old history. As its name suggests, it was built as a picturesque viewpoint, for the Duke of Cumberland, known to posterity as 'Butcher' Cumberland for the merciless way he put down Bonnie Prince Charlie's Jacobite Rising of 1745. Cumberland was ranger of Windsor Great Park from 1746 to 1757.

In its original incarnation Fort Belvedere consisted of a triangular tower with turrets at each corner. Cumberland's architect was almost certainly Henry Flitcroft, who was paid over £2,000 on account for works in the park in 1747–8 and who also designed a triangular viewing tower on the Stourhead estate for Henry Hoare in 1765. Although sometimes described as a military lookout, it was clearly always intended as a toy fort, for the duke's private use. Mrs Delany, who visited in 1757, described closets of blue and gold and green and gold, painted stucco festoons of fruit and flowers, and a chandelier of Chelsea china that cost £600. 'Nothing can be finer

Fort Belvedere: 'What could you possibly want that queer old place for?' George V asked the Prince of Wales.

than the prospects from all the windows,' she wrote.[24] The prospect included a faux-Chinese barge painted with huge dragons which the duke kept moored on Virginia Water.

In 1827–9, while Sir Jeffry Wyatville was remodelling parts of Windsor Castle for George IV, he extended Fort Belvedere to create a jumbled but undeniably picturesque collection of turrets and towers of different heights, besides building a single-storey octagonal drawing room and separate accommodation for staff. That staff included a unit of bombardiers, whose duties involved firing royal salutes from thirty-one brass cannon on a new terrace overlooking Virginia Water. The last bombardier died in his cottage at the fort in 1910, aged ninety.

Although yet more changes had been made to the fort early on in George V's reign, including the creation of a proper servants' wing, in 1929 Fort Belvedere was, said his son, a pseudo-Gothic hodge-podge, kept in perpetual shadow by overgrown yew trees and surrounded by wild and untended gardens. 'But the half-buried beauty of the place leaped to my eye.'[25]

Scaffolding went up that autumn. There were structural repairs, improvements to the plumbing, the installation of steel casement windows. The prince was adamant that he wanted the kind of modern conveniences he had enjoyed during visits to America: built-in cupboards, central heating, and plenty of bathrooms. In the basement he installed a Turkish bath and a shower; outside there was a new swimming pool and a hard tennis court. The gardens were laid out with lawns and long borders were planted with roses, delphiniums, irises and flowering shrubs to give colour from June through until November.

Around £21,000 was spent on the fort, most of it coming out of the prince's own pocket. It was ready for occupation by the end of April 1930, when he came back from a four-month safari to East Africa (on which, incidentally, he took a movie camera instead of a gun, observing that 'vanity had betrayed my friends into defacing the rooms of their otherwise handsome homes with unsightly stuffed trophies').[26] In his own mind, whatever credit was due for the fort's reinvention was due to him. 'Though I naturally sought professional advice,' he recalled later, 'the final result in the main represented my ideas.'[27] And again, 'Soon I came to love it as I loved no other material thing – perhaps because it was so much my own creation.'[28]

Nevertheless, the list of professional advisers associated with Fort Belvedere is a distinguished one, although since very little survives from the 1930s, it isn't at all clear who contributed what. The flowering borders owed a lot to Norah Lindsay, the society garden consultant whose planting schemes graced Sir Philip Sassoon's gardens at Trent Park and Port Lympne, the Astors' at Cliveden and the Marquess of Lothian's at Blickling Hall in Norfolk. At least three big names from the world of interior decoration were involved, or claimed to have been involved: Herman Schrijver, who also decorated York House for the prince; Sibyl Colefax; and Syrie Maugham. The two last certainly supplied individual items of furniture for the fort.

To judge from the photographs and visitors' accounts of the time, the prince and his helpers achieved an easy air of informality.

The octagonal hall had a black and white marble floor and eight chairs upholstered in yellow leather. The drawing room, also octagonal, had curtains of yellow velvet, low modern sofas and walls painted to look as though they were panelled in pine. There was a baby grand piano, and a gramophone to which guests sometimes danced after dinner. Good pictures hung on the walls: Canalettos in the drawing room, a couple by Stubbs in the dining room. The prince's bedroom, which was on the ground floor, had white walls and red chintz curtains. The six guest rooms upstairs were named, either for past and present associations – one was 'Prince George's Room', because the prince's youngest brother stayed there when he came for the weekend, while another was 'The Queen's Room', although no one could quite remember why – or for their colour schemes. Lady Diana Cooper stayed in 'The Pink Room', which lived up to its name: it was 'pink-sheeted, pink Venetian-blinded, pink-soaped, white-telephoned and pink-and-white maided'.[29]

Although the prince was understandably reluctant to publicise the fact, the ambience of the fort owed rather a lot to his mistresses, particularly Freda Dudley Ward, whom he had been seeing on and off since 1918. Freda, who was half-American, was the wife of William Dudley Ward, a minor courtier who led his own life, and was content for her to lead hers. Philip Tilden once called at their Mayfair flat to be let in by Dudley Ward with the greeting, 'Come in, there's nobody here but the Prince of Wales.' The prince leapt up from an easy chair and the four of them all went off house-hunting in his car.[30]

Freda enjoyed buying houses to renovate and sell. 'I doubt whether we were in any house longer than about two years,' her daughter recalled.[31] As a result she was on good terms with fashionable Mayfair decorators: it was probably through her good offices that Herman Schrijver worked for the prince at York House and the fort, and she was good friends with Syrie Maugham. Feted by *Vogue* as one of 'the Sophisticates of Mayfair', dressed by Cecil Beaton, and loathed by George V, who in references to her father's business as a Nottingham lace-manufacturer called her 'Freda

Loom' or 'the lacemaker's daughter', she was closely involved in the first stages of the renovation work at Fort Belvedere.

But she wasn't destined to enjoy weekends there. When the prince took up residence in the spring of 1930, he also took up with a new mistress, Thelma Furness, the twice-married American wife of a shipping magnate. They had begun to see each other the previous summer, and the relationship became more serious when she and her husband joined the prince's East Africa safari. So it was Thelma, rather than Freda, who acted as unofficial hostess at the first Fort Belvedere weekends.

They were relaxed, domestic occasions. 'He puttered in the garden, pruned his trees, blew on his bagpipes,' she remembered.[32] (The prince had learned the Highland bagpipe as a young man, and entertained guests with a tune after dinner, sometimes donning a kilt for the occasion.) There was no talk of politics. Bertie and the Duchess of York sometimes came over, and Prince George. They swam, and played tennis, and danced to the gramophone. One winter weekend they all went skating on Virginia Water. At other times Thelma's father, a retired US diplomat, came to stay. 'If a visitor had come upon us on any of these occasions he would have witnessed an unexpected and old-fashioned scene of bourgeois bliss,' Thelma wrote later, 'the prince and I busy with our needlework [which he had learned from his mother, Queen Mary], and Papa sonorously reading to us from a novel by Scott or Dickens.'[33]

The prince made no secret of his relationship, just as he had made no secret of his affair with Freda. In January 1932 some friends of Thelma invited the couple to dine with them at their London flat. The friends were an Anglo-American shipping executive, Ernest Simpson, and his wife Wallis. The dinner of black bean soup and fried chicken Maryland was a success; so much so that Thelma and the prince repaid the Simpsons' hospitality by inviting them to spend the following weekend at Fort Belvedere.

Subsequent events imposed an enormous and unlikely significance on this weekend. In 1934 Thelma Furness left for America to visit her twin sister, Gloria Vanderbilt, famously telling

Wallis to look after the Prince of Wales for her while she was away. 'It was later evident that Wallis took my advice all too literally,' she wrote acidly.[34] The latter's visits to Fort Belvedere, with and without her husband, were frequent, as she moved to occupy the centre of what the Archbishop of Canterbury would later condemn as 'a social circle whose standards and way of life are alien to all the best instincts and traditions of [the British] people'.[35] Judging from the visitors' book kept at the fort in 1935 and 1936, the circle was quite mixed. Besides close friends of both Wallis and the prince, weekend guests included Dickie and Edwina Mountbatten; Duff and Diana Cooper; prominent anti-appeasers like Anthony Eden and Robert Vansittart; minor diplomats from the American Embassy and major society hostesses such as Emerald Cunard and Sibyl Colefax.

One Thursday afternoon in January 1936 the prince was out shooting in Windsor Great Park when a note came from his mother to say that 'Papa is not very well'. It wasn't a surprise: George V had been in poor health for several years. But this time was different.

Queen Mary asked the prince to suggest his coming up for the weekend, casually, so as not to alarm the king. But he decided not to wait. The next day he flew up to Sandringham – he kept his own De Havilland Puss Moth at an airfield ten minutes from the fort – to find George V in his bedroom at the Big House, sitting in front of the fire in an old Tibetan dressing gown. The king was drifting in and out of consciousness and was clearly very ill indeed. Three days later, shortly before midnight on 20 January 1936, he died with his family at his bedside, his end hastened by a cocktail of morphine and cocaine administered by his doctor. Queen Mary immediately took her eldest son's hand and kissed it; the Duke of York followed suit. The man who had a moment before been Prince of Wales was now King Edward VIII.

In the last weeks of Edward's 326-day reign, Fort Belvedere, which was already a symbol of his suspect morals (especially among those who weren't invited to his house parties), loomed large in the nation's consciousness. 'Events have made it a house of destiny,' declared one newspaper.[36] As gossip about Wallis began to spread after her divorce hearing in Ipswich on 27 October 1936, she fled London and took up residence at the fort. It was there, on the terrace after dinner on the night of Wednesday, 2 December, that Edward told her about his crucial interview earlier in the day with Prime Minister Stanley Baldwin, at which Baldwin had told him the government wouldn't stand for his marrying a divorced woman, and that he must either give her up or abdicate.

The next day Edward packed Wallis off to the south of France, away from the gathering storm. Journalists descended in their hordes on Sunningdale, and Fort Belvedere became, in the king's words, 'a battle headquarters, with telephones ringing constantly and despatch riders on motor-cycles bringing state papers from London'.[37] Normal mail for the fort was usually brought by a postman on a bicycle: now the Post Office had to use a mail van to carry the sackfuls of private letters bringing support and accusation. Courtiers and lawyers and civil servants dashed back and forth. At one point Stanley Baldwin arrived with his suitcase. 'Good God!' the king muttered. 'Surely he doesn't intend to spend the night?'[38]

Harold Nicolson told Vita a rather pathetic little piece of gossip he'd picked up from Baldwin's son on 7 December. Apparently the previous day the prime minister and the king had been pacing round and round the gardens at the fort trying to reach some kind of solution to the crisis until eventually they agreed that Edward must abdicate. Exhausted, they went into the library and Baldwin asked if he might have a whisky and soda.

> The bell was rung: the footman came: the drink was produced. S.B. raised his glass and said . . . 'Well Sir, whatever happens, my Mrs and I wish you happiness from the depths of our souls.' At which the King burst into floods of tears. Then S.B. himself began to cry. What a strange conversation-piece, those two blubbering together on a sofa![39]

At ten o'clock on the morning of Thursday, 10 December, Edward's three brothers arrived at the fort and were immediately shown into the octagonal drawing room. They found the king at his desk, a red despatch box in front of him and aides and advisers all around. Sitting at his desk and watched by the three princes, he signed the Instruments of Abdication and then stood for each of his brothers in turn to sign as witnesses. Then he left the room and stepped outside into the morning air.

The following night Edward, now Prince Edward again, was taken by car from Fort Belvedere to Windsor Castle, where he was to make the abdication broadcast in which he famously told the nation and the empire that 'I have found it impossible to carry the heavy burden of responsibility and to discharge my duties as king as I would wish to do without the help and support of the woman I love.'[40] From Windsor he would go to Portsmouth and across to France and exile.

As he drove down the hill he caught a last glimpse of the fort. 'In that moment I realised how heavy was the price I had paid . . . The Fort had been more than a home; it had been a way of life for me.'[41]

He never saw Fort Belvedere again.

CHAPTER ELEVEN

Getting About

TRAVEL FOR THE country-house-owning classes was not a casual business. The 11th Duke of Bedford kept four cars and eight chauffeurs in London (along with two fully staffed houses in Belgrave Square, which he visited a couple of times a year). Guests invited to stay at the duke's country seat, Woburn Abbey, were picked up in town by a chauffeur, who arrived with a footman. Suitcases were carried in a second car, driven by another chauffeur accompanied by another footman. ('You never travelled with your suitcase,' recalled his grandson, 'that was not the thing to do.'[1]) On the outskirts of London this little entourage would be met by a third and a fourth chauffeur-driven car, both also equipped with footmen. Guests and luggage were transferred, and then they set off on the second leg of their journey. This odyssey, involving four cars and eight servants, took two or three hours: Woburn was less than fifty miles from central London.

In 1924, the year in which the Society of Motor Manufacturers and Traders began their annual analysis of the English market, just over 5 per cent of households owned a car.[2] By 1938 this had risen to 20 per cent, while the general speed limit of twenty miles per hour, in force since 1903, was relaxed with the passing of the Road Traffic Act of 1930, which imposed a thirty miles per hour limit on passenger and goods vehicles and removed it entirely from private cars. The Earl of Coventry at Croome Court in Worcestershire owned a Standard Twenty with deep red coachwork – nice enough, but not exactly a limousine. (His choice of car may have been motivated by loyalty to the city from which he took his title, which was also the home of the Standard Motor Company.) He also had a little blue 'hound van' which was used to transport his wife's pack of dogs to local meets, and to collect offal from the butchers and servants from the railway station. The Coventrys had a chauffeur, Roland, who also looked after Croome's water-pumping station and waited at table as a footman when they entertained; but the earl sometimes drove the Standard himself – at speed and uncertainly, since he was an alcoholic.

Sir Philip Sassoon had a shining Rolls-Royce, with a distinctive silver snake mascot on the bonnet. Sir Albert Richardson travelled in a black Rolls, a *sedanca de ville* of 1934 with walnut cabinets filled with pens, pencils and sketchbooks, reference books, brandy flasks of Georgian silver and emergency rations of grapes, nuts and sardines in case he and his chauffeur should find themselves stranded. The Duke of Westminster had a fleet of Rolls-Royces, several of which he had had steel-plated for use as armoured cars on the Western Front. In 1916 he commanded three armoured car batteries in the Libyan desert, each containing Rolls-Royces with reinforced bodies and machine-gun turrets where their boots should have been. Staff from Eaton Hall went with him to polish his shoes.

The adventurous traveller could forsake the country lanes and take to the air, something which happened with increasing frequency in the 1920s and 1930s. The Prince of Wales's personal pilot was Flight Lieutenant Edward Fielden, whom the prince appointed Chief Air Pilot and Extra Equerry in 1929. The prince had a pilot's licence of his own as well, although he rarely used it. Prince George and Prince Henry also took up flying, and the three brothers had raced to see who would fly solo first. The Prince of Wales won: 'I completed two extremely lonely circuits of the field and landed twice without cracking up the machine,' he wrote. 'Once out of the aeroplane, my first act was to telephone my two younger brothers. "I've beaten you to it," I announced to each in turn.'[3]

He owned several aircraft. Garden designer Norah Lindsay described how one day while she was working at Fort Belvedere she and a few others went out to a nearby airstrip and watched, collars turned up against the driving rain, as the prince clambered aboard his current favourite, a De Havilland Dragon. An overalled mechanic slammed the door shut and a moment later the engine changed its pitch and the gleaming red, blue and silver biplane began to bump across the grass. Just when the watchers thought it must disappear into the mist, the biplane abruptly rose into the air, climbing hard and wheeling round to pass over their heads, part roar and part ghostly outline. The prince was off to open a fete. And when in January 1936 he flew as Edward VIII from Sandringham to London, the morning after his father's death, he became the first British monarch to fly; George V never went up in an aeroplane in his life. 'A True King of the Air', said the headlines.

Flying was one of Sir Philip Sassoon's passions.* He served in government as Undersecretary of State for Air twice, in 1924–9 and again in 1931–7 and, like the Prince of Wales, he learned to fly himself. The prince wrote him an encouraging note in 1929, asking how he was getting on and saying 'There's no doubt but that it's tricky work but safer than motoring and far more fun.'[4]

The safety was a moot point. One Saturday in 1931 Mrs Philip Noble and her house party were waiting for her husband and another guest, the amateur aviator Violet Baring, to fly in for lunch at her Wiltshire country house, Chisenbury Priory, when a policeman came with the news that Mrs Baring's aeroplane had crashed in a field in Berkshire, killing both the pilot and her passenger. Instead of presiding over lunch, Mrs Noble was asked to come and identify her husband's body. At Trent Park Sassoon had a landing field of his own, but it was ridged and furrowed and surrounded by trees. His instructor, Flight Lieutenant Dermot Boyle, remembered an afternoon at Trent when the Duke and Duchess of York were lunching and Sassoon asked him to take the duchess up. 'I took off out of the appalling field, my mind filled with the horrific things that might happen if [it] lived up to its reputation.'[5]

A number of country houses had their own airstrips. By 1937, when there were about thirty commercial aerodromes in Britain,

* As were airmen, who were frequently invited to mix with the great and the good at weekend parties at Port Lympne and Trent Park. In one of Sassoon's rare hints about his sexuality, he confessed to being deeply upset by the accidental death of a young pilot he knew well. He kept a photograph of the young man, and bought his flyingboots after his death as a keepsake. Writing to a friend from Port Lympne in 1922 he spoke of his anguish at looking out over the marsh where they used to fly together: 'The heart is a wretched business.' (Stansky, 128.)

there were more than seventy in private hands. The Duchess of Bedford, until she died in a flying accident off the east coast in March that year, owned two: one at Woburn and another at Creetown in Dumfries and Galloway. Such private fields, unlicensed and unreported to the Air Ministry, varied enormously in size and quality. At one end of the scale was Ratcliffe Aerodrome, the creation of brewer Lindsay Everard MP, whose home was the early nineteenth-century Ratcliffe Hall in Leicestershire. Everard never learned to fly himself, but he was passionate about the need for Britain to lead the way in the development of aviation, and so in 1930 he built his own aerodrome at Ratcliffe. It was formally opened on 6 September 1930 by the director of Civil Aviation, Sir Sefton Brancker, who flew up from London in a bright yellow De Havilland Puss Moth with Amy Johnson, a huge celebrity after recently completing her famous solo flight from Britain to Australia. Five thousand people came to watch a hundred aircraft take part in a grand air pageant, with air races, aerobatics, parachute displays and a set piece in which three Royal Air Force planes 'bombed' some Chinese pirates, whose fake ship duly exploded.*

Throughout the 1930s Ratcliffe, which offered a smart clubhouse and an open-air swimming pool, was the only private aerodrome equipped for night flying. The field was floodlit, and facilities included a high-powered mobile searchlight mounted on the chassis of Everard's old Rolls-Royce.[6] There was an observation tower and Everard employed a full-time engineer to maintain his various aircraft. His personal pilots regularly flew him on business trips in England and Europe.

At the other end of the spectrum there were the Trent Parks – fields on a home farm or a piece of parkland landscaped by Repton or Capability Brown, with dangerously placed clumps of trees, rough ground and nothing but the hoops of a windsock to indicate

* Towards the end of the day one aircraft crashed, narrowly missing spectators and injuring a passenger, who had to be cut free and taken to hospital. Brancker died four weeks later when the R101 airship came down near Beauvais on its maiden flight to India. Amy Johnson died in 1941 after being forced to bail out when her plane ran out of fuel and crashed into the Thames Estuary in freezing conditions. Flying was a dangerous business.

their purpose. And in between there were the majority of private strips, hedges cleared and rabbit holes filled in, perhaps with some tarmac and a hut just big enough to house a light aeroplane with its wings folded. The Automobile Association published a handy register of airfields for its members, presumably on the assumption that anyone who drove a car might well harbour ambitions to fly a plane. It contained useful information on the grid reference, the maximum landing run – anywhere between a relaxed half-mile and a perilous 300 yards – and other things it would be good for a pilot to know. At Taunton, for example, cattle were often pastured in the field that served as an airstrip. 'If a circuit of the farm is made the owner, if at home, has consented to move any cattle that may be in the way.'[7]

FURTHER AFIELD, the spas of Germany, the antiquities of Italy, the peaks of Switzerland and the Tyrol, all had their appeal for the country-house-owning classes. 'Those suffering the penalties of excessive Mental Strain', predicted a 1922 guide, 'often, if the remedy is not too heroic for them, regain their tone and strength with marvellous rapidity by a residence of some weeks at a height of 5,000–6,000 feet.'[8] Even Spain, torn apart by war in the 1930s, launched a rather unexpected marketing campaign to attract tourists. In 1938, while the Spanish Civil War was still raging, the Franco regime offered nine-day bus tours of the battlefields in a fleet of twenty American school buses bought from Chrysler. For £8, the curious tourist got three meals a day, accommodation in first-class hotels, and a dangerous exercise in macabre voyeurism. 'I was anxious to prove that war and travel were not incompatible,' recalled the head of the Spanish National Tourist Board years later.[9]

But France was the destination of choice. 'We used to go on holiday to the South of France a good deal,' remembered the Duke of Richmond and Gordon. 'Your car came with you on the aeroplane . . . It was gorgeous, and so *cheap*.'[10] Two million foreigners were visiting France every year by the late 1920s. Many were there to remember friends and relatives killed in the Great War – the French Office National du Tourisme was planning a marketing campaign before the Armistice was signed, and Michelin actually published a motorists' guidebook to French battlefields *in 1917*.

The world was growing smaller. Increasing numbers of affluent travellers deserted their country houses each winter for the south of France, where, in the words of a 1927 traveller's handbook to the Riviera, 'the blue beauty of the Mediterranean takes its ease . . . and smart resorts . . . rise, from time to time, to an exuberant effervescence of marble pavilions and golden-domed casinos where the fashion of the world indulges its taste for luxury'.[11] Air Union offered a service which picked up passengers by car from central London daily, drove them to Croydon aerodrome and flew them down to Marseilles via Paris and Lyons for a fare of £18 10s. 6d. return. Flying time was seven hours, and lunch baskets were provided by the aerodrome restaurant. P&O had weekly sailings to Marseilles and Genoa – the voyage lasted seven days to Marseilles, and another day to Genoa.

It was also possible to drive, but one needed to complete a formidable array of paperwork: an International Certificate for Motor Vehicles, an International Driving Permit for each driver and a sixty-day pass from French customs. There was also the risk posed by Johnny Foreigner and his dangerous driving: Baedeker warned that on the winding coast roads of the south of France in particular 'very careful driving is necessary, owing to the impossibility of seeing ahead for any distance (keep close to the right when rounding curves and give warning of your approach) and owing to the high speed at which all motorists travel in these parts'.[12]

For those who yearned to play the tables at Charles Garnier's casino in Monte Carlo or stroll along the Promenade des Anglais in Nice, the boat train was the most popular route. From 1929 the first-class-only *Golden Arrow* left London Victoria station at 11 a.m. each day, crossing the Channel in a first-class-only ferry, the *Canterbury*, and arriving at Paris Gare du Nord six and a half hours later. Connecting trains took travellers down to the Riviera via Lyons and Marseilles.

And they went in droves. 'All is well with the Riviera,' ran a chirpy report in the *Illustrated London News* of 14 January 1922, elated to note that celebrities were starting to arrive in Cannes. Winston and Clementine Churchill were there, and Lord and Lady Grosvenor. A frisson of anxiety had been caused by the news that Lord Rocksavage, Sir Philip Sassoon's brother-in-law, had decided to leave his polo ponies at home this year; but that was replaced by sighs of relief as Baron Schroder came in from Chile with six and the Scottish all-rounder Leslie Melville brought some of his own. There would be sport at the polo ground at Mandelieu after all.

Prince Christopher of Greece and his wife Anastasia, widow of an Ohio tinplate millionaire, had taken the enormous Villa Kasbeck, built in the 1890s by Czar Nicholas II's uncle, Grand Duke Michael Mikhailovich, after his nephew exiled him for marrying beneath him, and named after a mountain in Georgia. Princess Anastasia's son was expected to join them with his new bride, the prince's niece Xenia. The famous Château Thorenc was let to the young cricketer Natwarshinhji Bhavsinhji, the Maharaja of Porbandar, who arrived with a large entourage. Nice was filling up, and there was an air of expectation about the preparations for Carnival, which after a couple of false starts was set to revive pre-war glories. Menton, said the *Illustrated London News*'s correspondent approvingly, 'is already an English place. In the streets, and tea-shops especially, our tongue seems to have swamped the French.'[13]

One or two British peers swapped their country houses for a permanent stay in the Mediterranean sun. The 16th Marquess of Winchester, premier marquess of England, sold up his Hampshire seat of Amport St Mary and, after a misunderstanding over the sale of some shares, decamped to Monte Carlo, where he gave his address simply as 'Palais de la Mer'.* The 2nd Viscount Bearsted, chairman of Shell, didn't move to the Riviera, but he kept a villa of his own in a spectacular hillside setting overlooking the sea at Cap Ferrat.

* Evidence at a later court case involving a squabble between his third wife, the daughter of a Parsee priest, and his ex-fiancée, a wealthy Nassau widow, included the memorable claim by his counsel that 'the first thing Lord Winchester required from a wife – and one to which affection had to take second place – was the provision of enough money to enable him to live in the style to which he had been accustomed' (*Manchester Guardian*, 27 November 1957, 4).

The Duke of Westminster was a frequent visitor to Monte Carlo, although he rarely stayed for more than a few days at a time. Fond of gambling, and sometimes playing three or four tables at once, he always took the same suite in the Hôtel de Paris next door to the casino. 'It was practically always on tap,' said Loelia, his 3rd duchess. 'I don't know what happened to it at other times. I suppose people were kicked out, or perhaps they never let it to anybody else.'[14]

THE RIGOURS OF INTERNATIONAL TRAVEL were softened by the servants, who put their master's or mistress's own crêpe de Chine sheets and pillowcases on their beds in the sleeper. 'You never had to worry about anything,' the Duchess of Westminster recalled, 'and never saw a ticket.'[15] The Countess of Rosse, recalling a trip on the Trans-Siberian railway in the 1920s, remembered caviar every day and perfect service. 'There was even a bath.'[16]

The conventional distinctions between master and servant were meticulously observed. When the Earl of Shaftesbury's valet went for lunch in the dining saloon during a Baltic crossing and was shown to the Countess of Shaftesbury's table, he refused to join his mistress, insisting it was inappropriate and he must be seated elsewhere. The empty seat beside the countess was then occupied by a black passenger, a situation which presented her with an even graver disruption of the natural order, so much so that she was unable to eat her lunch.

The Riviera wasn't the only destination of choice. In January 1929 the Earl of Shaftesbury, his two daughters, Lady Dorothy and Lady Lettice, and a small party of servants, including the earl's valet and the girls' lady's maid (who happened to be married to each other) set off for Egypt. They sailed from Tilbury Dock aboard the Orient Steam Navigation Company's SS *Oransay*. The party stopped off at Gibraltar, where they visited the new governor, Sir Alexander Godley, who was an old friend; and again at Toulon and Naples, before disembarking at Port Said and taking the train to Cairo. There they stayed for some weeks at the Semiramis,

stations. All the fires were electric, and a system of loudspeakers operated throughout the ship. The gymnasium on the shade deck contained an electrically driven mechanical horse and a rowing machine. Even in the galley everything was electrically controlled.

Lady Yule and Gladys both wore specially designed costumes which consisted of black trousers, berets and jackets. They brought their pet dogs, cats and monkeys with them when they sailed, along with a flock of birds which perched in dozens of gilded cages hanging on the upper and lower decks. 'The squawk of parrots and the chirping of canaries make a strange but not unpleasant symphony, echoing down the vessel's corridors,' wrote an Australian journalist when the *Nahlin* put in at Port Melbourne on a world tour in 1932.[25] The press reported gleefully on Lady Yule's annoyance with quarantine regulations when the authorities refused to allow her two poodles to come ashore with her.

The *Nahlin* carried a crew of fifty, all British except for Lady Yule's French chef, and all expected to conform to her strict ideas on teetotalism. When Edward VIII chartered the *Nahlin* for a cruise with Wallis Simpson along the Dalmatian coast in August 1936 (achieved this time without any tiresome interruptions from Mussolini), he took over the library on the shade deck as his cabin and replaced the books with bottles.

CHAPTER TWELVE

My New-Found-Land, My Kingdom

THE TRADITIONAL EXPLANATION for the appearance of Americans in the great halls and long galleries of England is that the special relationship was transactional; that it was the result of an unholy alliance between the socially ambitious mothers of heiresses from New York or Chicago and unscrupulous but impoverished English aristocrats who were happy to offer a title in exchange for a hefty dollar dowry to save an estate encumbered with accumulated debt. The poster girl for that discordant Anglo-American entente, the archetypal heiress-bride, was Consuelo, the daughter of railway magnate William Kissam Vanderbilt.

Consuelo has already appeared in these pages, restoring Crowhurst Place and divorcing Sunny Churchill, 9th Duke of Marlborough. She had been coerced into marrying Sunny in 1895 by her manipulative mother, Alva, who was determined to bag a duke. When Consuelo refused to go along with her plans, she reacted badly. In fact she swore to shoot the girl's preferred suitor dead, then locked her daughter up in the family's Newport mansion, Marble House, while feigning a heart attack which was caused, Consuelo was told, 'by my callous indifference to her feelings'.[1] Having secured her daughter's tearful acquiescence, Alva brought Sunny to propose in the Gothic Room at Marble House, 'whose atmosphere was so propitious to sacrifice'.[2] Consuelo cried all the way to the wedding. She cried again when her eleven-year-old brother told her Sunny was only marrying her for her money – as indeed he was. He received $2.5 million in railway stock as a dowry.

Consuelo spent eleven years lost in the marble halls of Blenheim Palace, surrounded by an army of blank-faced servants and condescending in-laws. The patronising began on her honeymoon as her husband explained that there were 200 English families whose lineage and titles and relationship she must learn. In much the same way, the banker Lord Revelstoke's proposal of marriage to another American heiress was laced with pride: 'Do you really think you could fill the position that would be required of my wife? You would have to meet Kings and Queens and entertain Ambassadors. Do you think you could do it?'[3] The object of Revelstoke's affections, Nancy Langhorne, decided she couldn't, and married Waldorf Astor instead.

Consuelo's lessons in inferiority continued when the newly-weds arrived at Woodstock station, and the robed mayor greeted them on the platform with the announcement that Woodstock had a mayor and a corporation before America was discovered. They were still going on years later, when the formidable octogenarian Dowager Duchess of Abercorn, Sunny's great-aunt, decided to have her photograph taken with 130 descendants. Any pleasure Consuelo took in being included was tempered by the way in which family members queued up to tell her what an honour it was for her, since 'I was the first American she had condescended to receive.'[4]

The Marlboroughs' unhappy marriage has become the stuff of legend. Guides at Blenheim Palace today point out John Singer Sargent's magnificent portrait of the couple with their two boys – 'the heir and the spare', they invariably say – and gleefully recount instances of their incompatibility. Their 1920 divorce, like their marriage, was played out on a public stage. Consuelo's one-sided and disingenuous autobiography, *The Glitter and the Gold*, stoked the flames with anecdotes of Sunny's odd behaviour – he spoke so rarely at meals that she took up knitting to pass the time between courses – and her own bewildered naivety: why were some of the Blenheim servants called 'odd men' when there was nothing odd about them? Why, when she rang for the butler to set a match to the fire, did he send for a footman to do it?

Consuelo claimed that the enormous public interest in her wedding was due to the fact that 'mine was the first international marriage that had taken place for some time'.[5] That wasn't true. By crossing the Atlantic in search of an heiress-bride Sunny

Marlborough was taking a well-trodden path to wedlock for the British landed classes. (He was also following in his father's footsteps: the 8th duke had married as his second wife a wealthy New York widow, the flames of his ardour stoked by her life interest in her first husband's $7 million fortune.) 'It has been roughly estimated that English noblemen alone have captured by marriage with American women, in round numbers, $50,000,000 of enviable American cash,' declared the *New York Times* in April 1893, listing forty-eight 'of the more important international weddings between England and America' over the previous twenty-five years.[6] The same month, the 4th Earl of Craven married sixteen-year-old Cornelia Martin and her fortune, which was reputed to be $1 million. Interest in that wedding was so great that when the doors of Grace Church on Broadway were opened after the ceremony for the bride and groom to pose on the steps, sightseers poured in, climbing over the pews and stripping the altar of its decorations in their rush for souvenirs. The police had to be called to clear the building. 'One of the most disgusting exhibitions of American snobbery I have ever seen,' wrote a senator's wife, describing the marriage as 'a palpable sale'.[7]

Between 1870 and 1914, 128 American women and three men married into the British nobility, although by no means all of the women – and of course none of the men – married titles or the heirs to titles. Thirty-nine baronets or their heirs married Americans in the same period, and in what can loosely be called the landed gentry, there were 176 Anglo-American marriages.[8]

The traditional view of the so-called 'American invasion' is that its spur on this side of the Atlantic was the series of depressions which hit British agriculture in the later nineteenth century, when falling rents and rising debts broke down the social barriers and snobbishness which had placed American brides beyond the pale. But it would be too cynical to suggest that money on one side, and social ambition on the other, were the only motives for the 'American invasion'. For one thing, in the British landed classes legal wrangling over money was an integral part of courtship, no matter where the bride came from. And yes, George Nathaniel

Curzon's marriage to Mary, daughter of retail emperor Levi Leiter, took place in 1895 only after lengthy negotiations about money between Leiter, Curzon, and Curzon's father. But those negotiations led up to a happy and loving marriage, and Curzon was distraught when his wife died, in his arms, after only eleven years together. In later life he used to say he wasn't afraid of death, because he would see Mary in heaven – a sentiment which perhaps contributed to the unhappiness of his second marriage, to another American, a diplomat's daughter Grace Duggan.

Curzon wasn't the only British nobleman to have two American wives. The 3rd Lord Leigh of Stoneleigh Abbey in Warwickshire, married a New Yorker in 1890; in 1923, as a widower, he married another. The 5th Lord Decies of Leixlip Castle in Kildare lost his first wife Helen, daughter of the railway magnate George Jay Gould, in 1931; five years later he married the widow Elizabeth Lehr, a member of the fabulously rich Drexel banking dynasty. In 1927 Decies' fellow Irishman, the 5th Earl of Gosford, deserted his ancestral seat of Gosford Castle in Co. Armagh, his wife Mildred, the daughter of the US minister to Rumania, and his teenage son; and went to New York, where he married a wealthy divorcee, set up a wine shop in Manhattan and joined the NYPD.

After his own divorce Sunny Marlborough immediately married again, and his second wife was also American. Gladys Deacon was a society beauty with a complicated past. Her father went to prison for shooting dead her mother's French lover in their suite at the Hôtel Splendide in Cannes, and then went mad. Her mother went off with an Italian nobleman. When Gladys was still a teenager, drifting around Europe, Proust and Rodin were captivated by her beauty. Bernard Berenson and the Crown Prince of Prussia wanted to marry her. She later claimed she had slept with every prime minister in Europe, and most kings.

In the 1890s, when she was sixteen, Gladys met Sunny, then just married to Consuelo, and decided that she wanted him. It took her nearly twenty-five years, but on 25 June 1921 she finally achieved her objective when the couple were married in Paris. Her bridal gown was 'of gold tissue specially woven in Italy for the occasion', announced *The Times*. 'The Court train is of gold tissue, and the veil, of old needle-point lace, [is] arranged like a coronet.'[9] That veil hid a slight but curious secret. Years before, Gladys had tried to improve on her considerable good looks by having paraffin wax injected in her nose. The procedure was not a success: the wax slipped and left her with a permanently bulky jaw.

The newly-weds settled in at Blenheim Palace and Carlton House Terrace, and Gladys took up the role of duchess with more ease than Consuelo had. There were house parties at Blenheim and receptions at Buckingham Palace. In 1923 she was presented to George V and Queen Alexandra, 'wearing a classically draped dress of silver lamé with a ceinture of silver embroidered in diamanté'.[10]

Gladys was forty years old when she married, and Sunny was fifty. After spending several decades consorting with some of the world's most distinguished artists and politicians in the capitals and casinos of Europe, the new duchess soon began to tire of Blenheim Palace and country life, while three miscarriages in four years put an end to hopes of motherhood. She turned to breeding Blenheim spaniels with more success, until they overran the palace and drove the duke to distraction. This, coupled with Sunny's conversion to Catholicism and Gladys's dangerously erratic behaviour – she once produced a revolver at dinner and, when one of her guests asked nervously what it was for, replied 'Oh, I don't know. I might just shoot Marlborough' – led to the break-up of the marriage.[11]

In 1931 Sunny fled Blenheim, and for several years Gladys and her spaniels had the place to themselves. But in 1933 he had the gas and electricity cut off. Gladys retreated to their London house, but he cut the power there too, and then had her evicted. Only his sudden death the following year prevented their divorce.

WITH SO MANY OWNERS of country estates unable to cope with rising taxes and falling rents, it wasn't surprising that the consolations of marriage to a wealthy American wife remained strong after the Armistice. But the tenor of the exchange was subtly different. Now, Americans brought glamour and dynamism, as well as money. When Iva Lawson bought Claude Lowther's

Herstmonceux, undeterred by tales of ghostly grey ladies and a phantom giant drummer who walked the battlements, the British press was delighted. 'Along Came a Brave American Girl Who Scoffs at Ghosts and Just Adores Haunted Rooms', ran one excited headline.[12] And sometimes glamour was enough without the fortune.

The Americanisation of British culture was felt at the highest levels of society. One thinks of the young Earl of Jersey's film-star bride Virginia Cherrill 'of Hollywood, USA', as *Debrett's Peerage* primly put it. In 1932 the 9th Duke of Devonshire's son married Broadway entertainer Adele Astaire, sister of Fred, who became Lady Charles Cavendish. George V and Queen Mary had private screenings of Hollywood blockbusters: in 1927 they watched Ben-Hur's legendary chariot race in the comfort of the Waterloo Chamber at Windsor Castle. The Prince of Wales, like many of his friends, used America as a yardstick by which to measure modern country-house conveniences: at Fort Belvedere he introduced 'many of the creature conveniences that I had sampled and enjoyed in the New World – a bathroom to nearly every room, showers, a steam bath, built-in cupboards, central heating'.[13] When as Edward VIII he left Windsor after his abdication speech, he drove into exile in a Buick.

But it wasn't just that America was becoming the dominant global culture. Post-Armistice Britain was a more cosmopolitan place, and some at least of the pre-war social barriers were coming down. Before he found Virginia from Hollywood, the Earl of Jersey was married to Patricia from Cootamundra in New South Wales. Thelma Furness's husband, the Yorkshire shipbuilder, colliery owner and iron and steel proprietor Marmaduke Furness, took as his first wife Daisy Hogg, who like his mother came from neighbouring Co. Durham. She died in 1918, and in 1926 Duke Furness married Thelma. Her father was American, her mother was half-Chilean and half Irish-American. When Thelma's affair with Edward Prince of Wales (and others) brought that marriage to an end in 1933, Duke married the twice-widowed Enid Lindemann, an Australian whose first husband had been a New Yorker and whose second was an English brigadier general. The days had gone when marriage among the country-house-owning classes was confined to a British elite.

The carved seventeenth-century staircase at Cassiobury Park, Hertfordshire, photographed before the house was demolished in 1927 and the staircase sold to the Metropolitan Museum of Art in New York.

And Duke married Thelma for love, not as a way of bailing out his finances or saving his country estate, which was draped around a well-maintained modern hunting box called Burrough Court near Melton Mowbray. In fact *he* tried hard to settle money on *her*, and couldn't understand when she refused angrily on the grounds that it was un-American and amounted to 'wife-buying'.

The other side of the coin was an American admiration for the Old Country. This found expression in some unlikely ways. Antique and architectural fittings dealer Charles of London established an office on 5th Avenue in 1904. White Allom & Co. had showrooms in New York and Montreal; Syrie Maugham had a shop on Michigan Boulevard in Chicago, where she was in partnership with cosmetics queen Elizabeth Arden, and another on East 57th Street in New York. Via dealers like these, stained glass from English country houses, fireplaces and plaster ceilings, even entire rooms, found their way across the Atlantic. When Cassiobury House in Hertfordshire, ancestral seat of the earls of Essex, was demolished in 1922 after the 7th earl's marriage to an American heiress had failed to restore the family fortunes, Edward Pearce's Restoration staircase was acquired by the Metropolitan Museum of Art; it is still there today, exquisitely beautiful but purposeless, leading up to nowhere. The 5th Avenue apartment of Judge Irwin Untermeyer, a noted collector of English furniture, contained two panelled rooms from demolished country houses, complete with Elizabethan chimney pieces and overmantels supplied by Charles of London.

In the 1920s firms like Charles, White Allom and Robersons of Knightsbridge were packing up cartloads of fixtures and fittings from English historic houses and shipping them across the Atlantic. Robersons' *List of Some of the Panelled Rooms Installed in America by Robersons of London* (c.1926) mentions twenty clients, including Edsel Ford in Detroit, William Randolph Hearst and Mrs Childs Frick, daughter-in-law of art collector Henry Clay Frick. Among the

items supplied were a 'George I Painted Drawing Room', 'late 17th Century Oak Room Christopher Wren period', 'Fine Henry VIII Linenfold Room for Living Room, with Stained Glass in Windows', and 'Pine Panelled Living Room, noted as from Stanwick Park'.[14] Stanwick Hall in Yorkshire was one of five houses owned by the dukes of Northumberland. It was sold to pay off death duties after the death of the 7th duke in 1918, and Robersons acquired at least four of the rooms.

The hall at Agecroft Hall, Lancashire, in 1903. Twenty-two years later Agecroft was dismantled and shipped across the Atlantic where it was reassembled in Richmond, Virginia.

It was even possible for the American Anglophile to acquire an entire country house by mail order. The timber-framed Tudor Agecroft Hall in Lancashire was dismantled in 1926 and re-erected beside the James River in Virginia. 'There seems to be a craze in the United States at the moment for this sort of thing,' said the bewildered secretary of the Ancient Monuments Society. 'No building of decent age and character is safe from the danger of kidnapping,' roared the *Manchester Guardian*.[15] Basildon Park, an elegant country house in Berkshire designed in 1777–83 by Carr of York, was acquired in 1929 by a property speculator named George Ferdinando, who offered to take it down and re-erect it in any suitable position in America in return for $1 million. It would be left 'ready for occupation as a Private Residence, or as a Museum, College Building, or Public Library', declared the sales brochure. 'Any patriotic American wishing to benefit his native State by presenting this imposing building is hardly likely to again meet with such a unique opportunity.'[16] In the year of the Wall Street Crash, Ferdinando's timing was bad. There were no takers, and he settled down with his wife and children to live in a wing of the house, although he sold some of the plasterwork to T. Crowther & Sons of the North End Road, and it found its way to the Waldorf Astoria in New York, which to this day boasts of its Basildon Room as having 'spectacular panelling and a frescoed ceiling taken from the British estate, Basildon Hall, and beautifully offset by a Parisian marble fireplace'.[17] British audiences who laughed at *The Ghost Goes West*, Alexander Korda's 1935 movie about an American businessman who reassembles a Scottish castle in Florida and finds that the castle phantom has come too, tempered that laughter

with the uneasy recognition that not everything about the film was fantasy.

On balance, a country house is best left where it is. Fortunately, that was the line taken by most American purchasers. They bought. They rented. Very occasionally, they built. For the wealthy outsider, even in the comparatively diverse and cosmopolitan society which had outstripped its Victorian ancestry, a country house remained an essential adjunct to acceptability, a badge of access as much as of success.

The Wisconsin-born entrepreneur Harry Gordon Selfridge, who had settled in England in 1906 and opened his eponymous Oxford Street department store three years later, harboured dreams of grandeur. In the last days of 1920 he rented the Adam-designed Lansdowne House on Berkeley Square, home to four British prime ministers and described in the press as 'the finest historical mansion in London'.[18] Selfridge already had his country house: four years earlier he had taken a lease on Highcliffe Castle, a sprawling monster on the south coast near Bournemouth.

Highcliffe was an architectural curiosity. Essentially a Picturesque Gothic creation by the prolific but pedestrian architect W. J. Donthorne, it incorporated elements of an early sixteenth-century French chateau brought over by its then owner, Lord Stuart de Rothesay, British ambassador at Paris between 1815 and 1824, and again from 1828 to 1831. The effect did not please the purists: Pugin ranted that 'Mr Donthorn could not have had the slightest idea of Gothic architecture as he has . . . made a sad havoc of everything';[19] although the episode is a reminder that in removing bits and pieces from British country houses and shipping them overseas, Ferdinando and his like were following a tradition in trafficking which had been around for generations. Stuart de Rothesay was accused at the time of 'Elginism', a reference to the 7th Earl of Elgin's recent looting of the Parthenon.

Selfridge liked Highcliffe's historical associations, which lent both romance and legitimacy to his tenure. He took the house furnished, and proudly showed off the writing table which had belonged to Marie Antoinette and had been used by both Napoleon and, bizarrely enough, Kaiser Wilhelm II, who spent a holiday at Highcliffe in 1907 when he couldn't find anywhere to stay on the Isle of Wight. But Highcliffe didn't belong to Selfridge; and as his retail empire grew, he wanted a country house of his own.

A castle of his own, in fact, in the same way that Highcliffe was a castle – that is, not a castle at all. Selfridge was in love with the pseudo-Gothic, 'the Walter Scott gothic, revived romantically through the influence of the Waverley novels', said Philip Tilden, who knew him well.[20] In 1921 Selfridge bought a 2½-mile stretch of coastline within sight of Highcliffe. It included Hengistbury Head outside Bournemouth, a beautiful promontory jutting out into the Channel, with views across to the Isle of Wight and the Needles. This headland was to be the site of Selfridge's castle.

Or more accurately, his castles. Selfridge commissioned Philip Tilden to design a Little Castle, which despite its name was to be the same size as Highcliffe, and would stand on the very edge of Hengistbury Head with only the sea beyond it. Above and behind it, a plateau encircled by four miles of turreted walls was the site of what Tilden labelled the Large Castle, and with good reason. It was to be the biggest castle in the world.

For Tilden this was a dream commission. 'Things had been arranged so that I was untroubled in my designing by the thought of money or the means by which to live,' he remembered artlessly; and with money no object, the only limits were imposed by the coastal site and his own imagination.[21] For more than a year he paid monthly visits to Selfridge at Highcliffe or Lansdowne House, bringing drawing after drawing of what was to be 'the most beautiful architectural effort of modern history'.[22] As the palace grew, each new tower or gallery or saloon was greeted by Selfridge with the same uncritical approval, each disbelieving question from outsiders – 'But how will you ever get it done?' 'What on earth does he want to do it for?' – with the same unsmiling confidence, the same 'cold, clear, blue and calculating eye'.[23] And slowly, inexorably, Selfridge's palace of dreams edged further and further away from reality.

One of Philip Tilden's designs for Selfridge Castle, Gordon Selfridge's palace of dreams at Hengistbury Head in Dorset.

Tilden's vision began with a gateway which pierced the bastioned wall, 'like the gate to a Spanish city'.[24] That was ambitious for Bournemouth, but it was only the start. From here the main drive wound its way upwards until it reached a piazza and a marble staircase hall with a dome almost as big as that of St Paul's. The central vista, 1,000 feet long, stretched out to either side of this hall which opened into a cloistered garden with a vast *galerie des glaces* based on that at Versailles on one side, which led to Selfridge's own apartments; and an equally vast tapestry gallery on the other. There were 250 guest suites, dining chambers that would seat hundreds, a theatre and tennis courts and picture galleries and

baths. Recitals would be held in a Gothic hall, 'where the organ would reverberate through the stone lace of screen and vaulting'. A winter garden led down through Piranesian archways to a covered lake fed with streams of clear water and filled with fountains which always played.

Dominating the palace was a great tower 300 feet high, which contained suites of rooms, studios, laboratories and observatories, culminating in a viewing platform on the roof. 'From here,' wrote Tilden with longing, 'one could watch the great liners gliding up the Solent to their berths; here one could forget the labour that went to the making of all man-thought things, and remember and appreciate only the results that man could achieve; or through some giant telescope learn more of the eternal vastness of space.'[25]

It was all bonkers, of course. A country house this size would take decades to build. (That was the reason for the Little Castle, which would be completed first so that Selfridge had somewhere to live during the years of construction work.) By 1923 Selfridge had given up Highcliffe Castle and abandoned his plans for a palace of dreams. He may never have taken the project seriously; he told *Building News* that it had always been meant as 'an imaginative exercise' only, and he sold Hengistbury and the rest of his coastal holdings, 700 acres in all, in 1930 without a stone being laid.[26] Philip Tilden, who certainly meant it as more than an imaginative exercise, was astute enough to note that in the early days as news of the scheme spread, Selfridge's neighbours along the coast treated him with a new respect. And everyone enjoyed themselves. The palace of dreams was born out of a new optimism. 'It was all a sign of the times,' remembered Tilden, 'a sign of hope that fear had been strangled, that culture was to be fostered, that men and women were to be happier.'[27]

A COUPLE OF YEARS after Harry Gordon Selfridge abandoned his dreams of an English castle by the sea, another American millionaire embarked on his. In the summer of 1925 Alice Head, editor and managing director of *Good Housekeeping* magazine, received a cablegram from her boss in California:

> WANT BUY CASTLE IN ENGLAND PLEASE FIND WHICH ONES AVAILABLE STDONATS PERHAPS SATISFACTORY AT PROPER PRICE BUT PRICE QUOTED SEEMS VERY HIGH SEE IF YOU CAN GET RIGHT PRICE ON STDONATS OR ANY OTHER EQUALLY GOOD HEARST

Newspaper tycoon William Randolph Hearst was at the peak of his career and in the middle of a frenzy of building and collecting. He already owned a New York apartment reputed to be the biggest in the world, and a 250,000-acre estate at San Simeon on the

California coast, halfway between Los Angeles and San Francisco. In the late 1920s he bought Sands Point, a castle on Long Island, for his wife Millicent; and built a 110-room 'beach house' at Santa Monica for his mistress, the film actress Marion Davies. At Wyntoon in northern California his architect Julia Morgan created an extraordinary group of brightly painted Hansel and Gretel cottages in a forest.

Hearst filled all these homes with precious things: Greek and Roman vases (he owned 450 of them); early Renaissance tapestries (he had the largest collection of important tapestries in private hands in the world); arms and armour; silver, paintings, manuscripts, fine furniture. His rage to collect led his *New York Times* obituarist to make the astonishing claim that at his peak, Hearst single-handedly accounted for a quarter of the world's art market.

Hearst began to think about renting or buying a country residence in Britain in the spring of 1925 and Alice Head, who acted as his London agent as well as managing the National Magazine Company, the British side of his publishing empire, went down to Kent to see Leeds Castle, but reported that it was in a poor state without a bath in the place. As the telegram suggests, the other leading contender was St Donat's, an imposing medieval fortress dating back in parts to the twelfth century, overlooking the Bristol Channel and about twenty miles west of Cardiff (and hence in Wales, rather than England – a distinction which was lost on Hearst). Victorian Gothic Revival architects Bodley & Garner had renovated St Donat's at the beginning of the century, leaving it in reasonable shape. It did at least have electricity from its own generator, and three bathrooms. The owners, Lady Winifred Pennoyer and her American diplomat husband Richard, had bought it in 1922; but now they wanted to sell, opting instead to live at Ingestre Hall, the Staffordshire ancestral home of Lady Winifred's first husband, who had died in the war.

On 16 August 1925 a *New York Times* headline announced 'Hearst buys 12th Century Castle in Wales for a Residence When He is Abroad'.[28] Alice Head had managed to buy the castle and

111 acres for £27,000, although she used company funds, so that strictly speaking, St Donat's always belonged to the National Magazine Company rather than to Hearst personally.

Why did he want it? 'Well,' he told the press on his first visit (which didn't take place until 1928 – he was in no hurry to see his new toy), 'I had seen some of your great castles, such as Caernarfon and Conwy, and they made such an impression on my mind that I decided to acquire something in the same way, only smaller and more domestic, as it were.'[29] That was only part of the story. He liked the idea of a place in the country where he and his mistress Marion Davies could entertain their friends, something which naturally didn't figure in his public pronouncements on St Donat's: in 1928, and again in 1930, 1931, 1934 and 1936, they spent the summer touring Europe, sometimes starting and always ending their trip there. 'We'd stay as long as we possibly could,' Davies recalled, and 'take life easy after the tour'.[30] Hearst's wife Millicent had visited the castle during a trip to Britain in 1926, but she and her husband never spent any time there together.

However, Hearst's real reason for buying an 'English' castle, as he persisted in calling St Donat's, had less to do with Marion Davies and rather more to do with finding the right setting for part of his growing collection of British and European art treasures. Before that happened there was work to do to bring the castle up to American standards. Mains water and electricity were laid on and Hearst's architect, Sir Charles Allom of White Allom & Co., demolished much of Bodley & Garner's recent work as not authentic enough. Allom created new bedroom suites and dozens of bathrooms, an outdoor swimming pool on the site of an old tilt ground, and two new halls, both of which made use of imported historic fittings. The carved and gilded early Tudor ceiling of the banqueting hall was bought by Allom after it had been removed from a church in Boston, Lincolnshire – not, as Marion Davies rather sweetly misremembered, from the Museum of Fine Arts in Boston, Massachusetts.

The second of Allom's great creations at St Donat's was the Bradenstoke Hall, so named because the timbers of its magnificent fourteenth-century roof originally graced the priory of Bradenstoke in Wiltshire. In a separate purchase Hearst also bought Bradenstoke tithe barn for £3,600, unwittingly becoming embroiled in a national scandal. When it emerged that the tithe barn was being dismantled and removed from its site, reputedly for shipping to America, there was a public outcry. 'An historical building cannot be severed from its site without destroying its spell,' said the *Observer*. 'In its new setting what it will most forcibly recall will be the misguided taste of its uprooter.'[31] Antiquarians wrote to *The Times* to complain about 'this stupid example of vandalism', and to mutter darkly that 'the name of a well-known American newspaper owner [was] associated with the transaction'.[32] The demolition was 'an attack on the soul-life of our people'. Questions were asked in Parliament; Prime Minister Ramsay MacDonald was urged to do something; Americans in England added their voices to the protests; and there were calls not only for the British government to ban the export of such treasures, but for the US Congress to ban their import.

When it was finally confirmed in October 1930 that Hearst was indeed the purchaser of the tithe barn and the priory buildings, but that both were destined for St Donat's rather than 5th Avenue, the Society for the Protection of Ancient Buildings, which had led the campaign to save them, was decent enough to thank Hearst for providing a proper home in Britain for them, and to recognise that 'this damage to our heritage is more the result of the action of our own people than that of citizens of the United States of America'.[33]

The introduction of historic elements into the castle was fundamental to Hearst's vision. 'Need ancient atmosphere at St Donat's', read one of his many telegrams to Alice Head.[34] On another occasion he urged her 'always to add old things' rather than making new.[35] A stone chimney piece and overmantel from Bradenstoke was installed in the Breakfast Room, and two sixteenth-century French chimney pieces in the Bradenstoke Hall. The Banqueting Hall had a gothic screen which had originally graced a West Country church, but which Hearst's agents had found built into the wall of a house in Bridgwater. 'We shall just increase [the castle's] historical interest,' he told reporters in 1930,

Urban Huttleston Broughton, 1st Lord Fairhaven, painted by Alexander Christie in 1942.

Bavarian giltwood cartouche supported by cherubs presided over the scene.

The 1st Lord Fairhaven enjoyed his wealth, and he enjoyed displaying it. He owned a fleet of Rolls-Royces, one of which was driven into Cambridge every afternoon so that his valet could collect his copy of the *Cambridge Evening News*. There was a full complement of domestic staff, including a male chef, a pair of yellow-waistcoated footmen and a butler in tails. Guests were said to have their shoelaces ironed before breakfast, and noted with astonishment that while lunch was being served, housemaids would brush the fitted carpets in the other rooms, so that when Fairhaven came out of the dining room 'there was the room once again as if nobody had ever been in it'.[45] In the evenings, he listened to the BBC news on a wireless that was brought in on a silver salver.

This opulence proved too much for many visitors, who found Fairhaven's transformation of Anglesey Abbey to be somehow un-English. 'More a fake than not,' was James Lees-Milne's verdict on the house after a visit in 1943, when he repaid Lord Fairhaven's hospitality by describing him as 'a slightly absurd, vain man, egocentric, pontifical, and too much blessed with this world's goods'.[46] Even the National Trust, which accepted Anglesey Abbey after Lord Fairhaven's death in 1966, was slightly nonplussed by the sheer exuberance and the variable quality of the contents. Staggering slightly under the weight of such riches, an early Trust guidebook led visitors out into the grounds – also Fairhaven's creation, and justly famous – with relief, declaring that 'not everyone will respond with the same enthusiasm to the rich interior of Anglesey'.[47]

Reactions like these missed the point of Anglesey Abbey. Lord Fairhaven's tastes were indeed un-English, but that didn't make them bad. They were Gilded Age tastes, turn-of-the-century robber-baron tastes, the tastes which Fairhaven's mother and Fairhaven himself grew up admiring in Long Island mansions and 5th Avenue palaces.[48] They are what makes Anglesey Abbey such an unusual example of the English country house between the wars, a fragment of an ancient religious house on the edge of the fens where two worlds met.

And Anglesey Abbey reminds us that America came to the English country house with more than just new bloodstock and a million dollars and an acquisitive admiration for the Old Country. It brought something of its own, a flamboyance and a joy in collecting.

CHAPTER THIRTEEN

A Queer Streak

Feeding the doves at Ashcombe: from left to right, Adele Astaire, Princess Polny, Tallulah Bankhead, Tilly Losch and Cecil Beaton.

FROM 1930 TO 1945 society photographer Cecil Beaton rented Ashcombe, the surviving portion of a late-seventeenth-century mansion which once nestled in a remote valley on the Wiltshire Downs. Beaton's Ashcombe exemplifies a different side of country-house culture between the wars, one which has nothing to do with tweeds and guns and panting retrievers, but with the ABC of Art, Bohemia and Culture, with masks and dressing-up and play-acting.

But the acts of reinvention and disguise which took place at Ashcombe hid an uncomfortable truth. Beaton's homosexuality, what he liked to call his 'queer streak', made him an outsider in that most conservative of English milieus, landed society. He and his gay friends led double lives. They were welcome in some houses and not in others, tolerated as oddities, whispered about as being 'artistic' – a common euphemism for homosexuality, just as 'oriental' was code for 'Jewish'. Some were outrageously camp, eager to shock. Siegfried Sassoon's lover, Stephen Tennant of Wilsford Manor in Wiltshire – part Peter Pan, part Dorian Gray, according to his biographer – caused outrage when he was photographed by Beaton in 1927 in the silver-foiled bedroom of his London house with make-up and marcelled hair, a flying jacket slung across his shoulders in a determinedly effeminate reminder of the masculinity that had been lost in the Great War.

Other gays were less flamboyant, more cautious, and with good reason. At the most visceral level there was a threat of physical and verbal abuse, even in the politest of polite society. In August 1927 Beaton, whose affected voice and long hair weren't calculated to endear him to hearty young heterosexuals, was tossed into the river at Wilton House by three of the other guests at a coming-of-age party for 'Sid' Herbert, heir to the 15th Earl of Pembroke.

Throughout the 1930s Beaton's Ashcombe was a place in the country rather than a fully fledged country house, a weekend retreat, although it was staffed all year round by a tribe of servants called the Betteridges, who cooked and cleaned and managed the gardens and were portrayed in Beaton's memoirs, like most of the local population of that corner of Wiltshire, as yokels, peasants and Starkadders.

In fact there was nothing of Cold Comfort Farm about Ashcombe. Beaton drove down from London on Fridays in his Ford, often bringing hundreds of flowers acquired at Covent Garden market – a gross of hydrangeas or lilies, bright speckled carnations and bunches of sweet-smelling sweet peas. The following day his house guests would arrive for the Saturday-to-Monday parties that were a feature of life at Ashcombe, their numbers supplemented

Cecil Beaton makes some final adjustments to his rabbit coat as Sir Michael Duff looks on.

mask, but not for long: he changed costumes at least three times in the course of the night, ending up in a flowered banyan. Even the supper tables wore fancy dress, in the shape of muslin tutus.

Everybody likes their party to go with a swing (although few would go as far as Chips Channon, who put Benzedrine in the cocktails at a formal dinner he gave for the queens of Spain and Rumania). Beaton provided non-stop entertainment, beginning long before his guests reached Ashcombe. As they converged on the valley where Ashcombe lay they encountered gesticulating papier mâché figures pointing them in the right direction; a bus which brought them in relays down the hill to the house was filled with libellous mock advertisements created by Gerald Berners. Villagers came to perform a rustic maypole dance, while the band from the Embassy Club in Old Bond Street were installed in the stables playing dance music. Local children dressed as gypsies wandered around, 'pulling a baby in a goat-cart, or letting off fireworks in their hands'.[8]

The highlight of the evening was a performance of *The Town Wench, or Chastity Rewarded*, a faux-Restoration comedy written by John Sutro and starring Gerald Berners as the lecherous Sir Jonathan Mock-Twitchett. Against the backdrop of the house and flanked by tall lime trees which glowed white in the arc lights, Mistress Sweetmeat, played by fashion model Olga Lynn in pink satin, did her best to resist Sir Jonathan's advances, to little avail:

> I will not listen to your threats nor prayers,
> You little West End baggage, come upstairs![9]

The party lasted all night, ending at 7 a.m. as a female guest dressed as a bacchante in a leopard skin tripped across the lawn and disappeared into the dawn.

SECTION II OF THE 1885 Criminal Law Amendment Act, usually known as the Labouchere Amendment after Henry Labouchere, the Liberal MP who presented it in the Commons, introduced a maximum penalty of two years in prison with hard labour for a man who procured, or attempted to procure, 'any act of gross indecency with another male person'. Section 11, which sent Oscar Wilde to Reading Gaol in 1895, criminalised any homosexual behaviour and in its vagueness it allowed considerable discretion to the police and the magistrates in deciding exactly what constituted an offence.

Prosecutions averaged around thirty a year, although the country-house-owning classes rarely figured. When they did, the consequences could be devastating. Sir Paul Latham, Bt, the MP who took over the rescue of Herstmonceux Castle in Sussex in 1931, was ruined by a wartime scandal. While still an MP, he joined the Royal Artillery on the outbreak of war in 1939. Two years later he was accused of indecent behaviour with three of his men. He tried unsuccessfully to kill himself by riding his motorcycle into a tree; resigned his seat in Parliament; and was court-martialled, cashiered from the army and sentenced to two years for 'disgraceful conduct of an indecent kind'. His wife divorced him and took their son to live in America.

More devastating than prison, particularly for a class whose status depended so much on social acceptance, was the disgrace. In the autumn of 1921 the Conservative politician Viscount 'Loulou' Harcourt, whose nickname might have set alarm bells ringing in some quarters, attempted to seduce the thirteen-year-old Edward James, who with his mother was visiting Harcourt's country house, Nuneham Court in Oxfordshire. James, who may or may not have been the illegitimate son of Edward VII, fought him off and told his mother, who indignantly repeated the story to her friends. Polite society, which already knew or suspected much about Harcourt's proclivities, began to feel uneasy at turning a blind eye to them. On the morning of 24 February 1922, Harcourt, who was married with four children of his own, was found dead in bed at his London house, 69 Brook Street. He had taken a large dose of a sleeping draught prescribed for a heart condition.

It would be 'grotesque' to suggest that Harcourt had committed suicide, announced the coroner at the ensuing inquest, recording a more kindly verdict of death by misadventure. Lord Esher, a friend whose son and daughter Harcourt had also assaulted – 'It is so tiresome that Loulou is such an old roué,' wrote Esher's daughter rather tolerantly. 'It is just ungovernable sex desire for both sexes' – quickly went through the viscount's personal papers and removed his child pornography collection, taking it off to his own house.[10]

The most notorious homosexual scandal of the 1930s concerned William Lygon, 7th Earl Beauchamp. That it is also one of the best known is due to the fact that the Lygons of Madresfield Court in Worcestershire were used by Evelyn Waugh as models for the Marchmains of Brideshead. Sebastian was recognisable as Hugh Lygon, whom Waugh knew at Oxford and who like his literary offspring was a charming self-destructive drunk. The household chapel at Brideshead where Charles Ryder kneels to say a prayer, 'an ancient, newly-learned form of words' in the final scene of Waugh's novel, is based on the Madresfield chapel, a riot of painted Arts and Crafts saints and metalwork which was created by Countess Beauchamp as a wedding present for her husband.

Happy families: Earl Beauchamp with his wife and their seven children.

And like Lord Marchmain, the head of the Lygon family lived in exile on the Continent, separated from his wife and children.

But whereas Marchmain's Venetian exile with his Italian mistress was of his own choosing, Earl Beauchamp's was not. The earl had a passion for male servants, which he indulged with reckless abandon throughout the 1920s. Harold Nicolson remembered a dinner at Madresfield where an astonished fellow-guest turned to him and asked, 'Did I hear Beauchamp whisper to the butler, "Je t'adore"?' Quick as a flash, Nicolson, whose own homosexual affairs were pursued rather more discreetly, said, 'Nonsense! He said, "Shut the door."'[11] Beauchamp openly slept with his young valet, George Roberts, during a visit to Australia in 1930 – so openly, in fact, that when he was preparing to travel from Sydney to Canberra, his hosts there let it be known that the valet would not be welcome.

At Madresfield he was caught in flagrante with his doctor; and in London, with an anonymous boy in a public bath (by Hugh Walpole, who told Virginia Woolf). Invited to Walmer Castle in Kent, where the earl as warden of the Cinque Ports had a household, Lady Christabel Aberconway was surprised to be introduced to a handsome young 'tennis coach' who didn't know how to hold a racquet. She was even more surprised to find the actor Ernest Thesiger, naked to the waist and wearing several strings of pearls. 'He explained that he had the right type of skin to heal pearls.'[12]

It was only a matter of time before the storm broke. Lettice, Beauchamp's wife and the mother of his seven children, seems not to have noticed his behaviour; she wasn't altogether clear what homosexuality involved, in any case.* But her brother, the 2nd Duke of Westminster, was all too clear. Explanations of Bendor's motive for outing his brother-in-law vary: he was homophobic, he was jealous of Beauchamp's successful public life, he resented the

* Or so the story goes. She later wrote to her children, confessing that 'for many years, I had strongly suspected that (with Daddy) all was not as it should be – and that one side of his life and desires went contrary to everything that is right, normal and natural' (Byrne, 148).

fact that the earl had fathered three sons while *his* only son had died when he was four years old.

Whatever the reason, malice, jealousy or moral indignation, in 1931 Bendor went to his sister and explained what her husband had been up to (with diagrams, according to one of the many legends that have grown up around the scandal). He then went to George V and told him that Earl Beauchamp, a senior politician, the Liberal Leader in the Lords and a man who had carried the sword of state at his coronation and served as Steward of the Household, was homosexual and that he intended to expose him and have him arrested. The prospect appalled the king, who is supposed to have muttered to himself, 'I thought men like that shot themselves.'

Countess Beauchamp had a breakdown and ran to her brother, an act of betrayal which her children, who remained loyal to their father, never quite forgave. Bendor pressed his brother-in-law to agree to exile and a formal separation, but for several months Beauchamp tried to ride out the approaching storm, behaving, in public at least, as if nothing had happened. He hosted a coming-out party for his third daughter Mary at the family's London residence, Halkyn House in Belgrave Square; and continued to fulfil official engagements, hosting political dinners and diplomatic receptions, speaking in the Lords. At the end of March he held a weekend party at Madresfield; guests included Stanley Baldwin, then the Conservative Leader of the Opposition, and Cecil Beaton's co-host at the Ashcombe *fête champêtre*, Sir Michael Duff. Lady Beauchamp was conspicuous by her absence, which her husband explained as ill health.

The story still didn't break. Beauchamp's second daughter Sibell later claimed it was because she was sleeping with Lord Beaverbrook, and out of consideration for her the press baron kept her father out of the papers. More likely it was due to George V, who was anxious to avoid public scandal. The king's bisexual fourth son, Prince George, had been romantically linked with Mary Lygon; he had stayed at Madresfield; and the thought that a prince of the realm might be called to give evidence in court horrified George

V. In any case, the age was more discreet, more deferential. What would the papers have said, exactly?

But Bendor would not let it go. He wrote to Baldwin, suggesting it might not be appropriate for the politician to weekend at Madresfield in future, and explaining why. He persuaded his sister to place an advertisement in *The Times* announcing that she was staying with him, and that she 'wishes her friends to know that she is very well and has been in good health for some time past'.[13]

Most damaging of all, Bendor pressed his sister into filing for divorce. There was to be no collusion, no chance for the earl to spend an uncomfortable night in a Brighton hotel with an obliging woman while the private detectives kept watch in the corridor. The grounds were that he was 'a man of perverted sexual practices', and that throughout their married life he 'has committed acts of gross indecency with the male servants and other male persons and has been guilty of sodomy'.[14]

Now Earl Beauchamp's reckless abandon came back to ruin him. The petition described in lurid detail the earl's sexual activities with ten men, nine of them named, at Madresfield, Walmer Castle and Belgrave Square. The earliest instance, an encounter in the chauffeur's room at Halkyn House, dated back to 1909; the most recent, an act of sodomy committed in the library at Belgrave Square with an unknown male, was said to have taken place in November 1927.

Lady Beauchamp's petition was filed on 14 May. The following day a brief item appeared in the press to the effect that her husband 'has been obliged on account of the unsatisfactory state of his health . . . considerably to curtail his engagements for the future'.[15] He resigned his post as Liberal Leader in the Lords and retreated to Madresfield, where one evening at the beginning of June three senior peers arrived to tell him that the king wanted him to leave the country, and hinting that if he did not do so immediately a warrant for his arrest would be issued. He crossed the Channel on 9 June. Bendor sent him a charming little note: 'Dear Bugger-in-law, you got what you deserved. Yours, Westminster.'[16]

*

The more obviously queer culture espoused by Beaton and his set tended to be confined to safe artistic and theatrical circles where make-up and cross-dressing might raise an eyebrow, but not a warrant for the victim's arrest; a world which was predominantly urban, metropolitan, at home backstage at a Cochran revue or listening to Ambrose's band in a Mayfair nightclub, but not, perhaps, weekending in the country. Or so you'd think. But the acquisition of a place in the country was still seen by many as a desirable adjunct to success, especially among those from bourgeois roots.

Take just two iconic gays of the period. Ivor Novello celebrated a contract with Gainsborough Films in 1927 by buying Munro Lodge, near Maidenhead, which he renamed Redroofs and kept as his country residence for the rest of his life. And Noël Coward bought Goldenhurst, a beautiful seventeenth-century timber-framed house, barn and cottage in Kent, tile hung and clad with ragstone.

Coward found Goldenhurst in 1926. He was twenty-six and, buoyed up by the success on both sides of the Atlantic of *The Vortex*, his sharp depiction of decadent Mayfair society, he came back from America with a vintage Rolls-Royce (which broke down so often that he reckoned it cost him as much as three brand-new Bentleys); a new business manager and lover, Jack Wilson; and a determination to find a place by the sea where he could move with an entourage that included Jack, his secretary Lorn Lorraine, his father and mother (who were not always on speaking terms), his younger brother Eric and his Auntie Vida.

All the houses he looked at were 'either too old and falling to pieces, or so new that they were horrible', he recalled.[17] Eventually a farmer, Mr Body, contacted him to say his farmhouse was available to let with six acres for £50 a year. Goldenhurst Farm was at Aldington in Kent, overlooking the Romney Marsh with views across to Dymchurch and the English Channel; on clear nights, the lights on the French coast sparkled on the edge of the horizon. But the house itself was poky with a Victorian feel to it, clad in red brick and filled with tiled fireplaces and awful wallpapers, surrounded by ponds and hedges and decrepit thatched barns, and boasting an eighteenth-century addition described by Coward as 'a square edifice wearing perkily a pink corrugated tin roof and looking as though it had just dropped in on the way to the races'.[18] No one was particularly impressed with the place, but at least it had electric light and a garage for the vintage Rolls; so the playwright decided to rent it while he scoured Kent for somewhere more suitable.

Coward lived at Goldenhurst for the next thirty years. When he and Jack found that behind the tiled fireplaces and awful wallpapers there lurked a rather lovely sixteenth- and seventeenth-century oak-beamed farmhouse, he bought the freehold from Mr Body; and between 1927 and 1930 they turned Goldenhurst into an attractive small country house, running together the farmhouse, the 'square edifice', one of the barns and an adjoining cottage. There were four reception rooms and six principal bedrooms, and a large studio or ballroom with a stage, the 'Big Room', where Coward would entertain house guests with performances of his latest works. It was at Goldenhurst that he wrote *Cavalcade*, the patriotic, jingoistic story of the Marryott family in the first thirty years of the twentieth century, which opened to huge acclaim in October 1931 and ran for 405 performances. ('It is sensational. It is staggering,' was how the *Observer*'s theatre critic began his review.[19]) Well-known figures, including Cecil Beaton and Joan Crawford, Somerset Maugham and Evelyn Waugh and Ian Fleming, would motor down for the weekend. The village postmistress went into shock one evening after putting through a call from Marlene Dietrich, phoning to congratulate Coward on his latest film.

Goldenhurst illustrates the blurred boundaries between farmhouse, place in the country and country house. When Coward found it in 1926, it was Goldenhurst Farm (although his mother, who could be difficult and didn't appreciate being moved from Coward's comfortable town house in Ebury Street, referred to it dismissively as 'the cottage'). Even after Coward and Jack Wilson had finished modernising the house, installing five bathrooms, a private electricity supply, garaging for four cars and oil-fired central heating, it was still a farmhouse. In 1937, when Coward's father died at the house, after having been relegated to a lonely existence in a room above the garage, it was Goldenhurst Farm, and Coward himself referred to it as 'a fine old 17th-century farmhouse'.[20] By 1956, however, when he put it on the market and moved to Jamaica, Goldenhurst had become a 'country estate' with a 'picturesque old manor house' and a 'home farm'. Its upwardly mobile metamorphosis was complete.

Neither Novello nor Coward were bred to country-house life. The former was the son of a Cardiff council rent collector; the latter's father was a clerk. Beaton came from a more solidly middle-class background: his father was a timber merchant, although that scarcely equipped him for life in landed society.

Others in their overlapping circles were born with a silver spoon in their mouth and a country house to call home. Stephen Tennant was the son of the 1st Baron Glenconner and Pamela Wyndham, a Soul who commissioned Detmar Blow to design Wilsford Manor. After inheriting Wilsford on the death of his mother in 1928 Tennant turned Blow's delightfully reticent essay in Arts and Crafts into a camp fantasy filled with mirrors and animal skins, gilded cherubs and Venetian grotto furniture, supplied by Syrie Maugham and much of it with a nautical theme, to reflect his enthusiasm for sailors. The stage designer Oliver Messel, a frequent visitor to Beaton's Ashcombe, was also familiar from birth with the country-house milieu. Oliver, who was born in 1904, was raised at Balcombe House, a lovely and very substantial Georgian rectory between Crawley and Haywards Heath; but on the death of his grandfather Ludwig in 1915 the family moved five miles down the road to Nymans, a country estate that Ludwig Messel had bought in 1890 with the profits from his City stockbroking business. Oliver's parents spent much of the 1920s remodelling the house, which metamorphosed from something rather ordinary into a romantic evocation of a late-medieval manor house, complete with two-storey great hall and minstrel gallery. Writing in 1932 Christopher Hussey mused that 'so clever a reproduction is it of a building begun in the 14th century and added to intermittently till Tudor times, that some future antiquary may well be deceived by it'.[21]

Gerald Berners' country house, Faringdon in Berkshire, was rather more substantial. 'Plain and grey and square and solid,' according to Nancy Mitford, who was a friend, Faringdon was 'a part of the rolling Berkshire landscape'.[22] It was built between 1770 and about 1787, when the inveterate tourist Viscount Torrington was already commenting on the plainness which was part of its charm: 'Mr Pye's house adjoining to Farringdon [*sic*] shews nothing particular, so I did not ask to see it.'[23] (The Pye in question was Henry James Pye, rightly described by Nancy Mitford as 'the worst poet laureate we have had'.)

By the time that Gerald Hugh Tyrwhitt-Wilson, 14th Baron Berners, to give Berners his full title, inherited Faringdon in 1931, he was nearly fifty. He was already well known as a minor composer – Diaghilev commissioned a ballet from him, *The Triumph of Neptune*, which was choreographed by Balanchine – and an even more minor painter and author. His homosexuality was not a particular secret among his friends, but he was never as obvious as Beaton or as flamboyant as Tennant, perhaps because his sexual appetite was not particularly strong. His partner, Robert 'Mad Boy' Heber-Percy, was bisexual, reckless and nearly thirty years his junior. When they met at Sir Michael Duff's Welsh country house, Vaynol, in the early 1930s, Heber-Percy was only twenty-one but already had a chequered past which included being asked to leave his cavalry regiment, working as an extra in Hollywood and helping to run a dubious London nightclub. Heber-Percy is supposed to have gone to stay at Faringdon for the weekend after the Vaynol meeting, but things didn't go well in bed. On the Monday he asked Berners if he should go, and Berners simply said, 'Don't leave. You make me laugh. I don't mind about the other.'[24]

Stories of Berners' eccentricities at Faringdon are legion, as are examples of his jokey sense of humour. Every month he dyed the pigeons magenta, copper green and ultramarine; fellow composer Constant Lambert used to claim that they only mated with pigeons of the same colour. He was also said to have experimented with

Belton House in Lincolnshire: 'almost overful with treasures', thought house-guest Chips Channon in 1935.

Welbeck Abbey, the Marquess and Marchioness of Londonderry, art historian Kenneth Clark and Conservative politician Lord Hugh Cecil.

Some house parties lasted no more than forty-eight hours. Others went on for an awfully long time: in Scotland, a long train ride from London, an invitation to shoot often meant a visit of three weeks. Besides meeting royalty and shooting, many parties were convened for a particular purpose. In January 1935, Chips Channon and his wife drove up to Lincolnshire to stay with Lord Brownlow, better known as Peregrine Cust, the courtier who the following year would take Wallis Simpson to France while her lover renounced his throne. Fellow guests at Brownlow's seventeenth-century Belton House were Duff and Diana Cooper,

Viscount and Viscountess Weymouth, and Lieutenant Colonel the Honourable Piers Legh and his American wife. Channon was a little overwhelmed by Belton; it was 'almost overful of treasures', he thought. And his fellow guests were 'frankly bores'.[2] (Being rude about the company was part of the fun: Harold Nicolson, staying with the Channons in September 1936, called them 'a trifle vulgar'.[3]) The real purpose of the gathering lay elsewhere. After dinner the party set out in cars for an invitation ball the Duke and Duchess of Rutland were holding for their two teenage daughters at Belvoir Castle, ten miles away.

Rex Whistler, Conversation Piece: The Family of the 6th Marquess of Anglesey, *1938.*

Channon was altogether more impressed with Belvoir. The ducal daughters both looked beautiful; coloured lights in the trees lit the way up to the house; and the ball, with music by Emilio Colombo and his orchestra, was 'a glorious Disraelian festival, and the castle illuminations could be seen for miles'.[4] Violet, the 78-year-old Dowager Duchess of Rutland (and mother of Diana Cooper) cut a particularly imposing figure in white, surrounded by her descendants, thirty of them, including a gaggle of small grandsons in black suits.

A fortnight after the Belvoir ball the Rutlands hosted a small house party for guests who were going to a charity ball in aid of nearby Grantham Hospital. It was common, usual even, to host a house party for events like this: a trip to the races, a ball, a political gathering. The Earl of Harewood hosted one every year at Harewood House for the Doncaster Races; the Duke of Westminster did the same for Aintree. In April 1932 Lady Warwick hosted a small party at Warwick Castle – Prime Minister Baldwin, Lady Warwick's brother-in-law Anthony Eden, then the undersecretary for foreign affairs, and their wives. They were also there for a purpose: to attend the opening by the Prince of Wales of the new Shakespeare Memorial Theatre at Stratford-upon-Avon, which took place on Shakespeare's birthday, Saturday, 23 April.

Like the Channons' visit to Belton and the Warwick Castle party, most country-house parties were weekend affairs. Born out of a burgeoning railway network – there was after all no point

in going away for a weekend if you spent the entire weekend travelling to where you wanted to be – and helped along by the rise in car ownership, the very word 'weekend' had only just joined the lexicon of leisure. A contributor to *Notes and Queries* at the end of the nineteenth century wrote that in Staffordshire, 'if a person leaves home at the end of his week's work to spend the evening of Saturday and the following Sunday with friends at a distance, he is said to be spending his *week-end* at So-and-so'.[5] Was this usage confined to Staffordshire, he asked?

By the 1920s the country-house weekend was an institution, although in polite circles it still wasn't actually *called* a weekend. The accepted phrase was 'Saturday-to-Monday'. The Duchess of Buccleuch recalled that it was 'awfully non-U to call them weekends. I remember being surprised that anyone should use the term.'[6] The phrase also distinguished the leisured classes from those who had to be at work first thing on Monday morning, and for whom a weekend began on Saturday afternoon and ended on Sunday evening. People invited you 'for a Saturday to Monday and that was precisely what they meant', said Loelia Ponsonby. 'It would have been very rude to leave on Sunday night.'[7]

HOW DID IT WORK? Whether a Saturday-to-Monday or a more extended stay, the country-house party began with invitations given and received.

Turn-of-the-century etiquette manuals were full of fiendishly complicated instructions on the theory and practice of invitations, how they must be worded, when they must be sent, how they should be responded to; and dire warnings of the catastrophic social consequences of transgressing them. 'To widely depart from any of these received canons of etiquette,' cautioned Maud C. Cooke in the classic *Manners and Customs of Polite Society*, 'is to commit a decided solecism and to discover an utter unfitness for the desired social rank.'[8] But the interwar years were changing times: by the early 1940s Stephen Tennant could ask Sibyl Colefax down to his Wiltshire country house for the weekend by simply writing 'Sybil [*sic*] dearest, do come to Wilsford soon. Suggest a day. I will meet you at the station.'[9]

To be sure, there were plenty of people who would regard *that* degree of informality as a decided solecism, if not a signal that

Philip Sassoon with John Singer Sargent, Lord Rocksavage and Sybil Sassoon at Port Lympne: 'the new etiquette is informal'.

civilisation was teetering on the edge of extinction; but the times were changing. Laura, Lady Troubridge, a baronet's wife whose books on etiquette and entertaining were best-sellers in the 1920s and 1930s, announced in 1939 that 'the new etiquette is informal':

> Remember you are of your day, and of your time, and therefore you will not be doing the wrong thing if you accept this new spirit, and waive any petty, cramping little rules which were intended for another, and far more formal, age.[10]

What did it matter if you felt sleepy and got up to go to your room at a house party before your hostess had authorised your departure from the drawing room, or invited friends to stay over the telephone rather than by letter, or used someone's Christian name when you had only just been introduced? 'Simplicity – that's the key-word for social demeanour nowadays.'[11]

Having accepted an invitation to spend a few days in the country, the next hurdle was deciding what clothes to take. 'One's clothes were a worry,' said Lady Marjorie Stirling, daughter of the Earl of Dunmore. Even for a seven-day shooting party, a woman was expected to dress for every day of the week. 'There were very rich people who had marvellous clothes, but on the whole one just scraped through.'[12]

Loelia Ponsonby suffered agonies on her first visit to the Duke of Westminster's Eaton Hall, going down to meet the rest of the guests in the library that evening in a recently bought chiffon dress, 'a singularly inappropriate choice for December', she remembered with a shiver; and appearing the following morning in a 'reach-me-down green tweed suit'.[13] (The Ponsonbys were always hard up. When Loelia came out, she had to re-cover her worn-out dancing shoes, dipping the heels in red ink and stitching black satin above the soles.)

Here again, Laura Troubridge was on hand with words of advice. Avoid anything too smart. Otherwise, when you get into a muddy lane 'you will wish you had chosen a classically plain tweed coat and skirt, the skirt wide enough to walk in, and the colour a soft tone to melt into the landscape'.[14]

Once the invitation had been accepted and the right clothes were packed, the next step was to get to one's weekend destination. If that destination wasn't too far from town, and sometimes even if it was, a leisurely drive was the usual option. In the summer of 1935 (and on a Friday – Saturday-to-Monday seems to have been a movable feast), the Channons motored down from London to Longleat in Wiltshire. It was quite a long journey, well over a hundred miles, and they took their time, stopping off on the way to picnic and have a snooze in a field. Everything was quite relaxed, as was their reception. 'We found the splendid domain lying in the full heat of a June day,' Chips wrote in his diary, 'with its amber-stone, gardens, dogs and almost overpowering beauty.'[15]

Loelia Ponsonby's arrival at the Earl of Lonsdale's Lowther Castle in the 1920s was anything but relaxed. She and her mother travelled up to the earl's Westmorland house by train, and they were greeted on the platform at Penrith station by a groom clad in buckskin breeches, high boots, a cloth coat in the Lonsdale yellow and a beaver hat. He conducted them to a coachman waiting in an open yellow landau drawn by a pair of cream-coloured horses, and when the two women were safely ensconced, the groom leapt up beside the liveried coachman and the landau set off on a stately progress through the town, leaving the Ponsonbys' luggage to follow in a yellow van.

When Marmaduke Furness invited Thelma Converse up to his shooting lodge near Inverness in August 1925 for the start of the grouse season, she also went by train. So did he, and his staff – valet, three footmen and two housemaids. Thelma had barely settled into her compartment before the valet knocked and informed her that dinner was ready. She found her host waiting in a sleeping compartment which his staff had converted into a temporary private dining room, with white tablecloth, champagne in ice buckets and a picnic basket packed with all kinds of delicacies. 'What, no plover eggs?' she asked, at which he took her in his arms and told her he loved her – a carefully planned stratagem, with a predictable outcome.

Lady Marjorie Stirling never forgot the social anxiety of arrival at a strange house. 'I always found it very alarming, driving up a long drive, not knowing what to expect,' she said. 'The door would be opened by the butler and you were ushered into a room full of people, nearly always strangers. It made me feel quite sick.'[16]

It was usual to arrive around teatime, or soon afterwards. When Wallis and Ernest Simpson drove down to Fort Belvedere to spend their first weekend with the Prince of Wales, they timed their journey to arrive at six on Saturday, bringing Wallis's maid Mary with them in the car. (Sometimes guests arrived with their own personal servants, sometimes they came alone, in which case a resident footman or maid would be deputed to look after them.) The Simpsons were greeted at the door by the prince himself. He took them into the octagonal drawing room and introduced their fellow guests: Thelma Converse, whose seduction on the night train from Euston had ended in her becoming Viscountess Furness, and who had been the prince's mistress for several years; Thelma's sister and brother-in-law; and Gerald Trotter, the prince's groom-in-waiting. After the introductions the prince personally showed them up to their room.

After dressing for dinner the Simpsons were back down for cocktails, where they found the prince dressed in a kilt (with a silver cigarette case tucked away in his sporran), working away at his needlepoint and with two cairn terriers at his feet, one of which promptly tried to bite Ernest Simpson's ankle. Dinner was simple: oysters, roast beef, salad, a pudding and a savoury. Afterwards, guests were invited to try their hand at a jigsaw puzzle, the pieces of which were spread out on a long table in the drawing room; or to play a hand of cards. Bored, Thelma suggested dancing: the gramophone played 'Tea for Two', and the prince took his mistress in his arms and whisked her away into the marble hall. After dancing briefly with Thelma's sister and Wallis, he announced he was off to bed. 'This being your first visit to the fort,' he told the Simpsons, 'perhaps I should tell you about the rules. There are none. Stay up as late as you want. Get up when you want. I go to bed early and get up early so that I can work in the garden.'[17]

They came down to breakfast on Sunday morning and looked out of the window to see their host advancing across the lawn in a sweater and baggy plus fours, and wielding a billhook. He invited them both to join him in hacking back the laurels. 'It's not exactly a command,' said Gerald Trotter diplomatically, 'but I've never known anybody to refuse.'[18]

Wallis, whose experience of country-house parties had included several stuffy weekends at Knole with the Sackvilles, was unprepared for the relaxed atmosphere at Fort Belvedere and the relatively simple domesticity of the prince, whose reputation as a

Wallis Simpson helping herself to some lunch on the terrace at Fort Belvedere, c.1935.

fast-living socialite was common knowledge. After a buffet lunch the prince showed the Simpsons round the fort. 'What fascinated me,' wrote Wallis later, 'was the architectural wizardry that had been exercised in imparting to the interior of this sprawling fort such an atmosphere of warmth and informality . . . For a bachelor's country house, the whole effect was astonishingly warm and attractive.'[19]

The Prince of Wales's easy-going approach to his weekend guests was in sharp contrast to the formality of entertaining in some of the great ducal houses, where many of the pre-war protocols remained firmly in place. Full evening dress had virtually gone out with the war, but dressing for dinner was still de rigueur, and black tie was the norm. Guests gathered in the drawing room at about 7.30 where a butler assisted by a footman served cocktails, 'the worst form of drinking', according to Viscount Astor, because they were taken on an empty stomach and appealed to women and young girls.[20] Particularly popular in the early 1930s were the White Lady (gin, Cointreau and fresh lemon juice) and the Paradise (gin, apricot brandy and orange juice), both said to have been invented by Harry Craddock, the legendary barman at the American Bar of the Savoy Hotel from 1920 to 1938. If it was a big party and most of the guests were strangers to each other, the hostess discreetly introduced each man to the woman he was to escort in to dinner.

At 8 p.m. the butler announced that dinner was served and the guests went in. At some of the grander houses and on more formal occasions, the strict order of precedence was followed, with the host leading the way and escorting the woman of highest rank, the woman second in rank with the man second in rank, and so on. The man of highest rank would come last, accompanied by the hostess. 'Always consult a *Peerage* or *Baronetage* if in doubt as to the precedence due to expected guests bearing titles', warned 'a Member of the Aristocracy' in the 1916 edition of *Manners and Rules of Good Society*, that bible of the socially insecure. 'Wealth or social position are not taken into account in this matter, it being strictly a question of date.'[21] With guests whose social rank was hard to determine, this raised all kinds of problems. Nearly two decades later Elizabeth Craig told 'the modern hostess' that 'there are no hard and fast rules about placing ordinary people like you and me at a dinner table'.[22] She advised that the only rules to remember where no titles were involved were to place the principal woman on the husband's right, and the principal man on the hostess's right, and to separate husbands and wives where possible.

Once everyone was seated, gloved footmen handed round the first course. They were supervised by the butler, who usually stationed himself close to his master's chair or by the sideboard from which he dispensed wines – sherry after soup, hock with the fish, champagne for the rest of the meal until pudding, and then claret, sherry, port and Madeira. White wine was served just chilled, champagne came ice-cold and claret with a very slight warmth, which was achieved by putting it on the hotplate in the server for a few moments.

The typical country-house dinner was a meal of Edwardian proportions. 'For a big dinner party, a really posh dinner party,' said Viscountess Hambleden, who entertained regularly with her husband at their country house outside Henley in the 1930s, 'you would have either thick or clear soup, followed by fish, followed by the entrée – chicken or quails. Then you had saddle of lamb or beef; you had pudding; you had a savoury; and then you had fruit.'[23] 'A Member of the Aristocracy' recommended that young women should steer clear of the more highly seasoned dishes ('middle-aged and elderly ladies are at liberty to do pretty much as they please'). They should also avoid artichokes, because it was impossible to eat them elegantly; and 'as a matter of course, young ladies do not eat cheese at dinner-parties'.[24]

Servants left the dining room after pudding, and the women set off for the drawing room ten minutes or so later. Coffee was sometimes brought in a silver coffee pot, and a woman would pour her own while the footman or maid held the salver. They were soon joined by the men: it wasn't fashionable any more to linger over the port for more than fifteen or twenty minutes, just long enough for the wine to go round twice and for the men to smoke a cigarette.

After-dinner entertainments depended on the party. Bridge was common, with several tables set up in the drawing room. 'In most country-house parties bridge forms the chief if not the only amusement,' declared *Manners and Rules*, 'and is played not only after dinner but in the afternoon also.'[25] Dancing to gramophone records was popular in some circles, as Wallis Simpson had found at Fort Belvedere. On her first evening at Eaton Hall Loelia Ponsonby was treated to 'that harmless, world-wide, after-dinner amusement, card-tricks'.[26] Major Basil Kerr, the Duke of Westminster's agent for the Eaton estate and one of his closest friends, was a genius with a pack of cards, and he and Bendor entertained everyone with their patter and their sleight of hand.

Musical recitals hadn't quite been superseded by the gramophone or the wireless. 'Mother and Sybil Thorndike used to play duets,' recalled Lady Molly Trevelyan's daughter Pauline.[27] That's why there were always two pianos in the drawing room at their house, Wallington Hall in Northumberland. John Christie, an Eton schoolmaster who took over the running of his family's 10,000-acre estate in 1922, was so fond of musical entertainments that he built a brand-new great hall at his rambling Sussex mansion to house a cathedral-sized organ so that a friend of his, the recently retired organist at the Chapel Royal in St James's, would have something to play. The Organ Room was the scene of concerts and operatic evenings for guests and local people throughout the 1920s, with Christie taking part along with professional and semi-professional musicians. He fell in love with one of these visiting performers, a young soprano named Audrey Mildmay, and after their marriage in 1931 conceived the idea of providing a larger space within the house as a showcase for her talents. The result was the Glyndebourne Festival, which opened its doors to the public for the first time in 1934 with a performance of *Le Nozze di Figaro*.

Sometimes more contemporary entertainments were on offer. Lloyd George was a great film fan, and he used to hold regular Saturday-night screenings in the study of his Surrey country house for friends, farmworkers and other local people. His chauffeur had lessons in how to operate the projector, and Lloyd George made the brave decision not to select the films which were sent down from London every Friday, preferring to take pot luck. 'At a recent Saturday night entertainment,' reported the *Manchester Guardian* in 1928, 'the film turned out to be one of the crudest of love dramas, and at another it was a Charlie Chaplin picture.'[28]

Breakfast was much more informal than dinner. Women guests often preferred to breakfast in their room, as did some hostesses. Men began to assemble when the breakfast gong sounded at 9.00 or 9.30, but it wasn't usual to wait until everyone was seated, and some guests might not appear until 10.00 or so. If she wasn't still in bed, the hostess would preside over the table, and footmen or maids were in attendance the whole time, serving eggs, sausages, bacon and devilled kidneys from a hotplate; and ham, tongue and game pie from the sideboard.

When breakfast was over, which might not be until 11.00 or 11.30, the host and hostess would set out the options for the day. 'The vital thing was to keep people amused without making them feel too organised,' said the Countess of Rosse,[29] a sentiment endorsed by the author of *Manners and Rules*, who noted that the good hostess's 'consideration and tact are so successfully exerted that somehow her guests always find themselves doing exactly what they like best and in company with those who are most congenial to them'.[30] At Holker Hall in Cumbria, Lady Moyra

Cavendish used to make a list of who wanted to go riding, who wanted to fish, or play tennis or golf. 'There were a great many activities to choose from,' her daughter Diana remembered. Jigsaws were popular, left out on a side table in the library or drawing room for anyone to contribute a piece or two. Guests might be taken to see an interesting local church or a picturesque ruin, or shown round the house where they were staying.

During her visit to Westmorland young Loelia Ponsonby found herself being conducted round Lowther Castle by the aged Earl of Lonsdale, whose anecdotes grew progressively more extravagant as he moved from room to room. Loelia was surprised when he pointed out a small chamber where Mary Queen of Scots had been imprisoned until she made a dramatic escape (Lowther was built by Sir Robert Smirke in 1806–14, more than 200 years after Mary's death); and she was frankly astonished when he showed her an iron sledge and told her he had travelled to the North Pole and back in it, pulled by six huskies. She later discovered there was a grain of truth in both stories: Mary Queen of Scots was held at an earlier Lowther after she crossed the border into England on her flight southward; and Lonsdale had undertaken an astonishing journey by sleigh to the Arctic Circle and up into northern Alaska in 1888–9.

Loelia was more impressed when her host, a keen racing man and a senior steward of the Jockey Club, showed her the Lowther stable yard:

> Every morning the grooms had to lay on it a sort of stencil of the Lonsdale arms with numbered partitions and into each partition they sprinkled coloured sawdust with the appropriate number. When the whole thing was complete the stencil was removed and there lay the Lonsdale arms in gorgeous Vistavision.[31]

And each morning the earl would come to inspect it, bringing with him his pack of pet dogs, who scrabbled around in the sand and ruined the grooms' work.

At Port Lympne, the hyperactive Sir Philip Sassoon rarely allowed his house guests to rest, careering around country lanes with them packed in the back of his Rolls, seeking out remote Queen Anne and early Georgian country houses. Philip Tilden, who used to take part in these architectural forays, described one occasion when Sassoon took it into his head that he simply had to gain entry to a lovely late-seventeenth-century house near Tenterden on the edge of the Kentish Weald. He strode up to the front door and told the maidservant who opened it that he was there to see Mrs Mackintosh; and when she told him that no one of that name lived there, he ordered her to go and look. 'Philip's smile, his introductions and his card (which, by the way, might have done the trick without all this scheming and plotting) led us to a pleasant meeting with hospitable people,' recalled Tilden, and to a memorable glimpse of 'faded rooms with their high, austere panelling, simple and dignified, the sweeping stairs, the old bits of furniture, the chintzes of fifty years before'.[32]

Frances Stevenson, who as Lloyd George's mistress and secretary frequently accompanied him to house parties in the 1920s, was exhausted by the Sassoon circus. 'There is always a spirit of restlessness about Philip's houses,' she wrote in her diary after she and Lloyd George escaped from a boisterous party at Trent Park in May 1921, 'always a crowd of people trying to be bright.'[33] Their flight may have been influenced this particular weekend by Sassoon's extending an invitation to the Dolly Sisters, identical twin dancers who were already as well known for their antics in the casinos and royal bedrooms of Europe as they were for their performances on stage and screen. In the late 1930s Stanley Baldwin told the Tory historian Arthur Bryant how Sassoon entertained large weekend house parties from London at Trent, with guests including 'ladies with painted toenails'. He wasn't present on these occasions, he added hastily.[34]

One constant in any country-house party was the way in which the day's activities were punctuated by lengthy pauses for meals. If there was shooting, the men often disappeared for the day, leaving at 11.00 and not returning much before 7.00 that evening: on a big shoot, the women guests would join them in the field for lunch and stay on to watch the sport or to join in themselves. Otherwise lunch was served in the dining room, usually at 1.00 or 1.30. It was a light meal: a soufflé, perhaps, followed by an entrée, followed by cold meats, followed by a pudding, followed by cheese and dessert.

Then there was afternoon tea at 4.00 or 4.30, just a little something to tide everyone over until dinner. Elizabeth Craig suggested a suitable menu: buttered crumpets, buttered date and walnut loaf, cream cheese and pimento sandwiches, maids of honour, coffee éclairs, chocolate sponge roll and queen cakes.

Early evening was taken up by the rituals of bathing, although the number and modernity of bathrooms varied wildly from one house to the next. The Earl of Strathmore's St Paul's Walden Bury in Hertfordshire, where Elizabeth Bowes-Lyon accepted

Rex Whistler, Mr and Mrs Robert Tritton taking tea in the garden at Godmersham Park, Kent.

a prince's proposal of marriage during a house party, had two bathrooms for twenty-five bedrooms. Drumlanrig, one of the Duke of Buccleuch's Scottish houses, also had two, and that was only because they had been installed when the mansion was taken over as a military hospital in the Great War. 'We wouldn't have had bathrooms otherwise,' said his duchess.[35] Other owners adhered to the Victorian principle that bathrooms were an unnecessary luxury when there were housemaids to carry up brass cans of hot water.

At the other end of the spectrum there was William Randolph Hearst's St Donat's Castle, which was fitted with thirty bathrooms, and the electric-lit marble-clad deco delights of advanced houses like Eltham Palace. Hot water supplied from more efficient central tanks meant that, as Arthur Oswald wrote in 1931, 'instead of a lukewarm trickle from the tap marked "Hot", a carefully tempered mixture of hot and cold wells up with a dance of bubbles'.[36] It was still rare for guests to find bathrooms en suite, though: at Flete, where Lady Mildmay converted some of the old dressing rooms, there still wasn't a bathroom for every bedroom, 'so you couldn't stay as long as you wanted', remembered her daughter rather wistfully.[37] At 7.30, bathed and refreshed and dressed, it was down to the drawing room again for cocktails and dinner and bridge.

AND SO TO BED. The great nocturnal pastime of the country-house party was sex, or so it seemed from the 'modern' plays put on in the West End in the period, and the testimony of the divorce courts. In the early hours, the bedroom corridors of England's stately homes were apparently filled with house guests padding along in their dressing gowns, intent on committing some act of adultery or fornication or betrayal. Exaggerations, no doubt; but it is certainly true that in some circles a Saturday-to-Monday was seen as a good opportunity for infidelity. Servants bringing the early morning tea discovered sleeping lovers; husbands and wives fell out of love with each other and into bed with strangers, and it was vulgar to mind. A 'don't ask, don't tell' policy ruled over all. One August night in 1933, a nursemaid at the Earl of Rosebery's

Dalmeny House in Scotland bumped into a young man carrying an electric torch and creeping down one of the corridors. Assuming he was a bedroom-hopping guest, she didn't challenge him. In fact he was a burglar and he got away with a pearl necklace worth £4,000.

Memoirs of the period are full of advances repelled, both above and below stairs. There is a story (probably told of several debutantes) about how one evening at Lisadell in Co. Sligo young Constance Gore-Booth was nonplussed to discover her dinner-companion's hand creeping up her thigh under the table. Lifting the offending hand high in the air, she said in a loud voice to the rest of the party, 'Oh, look what I've found in my lap!'

Rosina Harrison, who was Lady Cranborne's lady's maid, described in her memoirs an incident when she was staying at the British Embassy in Rome and an Italian footman tried to get into her bedroom:

> That night I was getting ready for bed and was standing in my voile knickers and vest when I saw a hand come round the edge of the door. I didn't stop to think. I was over in a flash and pressing the door against the obtruding hand with all my strength. I watched it go red and then purple and I could hear some nasty Italian words uttered from the other side . . . They began getting louder and as I didn't want to wake the house I relaxed my pressure. The hand was quickly removed and there was a scuffling of feet down the corridor. I was taking no chances though so I dragged a heavy chest of drawers and pushed it against the door. After that I slept easy.[38]

The next morning she found the footman in the servants' hall, looking reproachful and wearing his arm in a sling.

There is a darker side to this carry-on-up-the-country-house bawdy, though. The predatory nature of some encounters leaves an uncomfortable taste. For every Con Gore-Booth, confident enough to humiliate in public the man who was assaulting her, there were a hundred young women who weren't. For every Rose Harrison, prepared to slam a stranger's hand in the door rather than let him into her bedroom, there were a hundred scared maidservants who would rather risk their virtue than their job. And while there was a convention in some circles not to mind about a spouse's infidelities, it wasn't always possible to hide extramarital relationships. The marriage of publisher Sir Neville Pearson came to an abrupt end after a weekend at his country house in the summer of 1927. When the house party broke up, Sir Neville's wife left with one of the guests. Sir John Grey of Enville Hall in Staffordshire also saw his marriage founder after a house party at which his wife formed an attachment to a fellow guest. Whatever happened during their stay, when they got back to London Lady Grey advised her husband 'that she wanted a change in their relations',[39] and sometime later Sir John received a letter from her announcing that she and the guest were living together in the Felix Hotel, Jermyn Street. There was no doubt whose side the press was on when the story broke: 'Baronet freed from faithless wife' was the headline when Grey obtained his decree nisi.[40]

Oddly enough, the great country-house cause célèbre of the period involved only two people, and they were married to each other. It happened – or didn't happen, as the story will show – at Oakley House in Bedfordshire, a pleasant if unassuming thirteen-bedroom mansion built around 1750 for the dukes of Bedford. At the end of the Great War Oakley passed to a Bedford cousin, Arthur Russell, 2nd Lord Ampthill; and a few years later, it shot to fame as the scene of an event that rocked the nation and made legal history – nothing less than a virginal conception.

The virgin in question was Lord Ampthill's daughter-in-law, Christabel Hulme Hart. A Mayfair couturier, Christabel married the Hon. John Russell, heir to the Ampthill barony, in 1918, to his parents' dismay and, as it turned out, to his, because just before the wedding Christabel told John that she didn't want children for a while, and that therefore they weren't going to be sleeping together in the foreseeable future.

John took this news surprisingly well. But as the months went by and his wife began frequenting fashionable nightclubs without him and teasing him about her entourage of dark, sleek Argentines and Greeks who danced like dreams of perfection, the strain began to tell. In 1919 he bought Christabel a copy of Marie Stopes's *Married Love* and tentatively suggested they might use some form of birth control. She said 'no'. In 1920 he appeared in her bedroom brandishing a gun and threatening to shoot her cat if she refused him any longer. She remained unmoved. So he turned the gun on himself and said he would blow his brains out there and then if she did not consummate the marriage. It made no difference.

In the summer of 1921 Christabel told her husband she was expecting a baby.

That October she gave birth to a 10 lb 8 oz boy, Geoffrey. John Russell's response was to petition for divorce. The last time they had shared a bed, he said, was when they had been put into the same room while staying with his parents at Oakley the previous December. On that occasion, no physical contact of any kind had taken place. In fact Christabel hadn't even kissed him since August 1920. The child could not be his.

His wife gave a different version of events. She told the divorce court that while they were at Oakley, there had been 'Hunnish scenes' in which her husband had tried and failed to have sex with her. She had also had a soak in a bath recently left by John – perhaps this could have led to her pregnancy? Then her counsel dropped a bombshell: doctors who examined Christabel while she was pregnant would testify that her hymen was still intact. She was a virgin.

The arguments over what the press called 'the Russell baby case' dragged on through two divorce trials. At stake was the boy's future as heir to the Ampthill barony. Christabel's counsel urged the jury not to leave him 'branded with the infamy that cannot be redressed that his mother was a woman of no reputation, and he was a nobody's child'. John's barrister begged the jury 'to free this young man from a tie which he hoped would be a bond of pleasure but is nothing but a rusty chain that burns into his soul'.[41]

The first trial was inconclusive, and the second, described by one of the Sunday papers as 'probably *the* most talked of divorce case of a generation', ended in defeat for Christabel. The reputations of both husband and wife were in tatters. Their most private and intimate habits had been discussed at length in open court. John was widely regarded as effete and unassertive for allowing Christabel to dictate the terms of their relationship (and a revelation that he liked to dress up in women's clothes didn't help). His wife was seen as unnatural for refusing to accept her wifely duties. Both were condemned for having 'freakish' manners and morals. George V was so appalled at the details being aired in public that he lobbied for a change in the law: 'The pages of the most extravagant French novel', declared his spokesman, 'would hesitate to describe what has now been placed at the disposal of every boy or girl reader of the daily newspapers.'[42] As a direct result, the Judicial Proceedings (Regulations of Reports) Act was passed in 1926, prohibiting detailed press reporting of divorce cases.

In the meantime, though, Christabel appealed against the verdict. It was upheld by the Court of Appeal. So she went to the House of Lords, and in a remarkable judgement in May 1924 the Lords overturned the decree nisi on a legal technicality by a majority of three to two, thus legitimising the two-year-old Geoffrey Russell and his virgin birth.* The Ampthill heir's mother turned to fiction, if she hadn't already, and published a novel called *Afraid of Love*, 'the study of a woman who resolved to be dependent on no man'.[43]

When the house party was over and it was time to say goodbye to one's host, when the maid had packed the bags and the car was waiting at the front door, there was one more ritual to be observed. A guest had to tip the servants.

There was the chauffeur, if he drove them to and from the station; the groom, if he looked after their hunters; assorted footmen and maids if they performed any kind of personal tasks during the stay. Most important of all was the butler. If he had

* John and Christabel were finally divorced in 1937; she never remarried. Geoffrey inherited as 4th Lord Ampthill on John's death in 1973. His right to the title was contested by a son from one of John's subsequent two marriages, but although he refused to take a DNA test his claim was upheld by the Lords, on the grounds that they should not now overturn the ruling they had made half a century earlier.

unpacked for a guest, done any valeting or run any errands such as looking up train times or sending off telegrams, he could expect around ten shillings (50p), even for a Saturday-to-Monday. That is somewhere between £25 and £125 in today's money, depending on how one does the calculation. If the butler hadn't done anything at all apart from his normal duties, a guest could perhaps get away with five shillings. A footman who acted as one's valet deserved another five shillings, and if another footman carried up the breakfast tray, he might expect half a crown. Maids who performed any of these services in the absence of male servants merited only half the male rate. In some circumstances, a guest might also tip the head housemaid.

Choosing the right moment for this little ceremony could be awkward. Leaving money on the dressing table might be all right after a stay in a hotel, but it was a little cold for a private house. If you were tipping a maid, you might ring the bell and ask to see her. As for the butler, Lady Troubridge advised leaving things until he 'is putting the rug round you in the car. Then let the note slip from your hand into theirs, even though your friends are still waving from the front door.'[44]

But there were parting gifts for guests, too. At Woburn Abbey, a footman stood by the front door with a tray laden with cigars and cigarettes from which guests were invited to help themselves, something to smoke in the car or in the train on their way home. At Holker Hall, they were presented with a charming papier mâché attaché case filled with canapés and sweetmeats, little scones filled with Morecambe Bay shrimps and other delicacies. Each item was individually wrapped and labelled for the homeward journey, and each attaché case contained a label and postage stamps, so that when the treats had all been eaten a guest could simply pop into the nearest post office and send it back.

CHAPTER FIFTEEN

Field Sports

THE ORGANISED HOUSE PARTY played to one of the country house's great strengths: its role as a base for the elite's pursuit of leisure.

In some parts of England, life revolved around the hunt. In Gloucestershire, the Beaufort Hunt met six days a week from the middle of August through till 1 May in the 1920s, and there were fifty horses kept in the stables at Badminton. In the Midlands, where some of the country's most prestigious hunts met, the Meynell and the Quorn and Pytchley and the Belvoir, there was a ready market in country houses to let for the season. The day after the invitation ball at Belvoir Castle that Chips Channon enjoyed so much in January 1935, there was a special meeting of the Belvoir pack at the castle for the convenience of the guests.

Even so, when it came to organised country-house pastimes, the shoot was king, as it had been for three or four decades. So popular was the organised shooting party in the years before the

A meeting of the Beaufort Hunt at Badminton, c.1925.

First World War that it came to be *the* fashionable country activity. The numbers of birds killed in a single day, the Edwardians' marker of a successful shoot, could run into the thousands. The all-time record belongs to a party of seven guns, including George V and the nineteen-year-old Prince of Wales, shooting on the Hall Barn estate near Beaconsfield. On 18 December 1913 they killed 3,937 pheasants, three partridges, four rabbits – and one 'other'. Keen shots kept running totals of their kills. Looking back on his sporting life from the vantage point of the 1930s, the 6th Duke of Portland remembered with awe the prowess of the 2nd Marquess of Ripon, who died in 1923. Between 1867 and 1900 Ripon killed 370,728 creatures. The list included 142,343 pheasants; nearly 100,000 partridges; and two rhinoceroses, which Portland claimed to have seen him shoot dead, right and left, with a four-bore rifle from the back of an elephant in Nepal.[1] (*Are* there rhinos in the Himalayas?)

Portland recalled with relish other scenes from late-Victorian and Edwardian glory days, like the time when Winston Churchill's father, Lord Randolph Churchill, was shooting on the Marquess of Londonderry's Wynyard estate in the north-east of England and accidentally killed a fellow guest's pet dachshund. Anxious to make amends, Lord Randolph had the dog stuffed and presented it to its bereaved owner as a Christmas present. In a glass case.

The 9th Duke of Devonshire was notorious as an uncertain shot. There is a gate on the Chatsworth estate in Derbyshire which he would proudly show to friends as the place where he made a record bag with a single shot. A wounded cock pheasant was running past this gate and he fired at it and killed it. With the same shot he also killed a retriever that was pursuing the bird, wounded the retriever's owner in the leg, and hit his own chef, who happened to be on the other side of the gate watching the action. My, how everyone must have laughed.

The size of bag, in which dachshunds, chefs and rhinos were mercifully rare, was due to both a steady improvement in the efficiency of firearms and also the growing popularity of battue shooting, in which streams of birds were driven towards the waiting guns, as opposed to rough shooting, where the sportsmen walked in a line across stubble or root fields to find their prey. Battue shooting required careful and intensive game management. On the famous 23,000-acre Elveden estate in Suffolk, the Earl of Iveagh employed seventy men, and farming was subordinate to the all-important cultivation of birds. By 1911 there were around 25,000 keepers employed on estates in England, Wales and Scotland;[2] and the disadvantages to the tenant farmer of so much countryside – perhaps as much as 50 per cent of all agricultural land – being devoted to game conservation was causing disquiet in official circles. A Land Enquiry Committee Report of 1913 complained that the preservation of game was one of the reasons why the land was not producing its full yield. Under the law, the owner of land could reserve the right to kill and take winged game and to let this right to whoever he or she chose; tenant farmers couldn't take game, and had to live with the damage done to their crops by pheasants and other birds. Many weren't even allowed to shoot rabbits on their farms, in case they disturbed the birds. Under the Agricultural Holdings Act of 1908 they did have a theoretical right to claim compensation, but few chose to go down that route, as one Norfolk farmer explained to the committee:

> We have legal redress, but not many care to put it in practice. Very few landlords will pay willingly for damage done by game, and when they are forced to do so generally find means of resenting it. Generally some excuse is found for getting rid of the tenant.[3]

The sun set on this golden age in 1914. Keepers went off to the war. The guns found the stubble fields of Norfolk and the Home Counties replaced by the mud of Flanders. The 1914 Defence of the Realm Act made it illegal to feed grain to birds, which in turn led to smaller bags when shoots were organised. There was a brief renaissance after 1918, but then the sale and break-up of country estates began to take its toll. The stunning seventeenth-century Broome Park in Kent, once the home of Lord Kitchener but reduced piecemeal from 5,400 acres in 1908 to 650 acres in 1930, was still advertised in that latter year as having good shooting. But for those

The Duke of York shooting with Edwina Mountbatten, 1920.

who preferred their sports bloodless, the advertisement for Broome Park also noted that there was golf at Deal and Sandwich, and pointed out that the house boasted its own cricket pitch. Eighteen holes on the links and a summer afternoon listening to the crack of leather on willow were a good deal less expensive than maintaining a 5,000-acre shooting estate.

The fluid property market meant that some of the great game estates were let to syndicates, in a foretaste of the commercial shoots that are so common in the twenty-first century. The Duke of Portland looked at his Nottinghamshire neighbours in the 1930s and lamented the fact that at once-great houses like Clumber and Rufford, the shooting was either let or abandoned. At the same time there was a resurgence of interest in rough shooting as tenant farmers, once barred by fear and feudal obligation, bought their farms and began to shoot their own land – or to let it to new and enthusiastic sportsmen. 'The breaking up of estates has made shooting possible for the multitude, and has increased its popularity enormously,' wrote the author of a 1938 manual on rough shooting for the uninitiated. 'Anyone who has a second-hand gun and thirty pounds to spare can take "a bit of shooting" nowadays, and many who have no other qualifications do so.'[4] The definition of rough shooting varied wildly, from a couple of fields, one man, a shotgun and a dog, to a highly organised affair with half a dozen guns or more and five or six beaters.

There was general disagreement about the best way to rear birds. The Euston system, named after the Duke of Grafton's Euston Hall estate in Norfolk where it was perfected at the beginning of the twentieth century, was popular but labour-intensive. It involved taking eggs from game birds' nests in hedgerows, replacing them with dummies and putting the real eggs under bantams to incubate, returning them to nests in the wild for hatching. This was a full-time job, fraught with difficulties in finding the nests and getting the timings right. The advantages were that it reduced the risk of eggs being taken by vermin and increased the stock of wild birds, thought to provide much superior sport to hand-reared birds. 'In the main,' wrote the author of *Rough Shooting*, 'I have found that owners (i.e., those whose job it is to do the shooting and reap the rewards of their keepers' labours) are all for it, whilst the keepers themselves would rather leave it well alone, saying that it is a risky and unsatisfactory business at the best of times.'[5]

It was also rather a difficult system to keep up, especially in the years after the First World War when the number of gamekeepers fell by around 30 per cent from pre-1914 levels. This fall, coupled with a contraction in arable farming, led to a decline in game birds, particularly partridge. Fewer gamekeepers meant less management of the bird population, and more damage from predators; while as arable fields were turned to pasture they provided a less suitable habitat. By the 1930s the number of partridges shot per 1,000 acres had fallen by nearly half from pre-war levels. Bad weather and disease also took their toll: a particularly wet summer and outbreaks of strongylosis, a disease caused by parasitic nematode worms, wreaked havoc in the partridge population in 1930–31. The partridge bag at Welbeck in 1931 was 793, down dramatically on the previous year's 3,486. It fell again in 1932.

But other years told a different story. Driven partridges, 'the acme of good sport' in the opinion of the Duke of Portland, were often in good supply. The annual partridge bag on the Welbeck estate topped 3,000 on ten out of sixteen years between 1919 and 1936. In the 1934–5 season alone, 6,537 partridges were shot, along with 5,148 pheasants – all wild birds, since hand-rearing had been abandoned several years previously. So it would be a mistake to think that after 1914 the grand battue and the large-scale organised shooting party were consigned entirely to history and corporate entertaining.

NOT EVERY COUNTRY-HOUSE OWNER indulged in field sports, of course, and even among those who did there were wide variations. Some of the older and longer-established county families rode to hounds and shot because they were bred to it: such things were second nature. Newcomers did it because they thought it was expected of them, or because it would help them fit in. Some preferred tennis and bridge and to hell with what the neighbours thought.

The 2nd Duke of Westminster was one who took his sports very seriously indeed. He played tennis and golf. He owned racehorses, and hosted house parties each year at Eaton Hall for the Grand National at nearby Aintree. He stalked deer in the Highlands and fished for salmon on his vast estate on the River Laxford in the far north of Scotland, or travelled to Mimizan, the lodge in the Landes between Bordeaux and Biarritz which he used as a base to go after wild boar. He made fishing expeditions to Norway in his steam yacht, the *Cutty Sark*; or sailed down the Adriatic to Albania in his other yacht, the *Flying Cloud*, and roamed around desolate lakes in tweeds and Homburg hat, making friends with brigands and shooting snipe, woodcock and teal. Then he would take himself off for several weeks each winter to Saint-Saens, the small chateau he kept in Normandy, for more boar hunting. Several times in Scotland he achieved the so-called 'triple crown', by shooting a stag and a brace of grouse and catching a salmon, all on the same day.

The annual autumn shoots on the Eaton Hall estate were major events, and long after the end of the First World War they were still being conducted on an Edwardian scale and with Edwardian ritual and ceremony. There were about twenty keepers employed on the estate. On a shoot they all wore bowler hats and fawn leggings, and the head keeper wore a green velvet cutaway coat with brass buttons. His bowler hat was trimmed with gold braid to mark him out. Eighty estate workers acted as beaters, wearing wide-brimmed scarlet felt hats and calf-length white smocks. To see them emerging from the woods was like being in a Bruegel.

Guests arrived at Eaton on a Thursday night and left on Sunday, in contrast to the normal practice at other country houses, where shoots were usually held on Tuesday, Wednesday and Thursday. On the morning of a shoot, a horse-drawn wagon carried leather cartridge boxes to the stands, each marked with its owner's name, along with shooting sticks, extra coats, and cartridge bags. The stands were marked by up to twelve white numbered pegs driven into the ground, arranged in two staggered lines, one behind the other. The cartridge wagon was followed by a horse-drawn charabanc carrying the loaders, each with a pair of guns.

By the time Bendor and his guests arrived in chauffeur-driven motor cars at the pegs at 9.30, the loaders had sorted out the equipment. One loader in each team of two carried a pouch containing 200 cartridges, while the lad helping him carried another two pouches similarly filled. Pegs were assigned, everyone took their places, and at a shrill blow on a whistle from the head keeper, the Bruegelesque beaters began driving the birds – pheasants, although there was also some limited partridge shooting on the estate – towards the guns.

A stand lasted for about thirty minutes, during which time each gun might get through 200 cartridges. Then the cars and wagons appeared, everyone climbed aboard and set off for the next stand, followed by an elaborately painted horse-drawn game cart with the day's bag so far. Three drives, and the guns were taken back to join the women for lunch at Eaton Hall. 'The ladies find amusement in lawn-tennis, or in attending or assisting at some neighbouring bazaar or fancy fair,' declared one etiquette manual – slightly misleadingly, because by the late 1920s women did shoot occasionally.[6] The Duchess of Bedford, who died in 1937 at the age of seventy-one when the plane she was flying crashed into the North Sea, is still reckoned by *The Field* to be one of the hundred best shots of all time.

In the afternoon the women usually joined the men as spectators for two more stands. That evening, game cards with the Grosvenor crest were placed in front of each gun's place at dinner, announcing the size of the bag. It wasn't uncommon for 2,000 pheasants to be shot in a single day, or for 150 guests to be invited to dinner at Eaton Hall on one of the shoot nights.

In 1931, anxious that the Eaton woods were being shot out, the duke leased World's End, a remote valley near Llangollen, and introduced something like 10,000 pheasants. The site was spectacularly craggy, 'like the background of a Wagnerian opera', remembered Loelia Ponsonby. 'One would not have been surprised to see old Wotan perched on some boulder.'[7] There was a timber-framed farmhouse, Plas Uchaf yn Eglwyseg, which had once belonged to the radical millenarian regicide John Jones, brother-in-law of Oliver Cromwell. Local legend said that in the sixteenth century Elizabeth I retreated here to have an illegitimate baby.

The autumn shoots continued as before. Only now they took place twenty miles from Eaton Hall. The guns, the carts, the 180 beaters and loaders and keepers and dog handlers, all trekked across the border into Denbighshire, bumping along in a procession of cars. Once they got there, the terrain was too rough for cars or

The Duke of Westminster with guests during a shooting party at Worlds' End, Llangollen.

carts to move the guns from one stand to another. They had to walk: Winston Churchill, who shot with Bendor at World's End in 1931, a few months after he had been knocked down by a car in New York, was provided with a donkey to take him from stand to stand. Cooks brought half-cooked dishes which were finished off in the ovens at Plas Uchaf yn Eglwyseg. 'In these wonderfully wild surroundings,' wrote Loelia, 'we ate an entirely sophisticated lunch, washed down with mulled claret.'[8]

Shooting parties on this Wagnerian scale were rare after the Great War. But then they were rare before the war, too. More common was a grand battue – still big, but for seven or eight guns, with five keepers supervising forty or fifty estate staff. Lunch would be brought down to a keeper's house by the butler and a couple of footmen, sandwiches or stews, usually with plenty of cider or beer to wash it down. The opportunities to be shown up as an outsider were numberless: talking too much; talking at all, in fact; tipping too little (keepers' fees varied from ten shillings to £5, depending on the number of days shooting and the size of the bag – a sovereign to the head gamekeeper was the going rate for a day's partridge-shooting, and as much as two sovereigns for a good day's pheasant-shooting); shooting a bird that rightfully belonged to another gun; bringing along a badly behaved dog; wearing clothes which seemed just a little too new. Even *Manners and Rules of Good Society* jibbed at the prospect of predicting all the perils and pitfalls that awaited the inexperienced gun. 'There are numberless other points relating to field sports wherein the "inexperienced sportsman" is apt to give offence,' it declared; 'but [they] would take up too much space to enter into in a work of this description.'[9]

Cecil Beaton gave an atmospheric description of the shoots that were arranged on the Ashcombe estate on the border of Wiltshire and Dorset in the 1930s by his landlord, who until recently had also been the landlord of the Grosvenor Arms in Shaftesbury. Alderman Robert Borley JP had made a point of buying up adjoining parcels of land for shooting, and every autumn he held a big shoot for the county. Beaton watched and listened to the sound of the beaters moving through the undergrowth, pushing the birds on until they flew out to meet the assembled guns. 'Their squawks of fright were mingled with the ghostly calls of the beaters, "Over! Over!", the excited barks and whines of the retrieving dogs and the echoes of the shots throughout the valleys.'[10] After the inevitably massive lunch at long tables with starched white cloths – pies and joints and cheeses, all washed down with wine and port – the party set off again for the afternoon drive and the pheasants, 'like some clumsy bomber', took to the air, only to be brought down to earth in a flurry of feathers.

The beaters at these occasions were a motley crew, old men and boys in green frock coats, patched velvet breeches and billycock hats. They seemed to come from another time, and they returned to it at the end of the shoot. 'And as the years advanced and the shooting expeditions became poorer events, this strange army disappeared into the shades from which they seemed to come.'[11]

*

EVEN AS THEY DISAPPEARED into the past, another strange army was coming to take the place of Beaton's beaters and their like, another mob in curious costumes whose shouts rang out from undergrowth and fields and lakesides on landed estates all over England.

Golfers.

In May 1931 the Prince of Wales flew from Hendon to Hamble Aerodrome in his De Havilland Puss Moth to inspect a new Canadian Pacific liner, the *Empress of Britain*, at Southampton. Then he crossed Southampton Water in a speedboat to Hythe, where one of the new Imperial Airways flying boats was waiting for him. He took the pilot's controls and took off, roaring over the *Empress of Britain* as she steamed into the Solent, dipped low in salute, then handed over the controls to the pilot. Afterwards he returned to Hamble in a speedboat and flew in his own machine to Hendon. He was speaking at a charity dinner in London that evening, but he sent a message to say that 'I have been unavoidably delayed in the country, but I would ask that the dinner should proceed and I will join you in about half an hour.'[12]

It later turned out that the unavoidable delay was caused by his touching down at Walton Heath Golf Club in Surrey, so that he could play in a club competition.

In his youth the prince was a keen steeplechaser. But in 1924 he fell at the first fence in a point-to-point and knocked himself out, ending up in bed for a month and causing Ramsay MacDonald to write from 10 Downing Street urging him to be more careful. MacDonald's letter was followed by a less polite one from the king. 'You have shown great courage & horsemanship which everyone appreciates,' he told his son, 'but the time has come when I must ask you to give up riding in the future in steeplechases & point-to-point races.'[13]

The prince continued to hunt, but golf took the place of competitive riding. He had become captain of the Royal and Ancient Golf Club in 1922 with a fifteen handicap, and over the next few years he accepted the captaincy of the Royal Mid-Surrey at Richmond and the Royal St George's at Sandwich. He took lessons from professionals, including Open champion Ted Ray, and in 1933 he reached the final of a parliamentary handicap tournament, being beaten after he lost his ball at the first hole in the final. When he came to the throne in 1936, headlines in the foreign press announced that 'Golf is Favourite Sport of Ruler'.[14]

The prince's enthusiasm helped to position the sport in the pantheon of country-house pastimes. Proximity to a golf course or, even better, a golf course of one's own, was now a sought-after adjunct to country-house life. The property pages in *The Times* extolled the virtues of this country house or that, claiming it was 'practically adjoining golf course', or 'adjoining the links' or offered 'excellent golf'. Tadworth Court in Surrey was put on the market in 1925 as 'a genuine Queen Anne mansion . . . 1½ miles from Walton Heath Golf Course'. (In the event the purchaser didn't have much use for the golf course – it was Great Ormond Street Hospital, which used Tadworth as a retreat for children with respiratory difficulties.) Nine years later East Burnham Park in Buckinghamshire excited interest when it was offered for sale, partly because Mendelssohn and Jenny Lind had stayed at the house, partly because of the wealth of rare plants and trees, due to the fact that Sir Harry Veitch, the horticulturalist, had lived there – but mainly because 'golf courses near the estate are Burnham Beeches, a mile, Stoke Poges, two miles, Beaconsfield, three miles, and Denham, five miles'.[15]

Even better than living next door to a golf course was having one of your own. In 1926 the motor manufacturer William Morris, Lord Nuffield, bought the club in Oxfordshire where he played and ran it as sole proprietor until his death nearly forty years later. He moved into rooms over the clubhouse and lived there until 1933 when he was able to buy Nuffield Place, an Oswald Milne country house next door to the links. The Rocks, a nineteenth-century Gothic castle at Marshfield in Gloucestershire, boasted its own private golf course. Harrods offered an unnamed Queen Anne country house in the Sevenoaks area, with fifteen bedrooms, beautiful gardens and a fine park, in which there was a nine-hole golf course. At Meikleour in Perthshire, Lord Lansdowne created a nine-hole course in the park after his menservants, who had traditionally been allowed to use Meikleour's bowling green beside the local village pub, smelled of beer while waiting dinner after games of bowls.

Owners as disparate as the Duke of Portland and Sir Philip Sassoon built nine-hole courses in their grounds. Weekends at Sassoon's Trent Park went with a swing: on one occasion the house party trooped out after lunch to watch an exhibition of trick shots by the great Australian golfer Joe Kirkwood. Afternoon tea was followed by flights over the grounds in Sassoon's private aeroplane; and dinner, by a firework display over the lake better than anything seen in London during the season. Even then, the entertainment wasn't over: as the moon rose over the gardens, everyone assembled on the terrace to hear songs from the Austrian tenor Richard Tauber.

Perhaps the finest country-house golf course was the work of Viscount Castlerosse, the *Sunday Express* gossip columnist and eldest son of the 5th Earl of Kenmare. Castlerosse, described by his biographer as 'the best golfer who ever played the game without a right elbow' (he was badly wounded in France during the First World War), was a legend in the golf clubs of Kent, Sussex and Surrey, not least because of his erratic behaviour and the fact that he insisted on being accompanied on a round by a servant carrying a jug of whisky, and helped himself to a tumblerful at each tee. During a competition at Deal he buried his ball in a bunker: the crowd that gathered to see how he would extricate it watched as he cried to the skies, 'Oh God, come down and help me with this shot. And don't send Jesus. This is no job for a boy.'[16]

Castlerosse's family seat, Kenmare House in Co. Kerry, had burned down in 1913 and instead of rebuilding the vast Victorian mansion, his father had converted a surviving Georgian stable block into a house. In the late 1930s Castlerosse resolved to create a full-size golf course at the western end of the park at Kenmare, on a stunning site overlooking the lakes of Killarney. He enlisted the advice of Henry Longhurst, golfing correspondent at the *Sunday Times*; the golf course designer Sir Guy Campbell; and,

The Prince of Wales with Viscount Castlerosse at St Andrews in 1933.

having decided on a whim that each hole must be associated with a different flowering plant, William Macdonald Campbell, the new curator of the Royal Botanic Gardens at Kew. 'I am determined to call on the paintbox of heaven and draw a panorama of 150 acres in massed colours,' said Castlerosse. 'The thing is to be as loud and vulgar as God will let you . . . I am having three banks of one acre each of wild native flowers, then an Australian bank and also a New Zealand bank.'[17]

The Kenmare course, one of the loveliest in the world, was opened with a blessing from the Bishop of Kerry in October 1939. Along with the banks of flowers and lake views from every green, Castlerosse hit on a plan to do away with the need for a servant to follow him with a jug. He set up a series of locked huts at strategic points around the course, each containing a bottle of whisky.

CHAPTER SIXTEEN

In Which We Serve

ANY COUNTRY HOUSE, *every* country house, relied for its smooth running on a plentiful supply of cheap labour. Without servants, who would cook and clean and wait at table? Who would make up the fires and run the baths and raise the children? Who would answer the bell when one rang? 'No one will deny that servants are a necessity in every home,' wrote one commentator in 1906.[1]

So when in the years after 1918 the domestic service market seemed poised on the edge of collapse, it sent a shiver through the servant-keeping classes. The reasons for the crisis were many: women, who made up the vast majority of indoor servants, found they enjoyed the taste of freedom which war work had given them and were reluctant to return to a rigidly controlled environment where their evenings, and even their identities, weren't their own. Working-class women had acquired a 'restless desire for independence, which is a legacy of the war', said the *Daily Mail*.[2] The rise of popular education widened their horizons. The high casualty rate among servicemen gave them alternative job opportunities. And the social stigma, especially among their peers, was becoming a powerful disincentive to service. 'I have suffered untold misery by the name "only a servant",' a parlourmaid reported to a government inquiry into the supply of domestic servants. 'Invitations start out, "Be sure and don't let it be known you are a domestic. We shouldn't like our friends to mix with servants." It is the snobbery of our own class.'[3]

The shortage of servants was serious enough in 1918 for the government to act – or at least, to set up a committee of inquiry. Weeks after the Armistice was declared, the Ministry of Reconstruction invited a Women's Advisory Committee to look into the problem. Their report, presented the following spring, highlighted a lack of training, a lack of status and wide variation in pay and conditions.

Some of the committee's proposed solutions were quite innocuous: dispensing with caps, for example, and persuading employers not to call servants by their Christian names. This denial of identity was a common cause for complaint among female servants. Edith Lockwood's mistress called her 'Annie', because she already had a friend called Edith. Gordon Grimmett went for a job as a second footman to be told by his employer, 'If you come to me you'll be James, all my second footmen are called James, just as all my first footmen are called William.'[4] When Florence David went into service as a kitchen maid, her employers called her 'Mary' because that's what they called all their maids. They found it easier that way.

Other of the committee's proposals were more radical. It advocated 'a substantial reduction of the length of the servant's working day, definite time allowances for meals and outings, the latter to comprise a half-day every Sunday, and one afternoon and evening each week; in addition, the provision of from two to 2½ hours free time each day, with the right to remain in or leave the house; also a fortnight's holiday in a year with board wages'.[5]

The committee drew up a scale of weekly wages for different servants, ranging from twenty-five shillings a week with food for cook-housekeepers, down to a minimum of six shillings and sixpence for unskilled fourteen-year-olds. (Male servants didn't figure in this: the Women's Advisory Committee thought it wouldn't be appropriate to comment.) There were even suggestions that domestic staff should be paid overtime, and eventually provided with a trade union of their own. This was too much for one committee member. The Marchioness of Londonderry, who hadn't actually attended any meetings, refused to sign sections of the report, explaining that 'I regard any possibility of the introduction into the conditions of domestic service of the type of relations now obtainable between employers and workers in industrial life as extremely undesirable and liable to react in a disastrous manner on the whole foundation of home life.'[6]

The irony was that while it was certainly true the supply of domestic servants was declining – had been declining since the beginning of the century, in fact – the Marchioness of Londonderry really didn't have very much to worry about. 'The mistress of a small household will not be able to compete at all in the servant market,' a correspondent to *The Times* pointed out in response to the Women's Advisory Committee's report. But 'the position of the big house of the future will be better than it ever was'.[7] The shortage of servants was making itself felt, not in the Londonderrys' Park Lane town house or in one of their four country seats, but in the middle-class suburban homes of bank managers and shopkeepers, doctors and lawyers. Even they would soon find temporary respite from the awful prospect of doing their own housework, when the Depression of the late 1920s drove women back into domestic service.

The main problem for servants with households which kept fewer staff was simple: there was more work to do. However, there was also a question of status. In 1924 Lucy McLelland, who was born with the century, went to the Duke of Rutland at Belvoir Castle as first kitchen maid. It was her seventh job since going into service at the age of sixteen. She quickly worked her way up to cook, with four girls under her and a total indoor staff of twenty or more.

Belvoir was a community of its own. When the Duke of Rutland invited the estate workers to a screening of a Charlie Chaplin film as a treat one Christmas, there were nearly a hundred people present. Lucy started walking out with the groom of chambers, an Ulsterman twenty years her senior, and in 1926 they married and took a place as cook and butler with the novelist Agatha Christie, then living in Sunningdale with her first husband Archie. After working with a big staff at Belvoir, the Christies' house, Styles, was in Lucy's words, 'a come down'.[8] Apart from the McLellands there was a between-maid; a nursemaid, who didn't do anything but look after the Christies' seven-year-old daughter, Rosalind; and a gardener whose wife was sometimes brought in to help. Agatha was fond of entertaining, 'and poor me, I used to have to do the cooking and my own washing up', Lucy remembered.[9] Her husband had to wait at table and help her with clearing up afterwards, and he had to clean and polish the dining room. They only stayed for four months.*

In contrast, a big country house with plenty of staff maintained strict lines of demarcation. At Belvoir, although Lucy ran the kitchen, with four kitchen maids under her, there were also two still-room maids who did the baking. 'The kitchen never did toast. Never made no scones, no cakes, nothing of that. Tea, coffee – all came from the still room.'[10] Charles Dean, who was under-butler to the 2nd Viscount Astor from 1922 to 1925, remembered that the division of labour was just as clear-cut at Cliveden. 'Everything was separate,' he said. 'Nobody interfered. You couldn't dare to do other people's jobs as they would say, "What the hell are you doing?" if you did something without asking.'[11]

Cliveden, a palatial Italianate mansion overlooking the Thames, is a good example of how the bigger and wealthier country houses maintained a staff of Victorian proportions throughout the 1920s and 1930s.[12] It was designed in 1850–1 by Sir Charles Barry, architect of the Houses of Parliament, for the Duke of Sutherland, after a previous house on the site had been destroyed by fire only a few months after Sutherland bought it. By the First World War it belonged to Waldorf Astor, whose father William 'Walled-off' Astor presented it to him in 1906, a wedding present on his marriage to the wealthy Virginian divorcée Nancy Shaw.

The Astors' wealth, largely unconnected with land and so impervious to the agricultural depressions of the 1920s, meant that they were able to hold court at Cliveden in a style unaffected by the vicissitudes and fluctuations of the market. They also owned a town house, 4 St James's Square, where they lived from Monday to Friday when Parliament was in session. Astor was MP for Plymouth until 1919, when his father's death sent him to the Lords as the 2nd

* The Christies didn't stay much longer. Archie left his wife for another woman at the end of the year, at which Agatha famously disappeared, being found in a Harrogate hotel eleven days later.

Cliveden, Buckinghamshire.

Viscount Astor and Nancy was elected in his stead, becoming the first woman to take her seat in the mother of parliaments.* The couple also had a fourteen-bedroom 'cottage' at Sandwich in Kent, a house in Plymouth, and Tarbert, a shooting and fishing lodge on the Isle of Jura in the Hebrides.

The Astors used all five houses at different points during the year, but 4 St James's Square and Cliveden were their main residences, with most of the domestic staff travelling back and forth between them – London during the week, the country at weekends. Lady Astor had what she called her town style and her country style. Town style at St James's Square, where the majority of guests came from politics, was formal, with liveried footmen waiting at dinner and a reception for as many as 1,000

* But not the first woman to be elected. That honour went to Constance Gore-Booth, who as Constance Markiewicz was returned for Dublin St Patrick's in the 1918 general election, but who along with other Sinn Fein MPs refused to take her seat.

people afterwards. It was a big house.* The Astors were ardent teetotallers, and although there was usually wine with dinner, the receptions were sometimes rather dry affairs.

Country-style weekends at Cliveden were more relaxed. The atmosphere was that of a grand hotel, with folk coming and going and gathering in small groups. (When the house actually became a grand hotel in the 1980s, there was remarkably little to do by way of conversion.) Visitors were a mixed but illustrious bag: writers like George Bernard Shaw and Sean O'Casey, fellow aristocrats like the Marquess of Lothian who, like Nancy Astor, was a committed Christian Scientist; visiting European royalty, friends from America, film stars. Charlie Chaplin was a regular guest, as he seems to have been at most country houses between the wars. So was Lawrence of Arabia, by then known as Aircraftman T. E. Shaw. On one occasion Lawrence and Nancy suddenly leaped up from the Cliveden drawing room and ran outside, where they jumped on Lawrence's Brough Superior and roared off down the drive in a cloud of dust. A few minutes later they were skidding back. 'We did a hundred miles an hour,' shrieked Nancy. Her husband turned and walked away, speechless with rage.

Sir Charles Barry's creation was modified first for the 1st Duke of Westminster, who bought the house from the 3rd Duke of Sutherland, his brother-in-law, in 1869; and then again by the 1st Viscount Astor after he bought it from Westminster in 1893. By the time Astor handed it over to his son and daughter-in-law in 1906, Barry's Cliveden, although barely fifty years old, had acquired a clock tower and a porte cochère, and undergone some radical remodelling and redecoration. The house consisted of a main block nine bays wide, connected by curving corridors to flanking pavilions. This central section was dominated by a huge living hall, created for the 1st Viscount Astor by F. L. Pearson out of Sir Charles Barry's hall, morning room and library. Next door there was the French Dining Room, so called because the 1st viscount had it fitted with rococo panelling brought from the château of Asnières

* 4 St James's Square is now the Naval and Military Club, better known as the In and Out.

The Astor family walking on the terrace at Cliveden in 1921.

near Paris. A library and a drawing room completed the set of quasi-public rooms. Lord Astor's study and Lady Astor's boudoir were also on the ground floor. The main bedrooms above, for the family and important guests, were mostly named for flowers: the Rose, the Orange Flower, the Snowdrop, the Lavender. There were day and night nurseries on the top floor: by 1928, when the house was in its heyday, the Astors had five children aged from twenty-one to nine. Bobbie Shaw, Nancy's troubled son by her first marriage, also put in occasional appearances.

The east wing contained guest rooms: when the house was full, there were as many as forty people staying at a time. The domestic offices and staff bedrooms were in the west wing, the basement of which housed the kitchens; the servants' hall; the china room and wine cellar; the butler's pantry, with its teak sinks for washing the silver; and the silver safe. There was an underground passage connecting the service wing to the guest wing, so that servants could come and go about their business without being observed by guests or family. Rosina Harrison, who came to the Astors in 1928 as lady's maid to their eighteen-year-old daughter Phyllis, noticed that there were tramlines in the main kitchen passage, where food used to be wheeled along from the kitchen to a service lift. 'This practice had stopped before I joined,' she wrote, 'and the food was carried by the odd men on butlers' trays to the lifts and transferred to the large hotplate in the serving room next to the dining room.'[13]

Cliveden was designed to be run by a small army of servants, and the Astors employed thirty-three staff in the 1920s: a butler, an under-butler and three footmen; a valet for the viscount and two lady's maids for his wife and daughter; a housekeeper, four housemaids, two still-room maids and two women who came in daily but lived out; a chef, three kitchen maids, a scullery maid and another daily who helped in the kitchens; four laundry maids; two odd men and a hall boy; and a telephonist, a house carpenter and a nightwatchman. And that was just the indoor staff. There were another seventy-odd estate workers, everything from gardeners

The Cliveden manservants.

and gamekeepers to electricians, a boatman and a part-time clock winder.

The size of this army of labour fluctuated according to circumstance. When the children were young, for example, they were looked after by a nanny, Miss Gibbons, who ruled the day and night nurseries with a nursery maid to wait on her; there was also a succession of French or German governesses for the older children. The number of still-room maids, who baked the bread and cakes and made the breakfasts, had gone down from two to one by the later 1930s. There was a high turnover of staff, partly because Nancy Astor was a demanding employer, sometimes both mean and mean-spirited; but mainly because it was the nature of the domestic employment market for servants to move on, either to marry or to find a better place. And by the end of the 1930s even big, prestigious country houses like Cliveden were starting to feel the winds of social change blowing through their servants' halls. Noel Wiseman, who went to the Astors as assistant estate agent in 1934, remembered that a younger generation was less prepared to accept the terms and conditions of employment that their elders had taken for granted:

> It was alright when you got these older people who were willing to work these long hours, and happy in doing so, but once we'd lost that type and come out of that era, it was very difficult indeed to get people to stop.[14]

Theoretically, the responsibility for the management of the Astors' staff lay with their estate agent, H. J. Forster Smith. But as far as the indoor servants were concerned, they answered to one man, the Astors' formidable butler Edwin Lee, who had joined the staff as a footman in 1912 and worked his way up to the top job. Always immaculate, Lee was 'Lee' or 'Mr Lee' to the family, and 'sir' to the other members of staff. 'People have met him and thought it was Lord Astor,' remembered one of his colleagues. 'He acted like it.'[15] He was a constant presence at Cliveden and the St James's Square house, travelling between the two in a private car, separate from the other servants, who piled into a van. It was

Lee who interviewed prospective staff, although Nancy Astor also gave them a perfunctory once-over; Lee who maintained discipline below stairs. When Nancy's son Bobbie Shaw was gaoled for homosexual offences in 1931, Lee assembled the entire indoor staff in the servants' hall and explained in very general terms what had happened. Then he said, 'After you leave the servants' hall no one will speak about the matter. Anyone heard or suspected of doing so in or out of the house will be instantly dismissed.'[16]

Lee was the public face of the domestic machine, the primary point of contact with the family and their guests, greeting visitors during the day in a black alpaca jacket and bow tie, choreographing dinners in a dress livery of navy blue tail coat, black knee breeches and stockings and black pumps with gold buckles. And the Astors' dinners needed some choreography: at a dinner party and reception given in February 1922 to meet ex-prime minister Arthur Balfour, forty sat down at a table decorated with orange tulips in gilt plate. The diners included the current prime minister David Lloyd George, Winston and Clementine Churchill, the Duke and Duchess of Devonshire, the Marquess and Marchioness of Londonderry, the artist John Singer Sargent and a smattering of Souls. Eight hundred and fifty people came to the reception that followed.

Lee always supervised the table, ensuring that each diner was being attended to by the footmen, who were liveried in brown jackets, striped waistcoats, breeches and white stockings and gloves. Until after the First World War they also had powdered hair, an effect which they achieved with flour sent up from the kitchen. 'It was not resented by the men even though it made the top of your head feel as if it was in plaster,' Lee recalled.[17] He served the wines and brought in the port and liqueurs after dinner. As a teetotaller, Viscount Astor took no interest in the wines, leaving that side of things entirely to his butler. 'It's as well to limit the choice of liqueurs,' Lee believed, 'otherwise if you leave it to personal preference, you can be bobbing backwards and forwards all the time.'[18] He usually provided brandy, crème de menthe and kümmel.

Lee was a hard master. On one occasion a footman dropped a plate of savouries as he was about to take them into the dining room. Although the man pleaded afterwards that the plate was scalding hot, Lee was not sympathetic: 'You're hired to hold it and hold it you will in future, even if it burns you to the bone . . . Fingers heal, food doesn't.'[19]

When the Astors held big receptions at St James's Square, it was Lee who went round to Vine Street police station to ask for police help in controlling the traffic, and Lee and his footmen who received guests and took their coats and cloaks. He didn't personally announce the guests at these receptions, feeling the business required a professional announcer; he usually engaged a Mr Batley, who was noted for his clear voice and a delivery that 'could make even a plain Mr and Mrs sound important'.[20]

The cleaning was supervised by the Cliveden housekeeper, Mrs Ford, who was paid £45 a year when she started with the Astors in 1936, plus a weekly allowance of two shillings and sixpence for washing money, which in theory was to be spent on the regular laundering of aprons and other work-related clothes; and two shillings beer money. She had two weeks' holiday a year, and occasional weekends. Because she didn't travel up to London during the week like most of the other indoor servants, weekends were her busiest time. A day started at about 8.30, after the servants' breakfast at 8.00, when she would patrol to make sure that the housemaids were working on the downstairs rooms. They started work early, at 5.00 in the 1920s and 5.30 in the 1930s, since they had to be finished polishing, dusting, and laying fires by the time that guests started to surface. Then they would move upstairs to do the bedrooms. Interviewed in 1975, Mrs Ford remembered some of her other duties:

> I had all the linen to see to, well, see that everything in the house, to start with, was alright, that all the work was done, that the rooms were ready for the visitors and that kind of thing. Then I had all the marmalades and jams and that to make while I was there . . . I had to do enough for Cliveden

> for weekend visitors and also the London house as well, and jam making was a big job in the summer [with] fruit from the garden, and then bottling as well.[21]

Not surprisingly, considering the size and complexity of its domestic staff, Cliveden maintained the old Victorian hierarchies. Edwin Lee and Mrs Ford were the uppermost of the upper servants. Next in the pecking order, and still classed among the upper servants, were Arthur Bushell, Lord Astor's valet, and Rosina Harrison, Lady Astor's personal maid.

Bushell was the below-stairs clown. Valets were traditionally regarded with mistrust by other staff, as were lady's maids, and for the same reason: they had privileged access to their employer and were suspected of reporting to them on inappropriate behaviour in the servants' hall. At Cliveden, it was Bushell who was responsible for most of the inappropriate behaviour, mimicking the Astors' guests, up to and including Queen Mary and George V; and often dressing up in drag to entertain the other servants. Like some medieval court jester he pushed things to the limit, and sometimes beyond. After Nanny Gibbons and the Astor children were invited to an evening party in the servants' hall and Bushell dressed up as a woman and told some rather adult jokes, Nanny told him she found his behaviour left much to be desired. 'Oh, Miss Gibbons,' he said, 'what did it leave you desiring?'[22] Nor did he confine his antics to the servants. One Christmas he went to the Cliveden fancy-dress dance as the music-hall comedienne Nellie Wallace, and as he passed Nancy Astor he lifted up his skirt to show green knickers emblazoned with a Union Jack, and asked, 'How do you like my greens, my lady?' 'Arthur,' she replied, 'you're disgusting.'[23]

Rose (Rosina Harrison), who had been lady's maid to Lady Cranborne in London and Dorset before being poached by the Astors with an offer of £60 a year to look after eighteen-year-old Phyllis Astor, soon moved up to acting as lady's maid to her mother, and stayed with Nancy Astor until the latter's death in 1964.

As lady's maid, Rose's day was inextricably bound up with her mistress's activities. The day began at 7.30 when she went down to

Rosina Harrison, lady's maid to Nancy Astor.

Nancy's dressing room to collect her clothes from the night before, for pressing later. She ate her breakfast at 8.00, and half an hour later took breakfast to Nancy and ran her a cold bath. At 9.00 Nancy demanded solitude while she read her Bible lesson, after which she generally spent an hour or two with secretaries, correspondence and phone calls. Then she changed for her morning exercise – squash, tennis or golf – and again for lunch, for whatever she was doing in the afternoon, and for dinner. She usually got through five sets of clothes in a typical day:

> This required from me a deal of organizing, pressing, cleaning and repairing [said Rose]. Also there were perpetual messages to be run or delivered, shopping to be done either on my own or with her ladyship, and dressmaking or copying. I made many of her ladyship's things.[24]

A lady's maid led a relatively privileged life, in spite of being at someone else's beck and call round the clock. Rose had a big, comfortable bedroom of her own, well decorated and furnished with two easy chairs, a couch and two wardrobes. She didn't have to wear uniform. And she had opportunities to travel that most women of her generation and class could only dream of, with annual visits to Switzerland and the French Riviera, and trips further afield, to Bermuda, New York and Istanbul. Once, in 1936, when Lord and Lady Astor arrived in Yugoslavia as guests of Queen Marie, widow of the assassinated King Alexander I, Rose and Arthur Bushell were provided with a chauffeur-driven limousine of their own to take them to their destination, a palace outside Belgrade. 'Well, Rose, my queen, this is better than the bloody milk float,' said Arthur.[25]

The downside of this privileged existence was having to deal with Nancy Astor's moods. By Rose's own account her mistress was capricious, peremptory and occasionally violent. During one tantrum she tried to kick her maid. 'Whenever I am hurtful, I mean it,' she told her on another occasion, 'and I enjoy it.'[26]

The secret, as Rose found out, was to stand up to her. After one particularly bad spat, Nancy announced that the difference between them was 'that I was born to command and have learned through experience how to deal with people'. 'The difference between us, my lady,' countered Rose, 'is that you have money. Money is power, and people respect money and power so they respect you for having it.'[27] Their shouting matches became a byword at Cliveden: Lord Astor used to go his dressing room to listen in through the wall and have a good laugh, Rose found out later. And with the arguments came a closeness, an intimacy of sorts. When Nancy Astor's sister Phyllis Brand died of pneumonia in 1937, Nancy was distraught. But it wasn't her family she turned to for support. Rose remembered that the Brands' butler rushed in to her and said, 'Go to Lady Astor. She needs you.' She found her mistress screaming and crying and praying. 'I took her in my arms and comforted her as best I could.'[28]

It is always risky to generalise about domestic service, even at the grandest of houses. At Cliveden, the kitchens were controlled by the Astors' white-jacketed French chef, Monsieur Gilbert, who consulted closely with his mistress over the meals. The Duchess of Buccleuch at Boughton House in Northamptonshire left the ordering of the food and the menus entirely to her cook, who lived a strangely separate life, hardly ever coming out of the kitchen and eating alone in her own sitting room, served by the kitchen maids. At Croome Court in Worcestershire, the Earl and Countess of Coventry, who were finding it difficult to make ends meet, kept a cook-housekeeper, Winnie Sapsford, a thin, bird-like spinster in her late forties. She wasn't particularly able: meals in the stewards' room at Croome typically began with the butler, Mr Latter, looking at his plate and asking sadly, 'Winnie, Winnie, what have you done to this?'[29]

There were constants, however. At most big houses, the upper servants – butler, housekeeper, valet and lady's maid – signalled their status by eating the main meal of the day apart from the other staff. In some households the upper servants ate their meals in a separate room entirely, the stewards' room perhaps, while cook

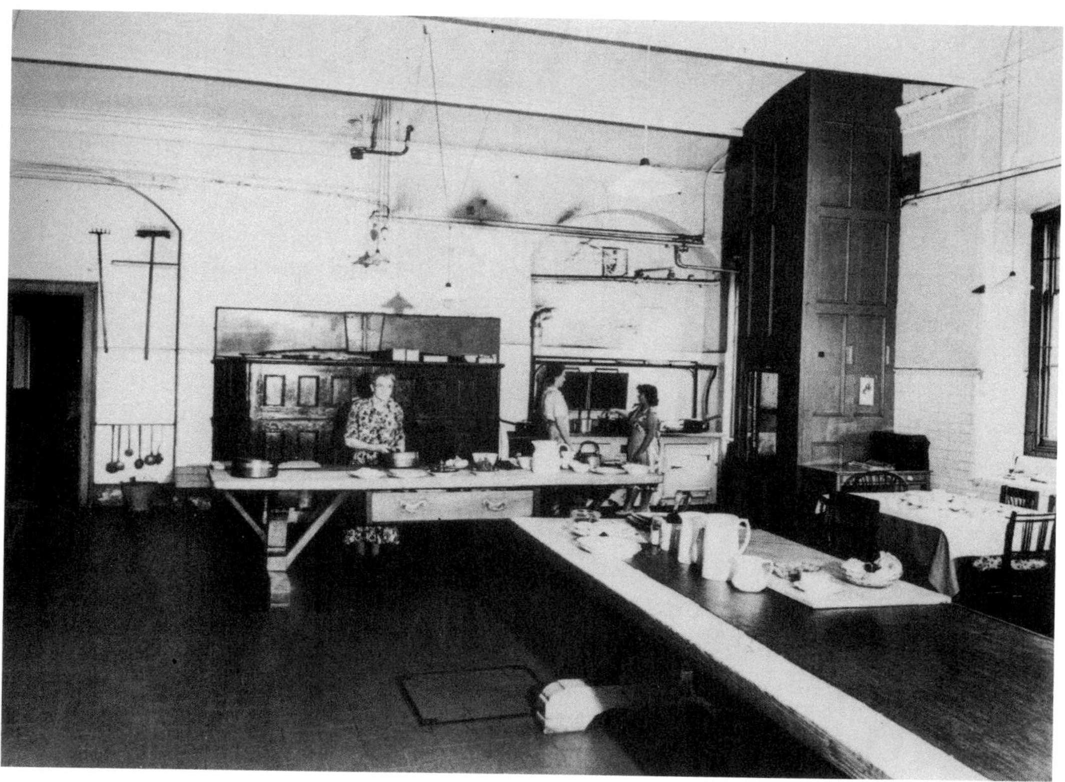

Domestic bliss: the kitchen at Ickworth in Suffolk in the 1930s.

and her staff ate in the kitchens, nanny was waited on in the nursery by the hall boy, and the governess ate in her own room or in the schoolroom. Oliver Messel's sister Anne recalled that when she went to Birr Castle as the new Countess of Rosse in 1935, there were six different lunches in six different rooms every day. At Cliveden there were two tables in the servants' hall, the upper table and the second table. Lee presided over the one and his immediate subordinate, Charles Dean the under-butler, looked after the other.

Dean was under-butler at Cliveden from 1922 until 1925, when he left to become butler to Lady Astor's niece Alice and her new husband, the divorced Russian émigré Sergei Obolensky. ('Prince Obolensky was a near-penniless Russian exile, so Alice Astor's millions came in useful,' observed Rose waspishly.[30]) Dean described his duties at Cliveden:

> My first job was getting up at 6.30 to 7.00 a.m. If there was a weekend party . . . it was my job to get everything ready to go up to the dining room as soon as the footman came along to lay the table [for lunch]. It was the footman's job to lay the table but my job to see that everything they wanted was there, like silver and things. It was my job to lay the dining room table for dinner; that was nothing to do with the footman or the butler, it was the under-butler's job. When there was a big crowd naturally other people helped you but in general it was your job to get everything ready so that they did not have to run around looking for a few knives or forks or salt or pepper or what have you. The butler would inspect everything . . .[31]

And, Dean added, Lee would invariably move a few things just to make a point, before putting them back exactly where they were.

The Astors acquired their servants through informal word-of-mouth recruitment, and also through the conventional London agencies which specialised in domestic servants. Although Rose's move came about after a casual conversation while on a visit to Cliveden with her mistress Lady Cranborne, she had found the job with the Cranbornes through Masseys of Baker Street, established in 1845 and one of the best known of all servants' registries, along with Mrs Hunt of Marylebone. There was also a more shadowy and entirely informal recruitment network, generally run by tradespeople. Lucy McLelland found her first post through Masseys, but as she moved up the career ladder she used to find her jobs 'through the desk' at Jackson's of Piccadilly, the famous tea house and grocery store. She got to know the staff at Jackson's on regular visits to collect coffee from the shop; when a chef or a cook came in and asked if the staff knew anyone looking for a kitchen job, they might recommend her. She had a similar arrangement at Fortnum & Mason.

Charles Dean found his job as under-butler with the Astors through the Mayfair Servants' Agency in North Audley Street, an agency which specialised in butlers, valets and footmen and which was used regularly by the Astors (or more accurately, by Edwin

Lee, who was in charge of recruiting the male servants). Their window was full of cards showing different jobs, and menservants in the area would keep an eye on that window even if they weren't looking for a change of job. 'It kept you in touch with the market price for menservants,' said Gordon Grimmett, who joined the Astor household as second footman in the early 1920s. Grimmett was seen initially by Lee and then interviewed by Lady Astor, if their brief conversation can be described as such:

> 'He looks a big strong boy, Lee. Where is your home, Gordon, and have you a mother and father?'
>
> 'I have a mother and father and my home is in Ascot in Berkshire, your ladyship,' I replied.
>
> 'Well now, isn't that nice. We have a country house at Cliveden, near Taplow in Buckinghamshire. You will be able to go home to your parents regularly.' Then she sped towards the door.
>
> 'How soon can you join us? We want you in one week's time. Good-bye, I must fly to the House of Commons.' And out she went.[32]

Lee was left to tell Grimmett his terms and conditions of employment – £32 a year with two shillings and sixpence beer and laundry money – and to arrange for him to be measured for suits and livery at the Astors' Mayfair tailors.*

Like the butler, footmen were public servants, operating at the interface between family, guests and staff. They had to look athletic – the Portlands made the Welbeck Abbey footmen do callisthenics to stay trim – and they were often matched for height, although this didn't happen at Cliveden, because Lee harboured a sad memory of once being turned down for a job because 'they wanted to match one of their footmen and I was an inch and a half too short'.[33] At Flete in Devon, the Mildmays' butler refused

* Tailors who cheated their servant-keeping clients, if Grimmett is to be believed. They charged the Astors for a pair of long woollen pants to go under his livery trousers, and quietly offered him a glass of whisky not to take them.

to have footmen who were taller than him. Fortunately he was six feet three, so new footmen had to be taller than six feet and not more than six feet two. One of their odder duties at Flete was to remove the electric lamps from the tables every morning and bring them in again in the evening, a relic of the time when oil lamps were taken down to the lamp room to be trimmed and filled each day. 'I can see them now,' recalled Lord Mildmay's daughter Helen, 'groping about under the big table in the library on their hands and knees, plugging in these lamps.'[34]

At Cliveden, there were three footmen, occasionally four. They had their own room in the basement of the west wing, near the servants' hall. The footmen greeted guests and served drinks before dinner and waited at table; they answered the bell and carried and fetched as needed. They may have acted as valets to the older Astor boys, who didn't have valets of their own, and they were required to valet visitors who came without their own servants.

The heavier work of the household was done by the two odd men who, as their title suggests, did odd jobs about the place, anything that wasn't the specific duty of another servant, from carrying luggage up and down to bedrooms and heavy trays from the kitchen to the serving room, to cleaning below stairs and helping out behind the scenes at receptions. The odd man was someone who hadn't quite made the grade, and never would. 'Some of them were not as other men are,' wrote Rose Harrison. 'By that I mean they were often lacking in brain power and had little ambition . . . Their interests were mostly limited to beer and baccy. I never knew one who was married.'[35] Lee used to say he could always recognise an odd man by the way he walked, as though he were carrying a heavy burden.

THE NETWORK OF SUPPORT that enabled the Astors to live as they did extended far beyond the basements and corridors of Cliveden. There was Ann Kindersley, variously described as the controller and Viscount Astor's head secretary. There were seven more secretaries, and three accountants, and resident housekeepers at the Astors' houses in Plymouth and Sandwich.

Five chauffeurs maintained their cars and drove them from place to place: one each for Lord and Lady Astor, and neither allowed to encroach on the other's duties; a horsebox driver, and two driver-mechanics who also looked after the mowers. A married couple, Mr and Mrs MacIntyre, looked after the Astors' lodge up on the Isle of Jura. On the Cliveden estate itself there were farm managers and cowmen, grooms both for the horses which the Astor family rode recreationally and for Viscount Astor's 450-acre stud farm; and of course a platoon of gardeners, more than twenty of them. It was their job to maintain the kitchen gardens and greenhouses and the breathtaking Thames-side pleasure grounds with their miles of walks and woodland rides.

One of the workers who crossed the divide between indoors and outdoors was Nancy Astor's 'decorator', whose job it was to provide and arrange the flowers at Cliveden and St James's Square. Frank Copcutt came to Cliveden as a gardener in 1928 from the Rothschilds' Waddesdon Manor, thirty miles north, and worked initially in the greenhouses until Nancy's existing decorator, George, moved on and he got the place. (For more than a year afterwards Nancy Astor called him 'George' and he didn't dare to correct her.) His day started at 7 a.m. when he walked up to the house to water, replace and arrange the flowers downstairs and then, when guests came downstairs, in the bedrooms. The rest of the morning was spent in the greenhouses, before he returned to the house to do the lunch flowers. The process was repeated in the evening, when he would put out fresh flowers on the dining-room table. If there was a party or a reception, the procedure was more complicated:

> The first thing to be thought about when decorating for a party [Copcutt said] was the general area: the hall, the staircase and the ballroom. These were large areas and could be set off with shrubs, forsythia, almonds, cherries, laburnum and wisteria, things of that kind. Standard fuchsias and standard geraniums were also useful and colourful. Planted around these would be primroses, polyanthus, forget-me-nots, the smaller border plants. These would be forced in the greenhouse. If I could

> get her ladyship marigolds at Christmas-time she was more pleased than if they'd been orchids. Medium-sized flowers we put in 'coffins', containers which are miniatures of the real thing. They were packed in with clay and overlaid with moss.[36]

Copcutt liked to use orange trees as decoration, although it was difficult to have them in blossom and in fruit at the same time. He hit on a simple solution – wire the oranges to the branches. No one noticed, not even the Astors.

THE DOMESTIC STAFF at Cliveden seem to have been quite content with their lot, although most of the recollections of below-stairs life with the Astors come from the upper servants, who carved out careers at Cliveden and came to identify strongly with their employers and their employers' values. Not much is known about the attitudes of the more lowly members of the team, the kitchen maids and scullery maids and odd men. But there is no doubt that the Astors were good employers. They did their best to create a model estate community at Cliveden between the wars, with a clubhouse that served alcohol, in spite of their commitment to teetotalism, and football and cricket teams for the staff. Indoor and outdoor servants had the use of a bowling alley and a gymnasium, and there were staff dances every two weeks. 'There would be a staff sports day,' remembered Tom Spuggard, whose father was a woodman on the estate, 'and they would have the Maidenhead town band up here, playing all the afternoon . . . And Lord and Lady Astor were amongst it enjoying it, really enjoying it.'[37]

The paternalism is hard to ignore and difficult to swallow today, but in the hard Depression years of the late 1920s and 1930s there were plenty who would gladly have swapped places with Edwin Lee and Rose Harrison and the rest. The view from the country house, even the country house basement, was still a good deal more attractive than the view from the dole queue.

CHAPTER SEVENTEEN

Serving Top Society

THE STORY OF CLIVEDEN and its servants offers a moment, a snapshot of below-stairs life in one country house. The career in service of Herbert Parker covers a lifetime.

Parker was a Victorian, born into a world of service and deference. His father was a gamekeeper on the Duke of Rutland's Belvoir Castle estate, and his most vivid childhood memory was of the time in 1906 when as a ten-year-old, he was put into a black suit and taken to see the body of his father's employer as it lay in ducal state in the great hall. He spent his life working in country houses, belonging and not belonging, a member of the army of domestic servants on which the mansions of England depended. His working life started in 1909, when Edward VII was king. It ended seven decades later, when Margaret Thatcher was poised to become prime minister and the England Parker had been born into was a history lesson.

Parker left school the day after his thirteenth birthday, to go as a live-in labourer on a local farm. But the outdoor life didn't suit him, and a year later he went as a houseboy to Fineshade Abbey in Northamptonshire and then after a few months to Cottesmore Hall, a good-sized Tudor country house in neighbouring Rutland.

His employers at Cottesmore, Cecil and Edith Noel, had three young sons and a household that was fairly typical for a middle-sized country house in the years leading up to the First World War. There were nine indoor servants: a nurse and a nursemaid who looked after the younger boys; a cook and a kitchen maid; two housemaids, two laundry maids, and Herbert, the houseboy. With no butler, below stairs was managed by the cook, Mrs Kemp. As the most junior servant and the only male, Herbert was given the heavy work. His daily duties included everything from scrubbing floors and chopping wood to waiting on the other staff and serving their meals in the servants' hall.

Cecil Noel, whose forebears had helped to establish the Cottesmore Hunt at the end of the seventeenth century, rode to hounds regularly during the winter. The habit often deterred domestic servants from taking a job, since it involved them in a deal of extra work cleaning the hunting kit.

After nine months at Cottesmore Hall, during which time he saw eight different housemaids come and go, Herbert climbed another rung on the career ladder by getting a post with the Rhodes family at Flore Fields in Northamptonshire. His new employers only kept seven indoor servants, but this time there was a butler, Mr Aulterey, and a liveried footman – Herbert Parker. The family employed a Swiss governess for their four daughters, the three eldest of whom were in their late teens.

It was a young staff. At thirty, Mr Aulterey was the eldest; the others ranged in age from the cook who was twenty-seven, down to fifteen-year-old Parker. The governess was only twenty-one.

The family entertained a lot, and Parker was kept busy waiting at table and cleaning the silver. 'This is when I got my first lesson in rouging silver with bare fingers until all the scratches were rubbed out,' he remembered.[1] And the family hunted: over the winter Mr and Mrs Rhodes rode out on three days a week, the three older girls on four. Parker and Mr Aulterey were kept busy with the hunting kit. Most days the women's riding habits were soaked in a soft-water tank in the stable yard, while coats and boots were cared for in a special cleaning and drying room.

Parker was at Flore Fields for less than a year before 'I entered the service of Top Society'.[2] And it was just about as top as it could get, in the shape of the distinguished 5th Marquess of Lansdowne, one-time Governor General of Canada and Viceroy of India. Lansdowne had been Secretary of State for War during the Boer War, and as Foreign Secretary he had negotiated the Entente Cordiale with France in 1904. Now in his sixties, he presided over an extended family and a formidable collection of town houses and country estates, the chief of which were Bowood, the family seat in Wiltshire, which had been remodelled over the years by a succession of distinguished architects from Robert Adam and

George Dance to C. R. Cockerell and Sir Charles Barry; and Lansdowne House in Berkeley Square, designed by Robert Adam in the 1760s.

Parker went to work first of all for the marquess's second son, Lord Charles Petty-Fitzmaurice, an equerry to George V with a young wife and a baroque country house in Berkshire. He had been with Lord Charles for a couple of years when he was poached – by the Marquess of Lansdowne's butler, John Burditt, who took him aside one day and said that while he wouldn't want the boy to be in any hurry to leave Lord Charles, when he did feel like moving on he should come to him.

Parker took the hint. He started as stewards' room footman to the Marquess, where he waited on the upper servants – Mr Burditt, Mrs Vennard the housekeeper, the groom of the chambers, the lady's maid and valet and under-butler. (A groom of the chambers announced visitors and made sure the reception rooms were presentable. 'As far as I can make out,' said the Earl of Pembroke's daughter, 'all he did [at Wilton] was to clean pens and put blotting paper and water on all the writing tables.'[3]) Within a matter of months Parker had risen to be second footman and finally first footman.

The marquess ran a household on a Victorian scale: Lansdowne House had a staff twice as big as any of the places where Parker had worked before. Besides his day livery, he was supplied with red plush breeches, white stockings and pumps, a white waistcoat and a short black 'coatee', all to be worn when he served dinner. Then there was a state livery which was only worn on special occasions and was kept in cupboards in the stewards' room. And a morning suit. And a wardrobe full of outdoor wear: a box cloth carriage coat, a waterproof carriage coat, top hat and gloves, a motor coat and cap and a black mackintosh for motor work.

Parker volunteered for the Grenadier Guards in 1915. By this time he had been in domestic service for five years, with five different employers. He had worked in Ireland, where the younger Lansdowne men went three times a year to fish on their estate at Derreen in Co. Kerry. He had served lunch to Queen Mary and the young Prince Albert and Princess Mary, helped to entertain ambassadors and politicians at house parties all over the kingdom; even earned a personal rebuke from Kaiser Wilhelm for not helping him with his overcoat as he left Lansdowne House after a visit to the marquess. (He didn't know about Wilhelm's withered arm.) He had presented the Marquess of Lansdowne with a War Office telegram and watched as the old man opened it, read it and collapsed; had personally given the news it contained to the marchioness, that her son Lord Charles had been killed at Ypres.

All this, and he was still only nineteen years old.

THIS RESTLESS PATTERN of movement from one house to another was typical of young men looking to make a career out of domestic service. Each move might involve slightly better wages, but that wasn't the only motive. There was the glamour of being part of a prestigious household. There were opportunities for travel, and for being close to the heart of things. Moreover, a larger, better-organised household had lines of demarcation between staff. And by and large, defined duties meant less arduous duties. At Bowood for a Lansdowne family Christmas, for example, Parker was detailed to carry trays up to the nurseries. There were three other footmen to help him. And that was all he did, apart from helping to clean the silver. The lunch and dinner silver, that is; two other footmen cleaned the breakfast silver and the afternoon tea silver.

Parker came out of the army in 1919, having spent the last part of it in Belgium acting as personal servant to the Grenadier Guards' commanding officer, Viscount Lascelles. He didn't go back to Bowood and the Marquess of Lansdowne. Instead, like Bulldog Drummond's manservant and ex-batman, Denny, he remained with Lascelles as his valet, continuing a master–servant relationship that had been forged in the trenches.

Lascelles, the eldest son of the 5th Earl of Harewood, introduced Parker to a restless round of country houses, shooting lodges and race meetings. The young valet (he was still only

or not it ever arrived, the widow from Ohio clearly didn't solve all of Huntly's problems, since there was yet another bankruptcy hearing, his fourth, in 1928, after a moneylender sued him for a debt of £615.

Orton Hall wasn't a happy place. In the three months that Parker and Gertie worked there, Huntly's chauffeur lost his licence after he ran over and killed a man, and one of the footmen died after getting stuck in a third-floor lavatory: there was no handle on the inside of the door, and he climbed out of the window, lost his footing and fell.

One day while the Parkers were eating their breakfast in the basement of the Grosvenor Square house, a man arrived at the door and announced discreetly that the Earl of Shaftesbury was in need of a butler. Would Parker come round to Chandos House in Marylebone and discuss the matter?

The interview marked the start of Parker's longest continuous period in service with one employer, twenty-three years. He took the job and on 26 August 1926 he travelled down to the Shaftesburys' Dorset estate in Wimborne St Giles. His wife didn't accompany him: this wasn't a married couple's post and Gertie had to take a temporary job as a lady's maid with a baronet's wife in Kent. It wasn't until the following year that Shaftesbury found the Parkers an estate cottage on the edge of the park. From then on Gertie worked occasionally for the family – several times in the late 1920s she travelled up to Scotland with them as a lady's maid to their two daughters – but in 1931 she gave birth to her only child, and from then on until the boy was almost ready to leave school, she stayed at home to look after him. When he was old enough, he would come down to St Giles House on Sunday mornings and father and son would walk to church together.

The household that Herbert joined was in the public eye for good and bad reasons. In February 1927 there was a public scandal when the Earl of Shaftesbury's son and heir, Lord Ashley, married a chorus girl, Sylvia Hawkes, very much against the wishes of his parents, who had continued to maintain that the marriage would not take place right up until the moment it did. As they predicted, it didn't last: Sylvia went into films, moved to Hollywood and began an affair with Douglas Fairbanks senior, who was cited as co-respondent in the Ashleys' divorce in 1934. She went on to marry Fairbanks, Clark Gable, and several others, and with a cheerful disregard for protocol, continued to use the name Lady Ashley for the rest of her life.

Happier for the Shaftesburys – and for Herbert Parker, who found the gossip about the Ashley marriage very painful – was the earl's role as Lord Steward of the Household to George V. One of the three Great Officers of the Household, the Lord Steward had to be on hand at important royal ceremonials. That meant regular attendance at Buckingham Palace, and Parker found himself constantly on the move. In any one week he might spend two nights at the Shaftesburys' London house; two nights at Buckingham Palace, where he had his own rooms; and the weekend at St Giles House, driving down with several of the staff on Friday evening and coming back up to London on Monday morning. When Queen Mary came to stay at St Giles for a fortnight in the summer of 1928, she told Parker that 'I hope you are as comfortable in our home as I have been here.'[15] The next time he stayed at Buckingham Palace he noticed a new bed had been put in his room.

Parker's duties varied dramatically over the years. That was partly because his role in the Shaftesbury household kept changing. He was engaged as butler; but when the earl's valet fell ill and left in the summer of 1927, he was asked to go up to London in the man's place to have the earl's uniform ready for a levee at St James's Palace. He was so competent that when he and his employer got back to St Giles, the earl asked if he should recruit another butler, or another valet? Herbert said he would rather be the earl's valet, an answer which earned him a rise. Soon afterwards he met up with an old friend from the war, a man called Standen who had been mess corporal in the Grenadiers; Standen came as butler and his wife moved in to the cottage next door to Gertie.

One of the most intriguing things about Herbert's time with the Shaftesburys was the rapid turnover in senior staff. (The lower staff didn't figure much in Herbert's memory, which is itself revealing.) Standen didn't stay long. He was followed by another, unnamed, butler, and then by a Mr May, 'a jolly chap but not very polished; I was amused at the way he announced breakfast in his apron. I saw his lordship often do a little titter at his funny ways.'[16] Then came Mr Moore; then Mr Thompson, who had been groom of the chamber to the Earl of Pembroke at Wilton. Then Mr Compton, 'a very nice man and well liked amongst the staff', who went off to work for the Duke of Rutland at Belvoir Castle. In 1937 a new, unnamed, butler was in post, but he went off somewhere for a time, so Herbert took over, as he had whenever there was an interregnum. After that Mr Stovold arrived; he was called up in 1940, and Herbert stepped up again. 'During the war years we had three other butlers,' he remembered. 'None of them stayed long.'[17] The faithful retainer who gave a lifetime of service to a single master was more common in literature than in life.

So was the fidelity, apparently: Parker described how after he left the Shaftesburys, another in the long line of butlers resigned and then came back to St Giles House one night, got some suitcases from the box room and with help from one of the footmen, filled them with silver, loaded them onto two bicycles and made off down the drive to where a lorry was waiting. 'He was a very naughty man,' said the Countess of Shaftesbury, with commendable restraint.

Parker resigned from St Giles House in 1949 and took a job with the fox-hunting Wiggin family of Honington Hall, a beautiful seventeenth-century country house in Warwickshire. The Parkers' decision to move back to the Midlands was influenced by the fact that their son had a place at Birmingham University – in itself a sign of changing times – and they wanted to be close to him (although after they took the job, he was offered and accepted a place at London University). Parker and his wife lived in, with Gertie helping out in the house. There was a chef at Honington Hall when they arrived there, but he left after a few years and his place was taken by a succession of temporary cooks, with Parker and Gertie taking over the cooking in the intervals. From Honington they went to their final country house, the Victorian Prestwold Hall in Leicestershire.

Looking back on his long career as a senior servant in

nearly a dozen great country houses, Parker had his fair share of upstairs, downstairs anecdotes. He remembered how at the Earl of Scarborough's Sandbeck Park near Rotherham, the butler grew mushrooms in all the disused cellars; and how while helping with lunch on a visit to the Chandos-Poles at Radbourne Hall in Derbyshire in the 1920s, he watched as the host's butler fell down dead drunk in the middle of carving a joint of beef. Colonel Chandos-Pole didn't bat an eyelid. He simply told Parker to roll him under the sideboard and carry on with the carving.

Sports of all kinds played a pivotal role in both his working life and his leisure time. He always seemed to be loading guns and organising lunches and waiting at table in endless marquees and tents while his employers and their peers blasted away at grouse and partridge and pheasant; or making sure the earl was properly turned out and serving hunting teas of eggs and bacon when the Portman Hunt met at St Giles. He also had the chance to shoot occasionally himself, and there were opportunities to play sports. Staff were encouraged to use the tennis courts in the park at St Giles, and after Shaftesbury's daughter married Lord Alington, who owned the neighbouring Crichel House estate in Dorset, Parker and the other servants were allowed to play golf on the Crichel links. And he became quite an expert at billiards. 'In the Stewards' Room Recreation Room [at Buckingham Palace] there was a very good table.'[18]

Parker was careful to maintain the old comrades' network established during his wartime service in the Guards. He often came across fellow menservants whom he had known in the regiment and whom he trusted and socialised with as a result, sometimes decades later. Mr Standen, the battalion HQ mess corporal, came to St Giles after being recommended by Parker. At Lowther Castle in Westmorland for a shooting weekend in 1927 he found that the Earl of Lonsdale's house steward was an old friend from the Guards, and the two men immediately struck up a working friendship. When Shaftesbury was replaced by the Duke of Buccleuch as Lord Steward of the Household after George V's death in 1936, Parker remarked that Buccleuch's house steward,

A labour day rally at Wallington, 1933.

People's Theatre of Newcastle was invited to regard Wallington as its second home.

Trevelyan's politics didn't pass without remark. After he lost his parliamentary seat in the 1931 election, the Lord Lieutenant's flag was stolen from its flagpole in the grounds, and statues in front of the house were tarred and feathered by midnight raiders who were thought to have driven up from Newcastle, although it was never clear exactly what these raiders were protesting about. All the time Sir Charles pushed for new ways to reconcile his politics with his pedigree. 'I still am not nearly content with the use we make of Wallington,' he told Molly in 1934. 'I want to try more definitely to make it a resort for socialist and international minded people.'[3]

In the summer of 1936 he found a solution. At a garden party for estate workers and their families that August he announced that he was bequeathing Wallington to the National Trust, lock, stock and barrel – the house, its contents and 13,000 acres of farms and moorland.

His motives were mixed. He didn't believe in private ownership of land, and he wanted to ensure that Wallington would always be available to the community and the wider public. He also acknowledged that the system of taxation which he supported made the continued existence in its traditional form of the country house difficult, if not impossible. And with commendable honesty he confessed that he wanted a way in which the Trevelyans could maintain their connection with Wallington: under the terms of the bequest to the National Trust his wife, and then their children, would continue to live there as tenants, a desire which 'will be understood by many who have no sympathy with my Socialism'.[4]

Trevelyan's decision met with widespread approval. Other answers to the country-house problem were being aired at the time. In France, La Demeure Historique had pioneered a public-benefit-for-public-funds option by which owners of historic houses opened their homes to the public in return for state grants towards their upkeep; and closer to home, the Marquess of Lothian, who was struggling to maintain his own ancestral seat, Blickling Hall in Norfolk, was busy advocating an annual grant from the state to the National Trust, enabling the Trust to buy endangered mansions and gardens and keep on the ex-owners as tenants. But Sir Charles's honesty appealed. As a good socialist, said *The Times*, he wanted the people to get all the benefit of Wallington. 'As a Trevelyan, he yields to a sadly unproletarian weakness for his family tradition.'[5] With a stroke of the pen, he had made the best of both worlds.*

Although in the lead-up to the First World War it was hard to find a member of the British government without a country estate and a house to go with it, after 1918 it seemed

* Sir Charles Trevelyan was a visionary, but he was no saint. His refusal to consult with his eldest son over the disposal of Wallington led to disquiet in the family, as did his close relationship with some of his tenants (he fathered a child by one of them when he was in his seventies), and his habit of walking naked on the Northumberland moors.

that the country house had less of a role to play in a more democratic world, where it was possible to climb to the top of the greasy pole without the validation of status, pedigree and economic worth which ownership of a landed estate brought with it. In 1922 Lord Curzon, with a string of country houses (one of which, Kedleston Hall in Derbyshire, had been in his family since the thirteenth century), was beaten to the job of prime minister by Andrew Bonar Law, who owned no country house at all and was born in New Brunswick, the son of a minister in the Free Church of Scotland.

But the country house continued to hold its own as a power base and, more importantly, as a congenial setting for the making of strategy and the breaking of political alliances. And still, despite the rise of the Independent Labour Party, the break-up of big estates and the Depression, throughout the 1920s and 1930s the country house as a political salon enjoyed something of a renaissance. Leading the way here, as in so many things, was Sir Philip Sassoon at Port Lympne and Trent Park.

Sassoon had served as private secretary to Douglas Haig for most of the war, and it was he who went to London in 1919 to negotiate directly with Lloyd George over his boss's earldom, which the field marshal would only accept if it came with a hefty pension. It did, and Sassoon returned to Haig's GHQ in France, as his friend Viscount Esher told him, 'with the plumes of Talleyrand and Metternich flowing from your red hat'.[6] His handling of the negotiations impressed Lloyd George, and the young man was careful to cultivate both the prime minister and, crucially, the prime minister's personal secretary and mistress, Frances Stevenson. 'Philip Sassoon dropped in for a chat,' wrote Stevenson in her diary in December 1919. 'He has become very attentive lately.'[7] And later that month, after Sassoon and Lloyd George had played golf together, she noted again how he singled her out. 'He seems to be fabulously rich, but is clever also,' she wrote, 'and can be most amusing. But one of the worst gossips I have ever come across.'[8]

In February 1920, after Sassoon had entertained Lloyd George and Frances Stevenson, this time at Trent Park, he was appointed as the prime minister's parliamentary private secretary. The move led to predictable sniping about Sassoon's Jewishness. The fascist leader Oswald Mosley, whose anti-Semitism in the early 1920s was of the common-or-garden British sort rather than the virulent race-hate it would become in the 1930s, criticised Lloyd George's habit of retreating to Port Lympne to consider affairs of state, with a sideswipe at Sassoon's origins. 'No longer are the abrasions of controversy to be soothed by a liberal application of precious ointment from the voluptuous Orient.'[9]

In fact just *because* he remained an outsider, Sassoon was perfectly placed to act as facilitator, hosting a gathering of international figures at Port Lympne or Trent Park; inviting the right combination of statesmen, financiers and industrialists to a discreet weekend house party; sometimes simply handing over one of his mansions to the prime minister of the day and leaving them to make their own arrangements. Mosley, who got on surprisingly well with Sassoon on a personal level (he first saw his future wife Diana while a guest at Sassoon's Park Lane mansion), wrote that Sassoon's 'amiable idiosyncrasy was to entertain the great, the bright and the fashionable'.[10]

Within weeks of Sassoon's appointment as the prime minister's PPS, the press was announcing that Port Lympne was to be the venue for a weekend summit between Lloyd George and the French prime minister, Alexandre Millerand. The summit was to be held in a marquee in the garden if the weather was good enough; in the event it wasn't, and the two premiers and their ministers retreated inside to the drawing room with its apt black and gold Sert allegory of France triumphing over German elephants, recently modified by Philip Tilden with gold-streaked walls and high mirrors of black and oyster-coloured glass. *The Times*'s correspondent reported, slightly hesitantly and not at all accurately, that 'the house itself is a modern antique, scarcely finished, in the rambling Old English style of architecture'.[11]

The object of the so-called First Hythe Conference, to agree an Anglo-French position on German war reparations, wasn't

The Second Hythe Peace Conference, 19-20 June at Port Lympne. Philip Sassoon stands on the far left; his chow, Herbert, takes pride of place in the centre of the photograph with Lloyd George.

achieved. But Port Lympne was established as a perfect meeting point for the two premiers. They walked in the gardens arm in arm; Sassoon motored them over to Canterbury Cathedral, where Millerand was shown the tombs by the dean and an enterprising schoolmistress persuaded Millerand and Lloyd George to pose for a photograph with fifty schoolchildren she happened to be shepherding round at the time of their visit.

As its name suggests, the First Hythe Conference was quickly followed by a second, five weeks later, and once again at Port Lympne. In a group photograph taken beneath the colonnade, Sassoon lounges to one side of Lloyd George, Millerand and the others, his arms folded, smiling but apart. His pet chow, Herbert, is less diffident, standing full centre in front of the British prime minister and staring straight at the camera.

Lloyd George holidayed at Port Lympne in March 1921, and presided over a third Anglo-French Hythe Conference there in April. 'The members of the Conference were entertained after dinner on Saturday night at a kinematograph performance,' reported the press, 'and much laughter was evoked by the antics of Charlie Chaplin in the trenches.'[12]

'Sir Philip Sassoon's villa', as Port Lympne was usually called in the papers, became a recognised venue for political weekends, often in its owner's absence. Lloyd George regularly used it when he was still prime minister, whether Sassoon was present or not. Frances Stevenson recalled a jolly evening in 1921 when she was staying there with her lover and he summoned Rufus Isaacs, Lord Chief Justice, and Gordon Hewart, the Attorney General, to tell them his plans for a minor government reshuffle. He wanted Isaacs to go out to India as the new viceroy and Hewart to take his place as Lord Chief Justice. The news pleased both men. They stayed on to dinner and afterwards Frances played the piano while Isaacs sang sea shanties and Hewart did a turn singing a comic song from the music halls. It would be rather hard to imagine senior figures in a twenty-first-century British government behaving with quite that abandon.

Sassoon didn't share in Lloyd George's fall from power in 1922. By 1924 he was serving as Undersecretary of State for Air in Stanley Baldwin's government. It wasn't a Cabinet post, but it was important enough, especially at a time when the role of air power in any future war was being keenly debated. Churchill wrote to congratulate him, telling him how well situated he was at Port Lympne to keep an eye on the various south coast air stations. 'I think you must have built your house there upon a prophetic inspiration.'[13]

THE WEEKENDS AT PORT LYMPNE gave Lloyd George a taste for a country house of his own within striking distance of Westminster. He found one, or rather a site for one, in the summer of 1921. That September Lord Ashcombe, the same Lord Ashcombe who once owned Bodiam Castle and who was the great-grandfather of the present Duchess of Cornwall, put his 2,000-acre Churt estate in Surrey on the market. Among the lots were sixty acres on a slope of the Downs near Hindhead, with glorious views across the Surrey Hills; and, so the story goes, the prime minister sent Frances Stevenson down to assess the site's potential.

She liked what she saw and reported as much when she got back to Downing Street. Lloyd George wanted sun and he wanted the view: when he asked Frances which way the slope faced, she said 'south'. Only after he had bought the site did they both realise she had made a mistake: the view faced due north. According to their granddaughter, Frances was close to tears, but Lloyd George merely laughed and said 'We'll call it Bron-y-de,' which in Welsh means 'slope of the south'.[14]

Lloyd George already had his architect. He had met Philip Tilden at Port Lympne during the Hythe conferences, and Tilden worshipped him. (It is another sign of a less formal age that Sassoon's architect could still be wandering around Lympne in the middle of an international summit, and no one seemed to mind.) 'Druidical and elemental . . . the most arresting figure of his time,' wrote Tilden, who was fascinated to find that in the flesh the prime minister lived up completely to his public image, dynamic, dramatic and filled with a passionate empathy for the countryside and his fellow human beings.[15]

Initially Bron-y-de was to be little more than what Tilden called 'a picnic home' – a country retreat for the weekend, although Lloyd George planted orchards with a view to doing a little gentle farming. He was still prime minister, and Tilden put a long army hut hidden away in the trees where the detectives who provided his personal security could sleep, unobtrusive but essential in the aftermath of Irish partition, when there were fears that Sinn Fein was poised to bring a campaign of bombing and shooting to the British mainland. (The fears were well founded: in June 1922 Field Marshal Sir Henry Wilson, one of the British Army's senior staff officers, was shot dead on the doorstep of his house in Eaton Square by two IRA men.)

Almost as soon as it was built Lloyd George outgrew Bron-y-de, and within the year Tilden was brought back to create additional accommodation, bigger kitchens and garage space for more cars.

Furniture, chosen by Tilden and Frances Stevenson, wasn't grand: it was mostly good solid oak, with bright curtains and comfortable beds. And from the first, Lloyd George loved being there. 'The centre of the political universe was moved from London,' wrote Tilden. 'Cars came and went, important people made long journeys, secretaries stayed in hotels, and a thousand inconveniences took place so that Lloyd George could smell the pine needles in the morning and wander out last thing to see the sun set behind the heathered hills.'[16] Frances Stevenson, ignored by Margaret Lloyd George but loathed by the prime minister's children, had to move out whenever the family arrived. To begin with she converted Old Barn, a disused farm building nearby. Then in 1935 Anthony Chitty, a founder member of Tecton, England's leading firm of modernist architects, designed for her a timber bungalow overlooking the orchards of Bron-y-de. She called it Avalon and installed her illegitimate five-year-old daughter by Lloyd George, Jennifer, with a nanny and a pair of discreet Scottish servants.

Lloyd George's coalition government collapsed in November 1922. He retreated to Bron-y-de with Frances to write his memoirs and dream of the day when the country would come to its senses and call on him again. (Is that why Frances named her new house Avalon, because she saw her lover as an ageing King Arthur?) That never happened; but he still sat as an MP, and Bron-y-de remained, if not the centre of the political universe, then at least one of its distant moons. Lloyd George held court there until almost the end of the Second World War. He summoned John Maynard Keynes to confer with him on industrial conditions; offered advice to progressive young Conservatives who came to find out how to win the next election; talked privately with Arthur Henderson, leader of the Labour Party, about his prospects if he should desert the Liberals and come over to them. Factions from all parties in Parliament still came to solicit support or sound him out on their plans for palace revolution. As Frances confided to her diary in 1934, her lover and employer 'now sits at Churt and welcomes all and sundry, and in this way gets a very fair account of all that is happening in the outside world whilst remaining far from it'.[17]

Lloyd George played the part of gentleman farmer at Bron-y-de with enthusiasm, installing modern irrigation systems and bringing in a giant mechanical gyro-tiller on caterpillar tracks to turn parts of the farm into a market garden. He went for long walks with Frances, hunting for holly in the woods near Christmastime. Occasionally the gardens were opened to the public for charity: one year Edward Fitzroy, Speaker of the House of Commons, came down to discuss the political situation and found he had to pay a shilling admission to come in.

PHILIP TILDEN cornered the market in politicians' country houses. In the spring of 1922, with Port Lympne and Bron-y-de still unfinished, he was commissioned to repair and remodel a rambling patchwork of a house, tumbling down with leaking roofs and dry rot, which stood in eighty acres outside the little Kent village of Westerham. The house was called Chartwell Manor, and Tilden's client was the 47-year-old Secretary for the Colonies in Lloyd George's government. His name was Winston Churchill.

Churchill had fallen in love with Chartwell, an awkward Victorian concoction, all high gables and ivy, in the spring of 1921, and he tried and failed to buy the house when it came up for auction that July. He persisted, without telling his wife Clementine, and in September 1922 his offer of £5,000 was accepted.

Churchill had already consulted Tilden, who had come to know him, as he came to know everybody, while working for Philip Sassoon at Port Lympne. Sassoon tried to persuade the politician to take Bellevue, a small early-eighteenth-century country house at Lympne which he also owned; but Clementine turned it down because it felt cluttered and contained too many antiques. Even before the sale of Chartwell went through in November 1922 Churchill was pressing the vendor for permission to start building work, estimating with wild optimism that the house could be remodelled and brought up to a decent standard for £7,000 or £8,000.

Over the next eighteen months Tilden virtually rebuilt

Chartwell, Kent: the entrance hall.

Chartwell. It wasn't his finest hour. He added a new east wing, which juts out awkwardly overlooking a valley, and introduced crow-stepped gables for no good reason. With neither the flamboyance of Port Lympne nor the easy informality of Bron-y-de, and no vision of what the finished work would look like, the house suffered from a piecemeal approach to remodelling. Any enthusiasm that Clementine Churchill may have had soon waned, although she retained a severely practical interest, commenting on the provision of servants' bedrooms, the balance between living-in and living-out staff (the Churchills employed both at Chartwell), the height of the new kitchen ceiling. And she was cross with Tilden for ordering the domestic arrangements without consulting her, as when he fitted a kitchen range without asking her first. After the Japan earthquake of September 1923 she suggested he might emigrate there, where he would be better employed in rebuilding Tokyo.

As Chartwell grew – at one stage the plan was for six reception rooms, twenty-two bedrooms, seven bathrooms and a servants' wing – so did the cost. Like many architects' clients before and since, Churchill's reaction to burgeoning bills was to look for reasons not to pay them. And he found them. After the family moved in just after Christmas 1923, they discovered that their new home was still plagued by dry rot and leaking roofs. There was damp, and plaster fell off the ceilings. The windows let in water. The timber was unseasoned. The newly installed electrical system was dangerously faulty. In September 1926 a glass chandelier fell down in the drawing room, 'fortunately not killing anyone', reported Churchill.[18] The tale of Chartwell's rebirth ended in a flurry of threats and solicitors' letters, with Tilden saying plaintively (and disingenuously) how sorry he was 'for Mr Churchill that Chartwell has proved so unlucky to him for I hope and wished it to be a really beautiful and well-built house'.[19]

Client, contractors and architect reached a settlement at the end of 1927. By then the Churchills were talking seriously of letting the house, or shutting it up and laying off most of the servants. They didn't; and for all its faults, Chartwell Manor, as it was still being called, became what they had always wanted it to be: a comfortable family home in the country for their four children and a setting for discreet weekend gatherings of leading figures in the political establishment, men like Philip Sassoon and Arthur Balfour and Lloyd George.

Chartwell also became a sanctuary. For ten years, from the fall of Baldwin's second ministry in June 1929 until the outbreak of the

The Churchills at breakfast at Chartwell, 1927.

Second World War, Churchill held no ministerial office. One of the ways he filled these wilderness years was by tinkering with his country seat. He created a heated swimming pool in the grounds, built an aviary and planned a butterfly house (the construction of which was interrupted by war). He acquired a parrot, an African Grey called Mr Parrot (or according to the Churchills' daughter Mary, 'Polly') who lived in a cage in the dining room and pecked anyone who ventured within range of its beak.* There were cranes and geese and budgerigars. Clementine brought home two black swans from a cruise to Australia, and threatened to introduce an opossum and a brace of wallabies. In the intervals between enthusiasms Winston toyed with the idea of selling up, going as far as to put Chartwell on the market in 1937. A couple of prospective

* In 2004 the owner of a Surrey garden centre claimed that his aged macaw, which shouted anti-Nazi insults, was 104 years old and was the very bird that had once belonged to Churchill. The story proved to be unfounded.

His ministers' country homes ranged from a modest but charming Gloucestershire manor house belonging to William Morrison, his Minister of Agriculture, to Chevening, the magnificent seventeenth-century seat of the Stanhope family near Sevenoaks in Kent, which Lord Stanhope, the president of the Board of Education, would eventually bequeath to the nation. The Home Secretary, Sir Samuel Hoare, owned Sidestrand Hall in Norfolk; although as we saw in Chapter 7, he disposed of it and built himself something more manageable, the Palladian Petit Trianon that was Templewood.

Lord Hailsham, the Lord Chancellor, lived in the picturesquely named Carter's Corner Place in Sussex, an Elizabethan house in fifty-six acres which he had enlarged in 1920, and which had been the scene of a minor cause célèbre in 1932 when Hailsham's stepson Edward Marjoribanks, MP for Eastbourne, was found shot dead in the billiard room. The Secretary of State for the Colonies, William Ormsby-Gore, had two country houses, the Greek Revival Brogyntyn Hall in Shropshire and Glyn Cywarch, a big gentry house of 1616 in Gwynedd; Chamberlain's Secretary of State for India, Lord Zetland, had three.

Some politicians were born into the country-house world. Witherslack Hall in Kendal had been in the family of Oliver Stanley, president of the Board of Trade, since 1485, although the current house was less than seventy years old. Others were newcomers. Sir Kingsley Wood was the son of a Wesleyan minister who had made good in local politics and the law before entering the Commons at the end of the war. The Minister for Health and then Secretary of State for Air in Chamberlain's government, he only joined the ranks of the landed classes in 1927, when he bought Broomhill Bank, a big Victorian pile near Tunbridge Wells.

One of the most distinguished members of Chamberlain's pre-war government, Edward Wood, 3rd Viscount Halifax, was born at Powderham Castle in Devon, home of his maternal grandfather the Earl of Devon, and at birth he had a silver spoon in his mouth and the front door keys to several ancestral seats in his hand.* Chamberlain's

* Almost, anyway. Edward was the fourth son; but before his tenth birthday his three elder brothers had all died, leaving him as heir to his father's fortune.

Lord President of the Council and then Foreign Secretary, known by friends and enemies as the 'holy fox' on account of his devout Anglo-Catholicism and his lifelong passion for hunting, was born into a prominent Yorkshire landowning family whose principal seat for the past hundred years had been Hickleton Hall, a Georgian country house near Doncaster with a park which his father, a whimsical man who was prone to seeing ghosts and building secret passages in his houses, stocked with yaks, emus and kangaroos. In 1904 when Halifax was in his early twenties an aunt died and left him Temple Newsam, a glorious Tudor house near Leeds known as 'the Hampton Court of the North'. In 1923 he sold the estate for £35,000, a good deal less than its market value, to Leeds Corporation, which opened it to the public. 'The house has now ceased to be a home of famous families and has become the heritage of the democracy,' declared the *Manchester Guardian*, reporting a speech at the opening ceremony by the Minister of Labour, Sir Montague Barlow, who hoped 'that Temple Newsam might in some degree restore a sensitiveness to beauty which English people seemed to him to be losing'.[28]

Halifax didn't need Temple Newsam because his father had already handed him Garrowby Hall, a family shooting box in the East Riding which had been vastly extended in the last years of the nineteenth century. Garrowby was Halifax's spiritual home: inviting Stanley Baldwin to stay in 1937, he wrote, 'Let us walk over a Yorkshire wold and smell the east wind and watch the gulls in from the sea following the plough on the bleak tops!'[29]

Garrowby was never a political salon. The East Riding of Yorkshire was too far from London for that. But with other Cabinet members disappearing up to their Yorkshire estates for shooting or for the Christmas holidays, it was natural that every now and then friends and colleagues would gather there for the weekend. Chamberlain was a regular visitor, as Baldwin was before him, and the prime minister only had to be in the same county as Halifax for the rumours of secret meetings and plots to begin. Halifax was known to be sympathetic to the cause of appeasement: Lord Birkenhead recalled a weekend at Garrowby where his host said Hitler 'reminded him of Gandhi'.[30] At the end of 1938, when

Chamberlain was staying on the Yorkshire estate of another of his ministers, Lord Swinton, the press began to report that the holy fox was to play host at Garrowby to a meeting between the prime minister and an emissary from Hitler. Both men were forced to issue denials: 'These rumours are absurd,' Halifax told reporters.[31]

There were other political houses. The Marquess and Marchioness of Londonderry, eager to further the cause of Anglo-German friendship, invited Ribbentrop, then the German ambassador to Britain, to spend Whitsun 1936 with them at Mount Stewart, their country house on the banks of Strangford Lough in Co. Down. The visit wasn't a success: Ribbentrop arrived in an aeroplane supplied by Goering, with an escort of noisy SS men who upset everybody. When the Londonderrys took him sailing on the lough he fell overboard.

At the end of April 1938 the writer and politician Philip Kerr, 11th Marquess of Lothian, spoke out publicly against rumours that he was part of a pro-fascist clique which met at Waldorf Astor's Buckinghamshire country house, Cliveden. A week later Astor himself sent an angry letter to *The Times*. 'For years,' he wrote, 'my wife and I have entertained in the country members of all parties (including Communists), members of all faiths, of all countries, and of all interests. To link our weekends with any particular clique is as absurd as is the allegation that those of us who desire to establish better relations with Germany or with Italy are pro-Nazis or pro-Fascists.'[32]

Many of the regular guests at Cliveden were journalists: Geoffrey Dawson, editor of *The Times*; James Garvin, editor of the *Observer* (which Astor owned); Robert Barrington-Ward, chief leader-writer on *The Times*. But active politicians also came along to enjoy the Astors' lavish hospitality. In June Harold Nicolson, his own flirtation with the ultra Right firmly behind him, spent a weekend at Cliveden in June 1936 and found himself in the company of the Foreign Secretary, the Speaker of the House of Commons, an Oxford professor of political theory, a Liberal MP, a Conservative peer, the Canadian high commissioner, Winston Churchill's aunt and a gaggle of forlorn Americans, Astor relations and assorted hangers-on.

History doesn't record what the house party talked about – the impending Berlin Olympics, perhaps, or Mussolini's annexation of Ethiopia. Nicolson remarked on the 'great groups of delphiniums and tuberoses, great bowers of oleander', the work of the Astors' decorator Frank Copcutt.[33] But apart from the flowers, Cliveden wasn't to Nicolson's taste. 'I simply do not want a house like this where nothing is really yours, but belongs to servants and gardeners,' he reported to Vita. 'There is a ghastly unreality about it all . . . I enjoy seeing it. But to own it, to live here, would be like living on the stage of the Scala theatre in Milan.'[34]

Sections of the press saw the Astors and their friends as leading players in the horror that was unfolding across Europe in the late 1930s. When Lothian and Astor made their denials in the spring of 1938 they were responding to what Nancy Astor tried to dismiss as 'a false and stupid story published in a Communist rag'.[35] For months a small-circulation paper called the *Week*, edited by the left-wing journalist Claud Cockburn, had been suggesting that a group of pro-Germans in positions of power were using their influence to move the government towards an alliance with Hitler and Mussolini, allowing Germany to achieve its territorial ambitions in Eastern Europe. It was this group which had forced the resignation of Foreign Secretary Anthony Eden, who was opposed to Mussolini's expansionist policies; this group which had engineered his replacement by the pro-Hitler Lord Halifax; this group which was pushing Chamberlain into appeasing the Nazis. And this group met at Cliveden.

The campaign gained strength over the winter of 1937–8. When Chamberlain spent a weekend at Cliveden, the Labour politician Sir Stafford Cripps declared that 'the Cliveden set . . . are the people who are running policy today behind Neville Chamberlain and they are the people who would like to see Great Britain a Fascist State as well'.[36] In the *Evening Standard* cartoonist David Low portrayed Nancy Astor, Lothian and Geoffrey Dawson of *The Times* as the

'Shiver Sisters', dancing as they held high a placard reading 'Any Sort of Peace at Any Sort of Price'. The Set was lampooned on the stage and in the press. US ambassador to Britain Joseph Kennedy, back in New York to report to Roosevelt on Germany's anti-Semitism, was quizzed by reporters about his sympathy with them. 'I have never met any of that set,' he told the *New York Tribune*.[37] When George VI dined at the American Embassy and was served Virginia ham and Georgia pickled peaches, the *New York Times* jokingly put the menu down to the malign influence of the Astors, who were on the guest list. 'The chief engineer of the Cliveden set has been pulling the string again,' it reported. 'It is a well-known fact that Nancy Astor of Virginia gets in her deadliest work around the dinner table. This time she has been rigging things for her native Southland.'[38]

Less amusing was the hate mail. 'You blasted American whore of a chorus-girl,' ran one example. 'Go back to your own country.' Another accused Nancy of having Hitler's bastard child. When she was finally introduced to Claud Cockburn in the lobby of the Commons, she spat at him.

There are two questions to ask about the Cliveden Set. Perhaps the easiest is, was Cliveden really a hotbed of appeasers and pro-Nazis? Nancy and Waldorf welcomed all sorts to their weekends. George Bernard Shaw, then pro-Stalin and a self-styled Communist, dismissed the furore about the Set as 'senseless', pointing out that 'I could prove that Cliveden is a nest of Bolshevism, or indeed of any other bee in the world's bonnet.'[39] Astor's valet said the story was a pack of lies. 'Whoever invented them ought to come and work here for a week as a housemaid. They'd find no Nazis under Cliveden beds.'[40] But Lothian, Dawson, Garvin, Nancy Astor and others of their friends *were* pro-German and remained so long after it was obvious that Hitler was a very bad thing indeed. Nancy was an outspoken and bigoted anti-Semite. At different times and in different degrees, members of the Set believed that the Treaty of Versailles had left Germany with legitimate grievances; that what Hitler did in pursuit of *Lebensraum* in Eastern Europe was no business of Britain's; that the Nazis would prove a formidable bulwark against the creeping Bolshevism of the Soviet Union. That another world war must be avoided at all costs.

A lot of people in Britain believed these things. A lot of people envied Germany its strong leadership and disliked the Jews and cheered when Chamberlain sold Czechoslovakia down the river and promised peace in our time. This raises the second question. Did the Set really wield much power? Did those country-house weekends make a difference to British policy? And here the answer is a qualified 'no'. Individual members of the Set had some little impact, particularly Dawson, who kept *The Times* to a pro-German line for far too long. But they just weren't that important. Prime Minister Chamberlain and Foreign Secretary Halifax needed no encouragement in their appeasement of Hitler; and when they saw there was no help for it and that war would come, they disregarded calls to give up on Poland and sue for peace at any price.

Harold Nicolson put his finger on the hubristic heart of the Cliveden Set in the spring of 1939. As war loomed, he railed at Nancy Astor for being one of those 'silly selfish hostesses' who do immense damage by giving the impression 'that policy is decided in their own drawing-rooms'.[41] By now, most of the Set was revising its opinions. Lothian read *Mein Kampf* and belatedly decided that Hitler was a gangster who would stop at nothing. Astor stood up in the Lords and urged Chamberlain to think about negotiating with Stalin. 'I think', he said, 'we should be big enough to admit that during the past year or two each of us and all of us as individuals and as parties have probably made some mistakes.'[42]

The last of the Cliveden political weekends, and one of the last great country-house parties of the decade, took place at the beginning of June 1939. The Astors had thirty-odd guests, including Halifax, Lothian and Dawson. They had gathered to meet Adam von Trott, a German diplomat who was in England to rally support for a strategy to avoid war. Trott was no friend to the Nazis, but his proposals didn't go far enough to satisfy most of the Cliveden Set, now firmly opposed to appeasement. He went back to Germany. And Britain went to war.

POSTSCRIPT

The Old Order Doomed

On 16 June 1939, an announcement appeared in the letter columns of *The Times*. It was from Lord Derwent, chairman of the Georgian Group. Owing to the great kindness of Lord Jersey, he wrote, the Georgian Group planned to hold its first annual ball at Osterley Park in Middlesex. This would be a Georgian-themed *fête champêtre*, and it promised to be the event of the season.

Osterley had been in the news a lot over recent weeks, the result of the Earl of Jersey's decision to open the family's Adam mansion to the general public for three days a week, at sixpence for admittance to the grounds, and another shilling to see the house. When asked why he was doing it, Jersey said 'it was sufficient answer that he did not live in it and that many others wished to see it'.[1]

So they did. Twelve thousand visitors came in the first month, and the papers were full of praise for both the owner and his house. An exhibition of work by contemporary English artists from Augustus John to Duncan Grant and Charles Cundall was an added attraction. 'In these days, when the great country houses which once surrounded London are for the most part empty, pulled down, or turned into institutions,' said *The Times*, 'it is highly satisfactory to know that the public will be able to see a country house of Middlesex not only in all its glory but in its natural setting.'[2]

At twenty-five shillings a head 'including buffet, beer and cup', the *fête champêtre* was a more exclusive affair, a fund-raiser with profits going towards the Georgian Group's work of preserving the architecture of the eighteenth century. Guests were invited to come in costume. The film-star Countess of Jersey (Virginia from Hollywood) wore a pale blue lavender and rose net gown designed for her by Oliver Messel, who did most of the organising and was also in charge of decorating a vast lakeside pavilion for the ball. She had a diamond tiara in her powdered grey hair and a diamond bracelet on her wrist, although she had managed to lose the £250 bracelet by the time the sun came up, 'a dramatic climax', wrote one society columnist, 'to a season which has been remarkable for the mysterious "disappearances" of jewels and furs at almost every function'.[3]

Oliver Messel's sister, the Countess of Rosse, wore aquamarines at her throat and blue-dyed hair piled high, like Madame Pompadour. Diana Cooper wore a wimple. Actor and director Peter Glenville spurned the eighteenth-century theme altogether and came as the Trojan prince Paris, in another Messel costume designed seven years earlier for a production of Offenbach's *La Belle Hélène*. Cecil Beaton wore a coat of tapestry, and Lord Antrim, a Northern Ireland Protestant, chose the bright red robes of a cardinal.

Footmen greeted the 1,000 or so guests on the steps of the floodlit portico wearing powdered wigs and period livery. There were fireworks across the lake, which was floodlit in a purplish green for the night; an eighteenth-century beer garden; and displays of open-air wrestling. An orchestra dressed as eighteenth-century peasants played sprightly minuets, 'to which the guests, instead of dancing, listened with religious solemnity', before retiring to Messel's pavilion, where they danced till dawn to a modern swing band.[4]

That day, the government distributed 15 million leaflets to households all over the country – 'Your Gas Mask: How to Keep and Use It'.

As the world shambled towards war that summer, the stately homes of England kept calm and carried on. Nancy Astor hosted the annual rally of the local branch of the National British Women's Total Abstinence Union at Cliveden. The tea arrangements, reported the local press, 'were carried out to the satisfaction of all'.[5] The guest of honour at Blenheim Palace's annual garden fete was Sir John Simon, the Chancellor of the Exchequer. War may never come, he told the crowd. The strong heart and cool head of the British people would 'see this business through'.[6] Ginie Courtauld entertained members of the Anglo-French Art and Travel Society at Eltham Palace, while four huge barrage balloons hung in the sky above them. At Harewood House, the Princess Royal's two teenage sons received a reprimand from the War Office after the *Harewood News*, a news-sheet they produced on a typewriter in the school holidays, described an anti-aircraft battery in too much detail.

Three hundred guests danced in the ballroom of Castle Howard to celebrate the coming-of-age of Mark Howard, 'tenants rubbing shoulders with titled persons'.[7] Major Mark Howard of the Coldstream Guards died in Normandy five years later, a few months before his younger brother, a bomber pilot, was killed in a daylight raid over the Rhine. At Chatsworth, the Duke of Devonshire threw a garden party for 2,800 people to mark the coming-of-age of his son and heir, Billy Cavendish, with troupes of circus ponies performing for their entertainment. As darkness fell, Chatsworth was floodlit, and hundreds of cars were parked along the lanes overlooking the park to catch a glimpse of the spectacle. Billy Cavendish was killed by a sniper in Belgium in 1944.

The octogenarian Duke of Portland and his duchess celebrated their golden wedding that hot, humid August with a pageant at Welbeck involving 800 of the duke's estate workers in costume, enacting scenes from the abbey's past. Robin Hood and his merry men put in an appearance, as did two kings: Charles I, who visited the abbey in 1633, and William of Orange, who came in 1695. There was a ballet and an elaborate prologue in which local women represented the three Fates spinning the web of life, and schoolchildren from the surrounding villages playing the part of the threads. The Archbishop of Canterbury came to watch.

COUNTRY HOUSES were in the news that summer for other reasons. Schools were poised to occupy empty mansions in an emergency, preparations were made to set up camps for evacuees in their grounds. Big companies were buying up country houses as out-of-London accommodation if the worst came to the worst. Milton Hill House in Oxfordshire became Esso House; Chesterton Lodge, an enormous Italianate mansion outside Bicester, was bought by the Royal Exchange Assurance Corporation; the early Georgian Alresford Place near Winchester was sold to the Provident Mutual to serve as their headquarters in the event of war.

Sensitive to criticism that owners like the Jerseys were playing at dressing-up games while Europe stood on the brink of Armageddon, *Country Life* was protective about the Osterley *fête champêtre*, suggesting that it was just such events that we were about to be called upon to defend, 'for a great country-house ball on a July night is, in a sense, the fine flower of one aspect of civilisation'.[8] At the same time, the magazine began to carry advertisements which offered advice on air-raid precautions 'for fire protection of country mansions'.[9]

And advice was coming thick and fast, as the government instructed the population on everything from how to black out windows to procedures for the evacuation of children, expectant mothers and 'adult blind persons who can be moved'.[10] Incendiary bombs were considered to be a major threat to country houses, and owners were urged to clear junk out of attics and roof spaces, where a fire from an incendiary was most likely to start, and to keep fire-fighting gear – buckets of water and sand, a handpump and a bath or tank of water to replenish the buckets – on the top floor. 'If you throw a bucket of water on a burning incendiary bomb it will explode and throw burning fragments in all directions. You may be able to smother it with sand or dry earth.'[11]

The Air Ministry announced plans to turn part of the Stourhead estate into an aerodrome, then abandoned them. Enterprising firms marketed concrete air-raid shelters with outer walls of wattle hurdles; circular and domed, it was claimed that they might be mistaken for a rustic garden temple. In fact they looked more like public conveniences.

War was declared on the morning of Sunday, 3 September. Harold Nicolson, now an MP, drove down from Westminster to Sissinghurst that afternoon, passing convoys of lorries filled with evacuees from the East End. He was shocked when an old lady in one of the trucks shook her fist at his passing car and yelled that the war was all the fault of the rich. When he reached Sissinghurst on

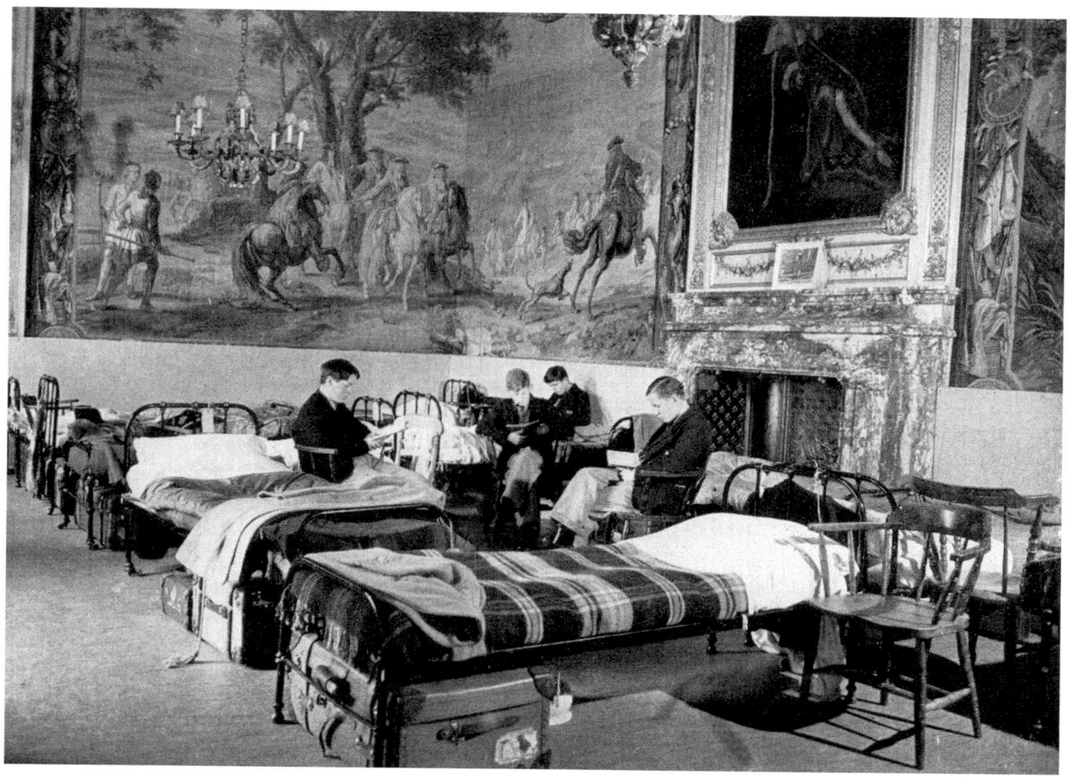

A stateroom at Blenheim Palace becomes a school dormitory.

a day redolent with omens he found that the Sackville flag which flew from the top of the tower had been taken down.

Almost before Neville Chamberlain had come to the end of his famous radio broadcast to the nation at 11.15 that morning – 'It is the evil things that we shall be fighting against – brute force, injustice, oppression and persecution – and against them I am certain that the right will prevail' – country houses were being put to new uses. By the end of the month Blenheim Palace and Attingham Park, the Marquess of Lansdowne's Bowood and Lord Methuen's Corsham Court, were all playing host to boarding schools. The Earl of Harewood offered Harewood House for use as a hospital. Many owners of large houses took similar steps. Donington Hall in Leicestershire was set up as a prisoner-of-war camp, although there were as yet no prisoners of war. The Earl and Countess of Pembroke took in forty nursery-school evacuees at Wilton: Cecil

The Countess of Carnarvon playing with evacuees from the East End on the lawn at Highclere Castle.

Beaton, still at Ashcombe, came over and photographed them, beaming and bewildered, huddled together on Wilton's Palladian Bridge.

'The most unmanageable white elephant of a mansion is now securely harnessed to the wartime machine,' commented *Country Life*. 'Indeed, the more rooms and wings and outhouses a residence possesses the more desirable it has seemed.'[12]

HOW HAD THE COUNTRY HOUSE changed in the years between the Somme and the Second World War?

For one thing, it had changed its purpose. In 1944 Robert Lutyens reckoned there would be no more ancestral houses after the war was over. 'Fluctuations of income between generations, and extensive recruitment to the possessing classes, on the one hand, and the gradual dispossession of the territorial families on the other' meant that this time the Old Order really was doomed.[13]

That didn't mean the country house was doomed as well. As we've seen, the dismantling of traditional bonds between family, mansion and local community, the breaking up of estates and the sales of houses and their contents often led simply to a change of ownership and a less traditional approach to life in the country house. But the perception of doom was there, and the 1930s and early 1940s were dominated by the quest to find a future for historic mansions that were no longer financially viable. At the 1934 annual general meeting of the National Trust, the Marquess of Lothian called on the Trust as a private charity to extend its protection, until then confined to areas of countryside and smaller historic buildings, to 'another part of our national treasure now threatened with potential destruction – the historic dwelling houses of this country'.[14] He told his audience that English country houses were under sentence of death, and that the axe which was destroying them was taxation. They cheered.

Lothian proposed that the National Trust should take on a number of furnished historic mansions. (It currently owned two, Montacute and Barrington Court, both in Somerset; and it wasn't at all sure what to do with them.) He also urged that historic houses should be exempted from death duties unless they were sold; that the Treasury should allow all maintenance claims for sums spent on upkeep and restoration; and that country houses could be exempt from death duties even if they were sold, providing that house, garden and contents were preserved as a whole, and provision made for public access from time to time.

Lothian's remarks struck a chord. Three months later, at the national conference of the Council for the Preservation of Rural England, the pioneering town planner William Harding Thompson called for the setting up of an owners' association to lobby for the 'remission of duties in approved cases in exchange for regulated public access at specified times'. And the National Trust's chairman, Lord Zetland, proposed that in return for an undertaking by owners to open their houses to sightseers, 'the Government should be asked to make easier the upkeep and preservation of the houses by remitting some of the taxation that now burdens them'.[15]

The government wasn't about to give these kind of concessions to the owners of country houses, particularly in the middle of a depression; but the notion of public money for public benefit was one that would eventually come to inform the entire stately-home business in Britain. In the meantime the National Trust lobbied Parliament to pass new legislation which would allow the owners of historic houses to hand them over to the Trust while continuing to live in them – something prohibited by charity law. In the summer of 1937 the National Trust Act passed into law and the Trust launched its Country Houses Scheme.

> The essence of the scheme [reported the *Observer*] is that owners will be able to transfer the ownership of approved country houses to the National Trust while retaining the right for themselves, and for their families and successors, to continue in occupation as long as may be desired. Places so transferred will be preserved for all time, not as dusty museums but as inhabited houses with their rooms and contents in constant use, possibly by the families who have been associated with them for centuries.[16]

Prominent figures lined up to promote the scheme. There was no alternative, said Vita Sackville-West, whose romantic ruined tower at Sissinghurst would come to the Trust thirty years later. Owners might feel 'that they could not bear to do it, but what else was there for them to do when upkeep alone cost a fortune?'[17] Lord Lothian, whose 1934 speech started it all, left Blickling Hall to the Trust when he died in 1940. Sir Charles Trevelyan handed over Wallington in 1942, and in the same year the Astors gave Cliveden, along with a large endowment. Sir Henry and Lady Alda Hoare, whose son Harry had died so tragically in Palestine in the First World War, began negotiations over Stourhead during the Second. The house and garden finally came to the Trust in 1946. Sir Henry and Lady Alda died a year later, on the same day.

There had never been a proper national survey of country

houses, but at the time conservationists reckoned there were fifty-seven 'great mansions' and 550–600 smaller country houses 'which are worthy of preservation for their historic or architectural interest or their natural beauty'.[18] That was a wild underestimate, no matter how one defined 'worthy'. In any case, even when the trickle of mansions that came to the Trust before the Second World War turned into a flood after 1945, the Country Houses Scheme could only account for a fraction of the whole. By the early 1950s the Trust opened a total of ninety-eight houses and gardens to the public. That left several thousand in private hands.

Many country-house owners continued in the 1940s as they had for decades. They stayed put or sold up. Some hung on by getting rid of yet another 'outlying parcel of land' or some rare books or a portrait of an ancestor; others took the place of those families who had gone and bought themselves a past and a place in county society. They installed electricity plants and bought labour-saving devices to help them cope with the shortage of servants. They complained about taxes and cursed the government and took in evacuees and sent their sons off to die for their country.

On the outbreak of war, smart owners were quick to offer up their mansions for the war effort. There was a feeling that being able to choose one's tenant gave a degree of control: better a girls' boarding school than an army camp. And they were right: it has been estimated that more than 1,000 country houses were demolished in the decade after 1945 as a direct result of wartime mistreatment. Classical garden statues were smashed by servicemen who couldn't care less about what Lothian had called 'the national treasure'. Rococo panelling was defaced, baroque staircases were broken up for firewood. Port Lympne, which Philip Sassoon had left to his cousin Hannah Gubbay on his death in 1939, was requisitioned as accommodation for British and foreign airmen, who vandalised it comprehensively. Tyneham House in Dorset was requisitioned for gunnery training by the Ministry of Defence and never given back to its owners. The forecourt at Lowther Castle, where Loelia Ponsonby had been regaled with stories of Arctic expeditions by the Yellow Earl, was peppered with concrete pillboxes; its elaborate gardens vanished under a wilderness of weeds, 'with just the faintest outline of the one-time paths and rides, and here and there a pagoda or a summerhouse as a pathetic relic of the romantic past'.[19]

More serious for many country houses were six years of neglect, so that by the time the Second World War was over and the Ministry of Defence began to hand back requisitioned mansions, leaking pipes and sagging roofs and dry rot had achieved the kind of destruction only dreamed of by Hitler's bombers. Many owners never occupied their homes again.

Their fate is all the more ironic because all through the war the government exploited the idea of the country house as the epitome of British values, ancient and romantic and ivy-covered – in contrast to the hard, mechanised inhumanity of the enemy. These were the values that featured in dozens of wartime films from *Mrs Miniver* to *The Tawny Pipit*. They portrayed Britain – or rather England, and a quiet, Cotswolds-type of England at that – as quintessentially rural, individualistic to the point of eccentricity, above all humane and rooted in the past. The country house, moated and timber-framed or stately and magnificent, was an emblem of this particular brand of Englishness, a symbol of what the historian G. M. Trevelyan eulogised in 1945 as 'the rural and agricultural life and the natural and historic beauty of England'.[20] It was precious, and it seemed to represent a common cause. A war widow told Christopher Hussey that before her husband's death in North Africa he had found a copy of *Country Life* and written to her 'that it was so lovely to read what one was fighting for'.[21]

There is an echo of this in the story told by novelist Elizabeth Bowen, who was staying with Gerald Berners and Robert Heber-Percy at Faringdon when Allied victory in Europe was declared in May 1945. After lunch they all went out and stood on the terrace, overlooking the fountain which had been turned off at the beginning of the war and, beyond it, an impossibly long vista across the rolling English landscape:

> Robert did something to the fountain; there was a breathless pause, then a jet of water, at first a little rusty, hesitated up into the air, wobbled then separated into four curved features of water. It was so beautiful and so sublimely symbolic – with the long view, the miles of England, stretching away behind it, that I found myself weeping.[22]

Sir George Vernon of Hanbury Hall was the last in a long line of country squires. His ancestor, Richard Vernon, had been rector of Hanbury in Worcestershire before the time of the Spanish Armada. In the reign of Queen Anne, Thomas Vernon, a successful chancery barrister, marked that success by building Hanbury Hall, an exquisite essay in red brick with dormers and white sash windows, its interiors filled with murals by the court painter Sir James Thornhill. Victorian Vernons added to the estates, and by the 1920s Sir George owned and managed 5,000 acres of good Worcestershire farmland.

He was of his class and of his time. He served as a local magistrate for thirty-five years, resigning because he thought his colleagues on the bench were too lenient with speeding motorists. He was a leading figure in the National Farmers' Union, and like so many country-house owners he did his duty and opened the gardens at Hanbury Hall once a year in aid of the Queen's Institute of District Nursing. He wrote angry letters to the papers complaining about the punitive effects of taxation on farmers, he protected his tenants when times were hard, and every now and then he discreetly sold off the odd pieces of jewellery and family silver, or a few books and manuscripts from the Hanbury Hall library, to keep things ticking over.

In so many ways Sir George Vernon was the archetypal English squire – irascible, always grumbling that the country was going to rack and ruin, while he struggled to keep his ancestral seat and his place on the creaking boughs of a family tree which stretched back for hundreds of years and was rooted in community and county.

In other ways Sir George was less typical. In 1905 at the age of forty he had married Doris Allan, the 22-year-old daughter of a neighbour. But the marriage wasn't a success. There were no children, and in the 1920s Doris moved out of Hanbury and went to live in the couple's town house in Chelsea. Sir George was left alone in his Queen Anne mansion.

One day in 1928 he walked into the house of his estate manager, Edward Powick, and announced that he wanted to borrow the man's daughter for six months. 'Things are in a mess at the Hall,' he told him. So sixteen-year-old Ruth Powick went to live with the baronet as his secretary.

She never left. Ten years later, Sir George changed his will in her favour and Ruth changed her name to Vernon. Among those who weren't aware of their real relationship, the couple passed her off as his daughter.

In the mid-1930s Sir George took up the cause of the Tithe Campaigners, who were protesting against the fact that the established Church was able by law to extract tithes from many farmers, payments which were unrelated to their profits. He attacked the Church of England in print and on platforms, telling his audiences that he refused to be buried in consecrated ground: 'No snivelling parson is going to read any service over me.'[23] And in common with other landowners and farmers across the country, he refused to pay his tithes. In June 1935, in front of hundreds of supporters, he stood on the steps of Hanbury Hall as bailiffs carried out a distraint sale of its furniture. Afterwards he addressed the crowd, telling them that 'we English have always regarded it as our most sacred duty to resist oppression and injustice from whatever quarter it comes'.[24]

Sir Oswald Mosley and the British Union of Fascists also embraced the Tithe Campaign, with blackshirts disrupting sales and barricading farms against bailiffs and the police. This brought the baronet into contact with Mosley, and when the latter wanted to put up a local man as a fascist candidate to oppose Stanley Baldwin in his Worcestershire constituency, Sir George approved the plan and told Mosley he would use his influence to help the movement. He never joined the BUF, but he flirted with fascism, which proved a good fit with his own highly individual brand of right-wing politics.

Then came the war. In the last week of May 1940 Mosley and hundreds more fascist sympathisers were rounded up and arrested under Defence Regulation 18B. In the days that followed, Sir George worried that his pre-war links with the fascists, insubstantial though they were, might be enough to bring Special Branch detectives to Hanbury Hall. He was also depressed about a heart condition and convinced he had not long to live.

At noon on 14 June 1940, Ruth heard the crack of a pistol shot from a small room leading off Sir George's bedchamber. She dashed in and found him lying dead, his revolver next to his body, and a letter which read: 'My heart is causing me great and increasing trouble at night, so instead of enduring what can only be two or three weeks' more misery, I take the short cut.'[25]

There were other things to claim the attention of the public that June. The demoralised remnants of the British Expeditionary Force had just been evacuated from Dunkirk. Paris and Norway had fallen to the Germans. Chamberlain had gone and Churchill was standing defiant in his place and telling the Commons that 'we shall never surrender'. The suicide of a 74-year-old baronet didn't merit much coverage in the press.

But the death can serve for other endings. There was no place any more for Blimpish country squires like Sir George Vernon. With this new war, the old order, whose demise had been so confidently predicted at the end of the last, really would disappear, quietly and without protest.

There was no snivelling parson to stand over Sir George at his burial. On Monday 22 June his coffin, draped in a Union Jack, was taken from Hanbury and placed on the back of a farm lorry. The makeshift cortège drove to a clearing in nearby woodland, the site of an old summerhouse, and he was buried there without any ceremony.

Ruth was the only mourner. And whether she knew it or not, she mourned for more than a lover, more than an irascible country squire. She mourned for a past. For a way of life. She mourned for an England. The long weekend was over.

NOTES

INTRODUCTION
Everyone Sang
Appearing between pages 1 and 14

1 'Stourhead Annals'.
2 Ibid.
3 Ibid.
4 Ibid.
5 Ibid.
6 Mosley, *Julian Grenfell*, 265.
7 Thompson, interview 23, 12.
8 *Times*, 12 November 1920, 15.
9 Forbes, 130.
10 Buchan, http://gutenberg.net.au/ebooks12/1201761h.html#ind.
11 Ibid.
12 *Manchester Guardian*, 29 December 1920, 3.

CHAPTER ONE
It Is Ours
Appearing between pages 15 and 33

1 Nicolson, *Vita and Harold*, 67, 113–14.
2 Walpole, *Letters*, vol. 2, 445.
3 Nicolson, *Vita and Harold*, 227.
4 Ibid., 228.
5 Nicolson, *Diaries*, 47.
6 Ibid., 48.
7 Ibid., 247.
8 Ibid., 311.
9 *Country Life*, 9 August 1930, 190.
10 Ibid., 19 July 1930, 94.
11 Ibid., 12 April 1930, 541.
12 Ibid.
13 Ibid., 28 December 1918, 614.
14 Ibid.,10 January 1920, 58.
15 *Times*, 31 December 1919, 4.
16 *Country Life*, 1 March 1919, 236.
17 Ibid., 4 January 1919, 24.
18 Ibid., 11 January 1919, 50.
19 Ibid., 8 March 1919, 264.
20 *Times Literary Supplement*, 28 May 1925, 372.
21 *Times*, 5 August 1925, 10.
22 Ibid., 10 May 1927, 17.
23 Ibid., 8 November 1919, 7.
24 Harris, *Moving Rooms*, 252.
25 *Times*, 1 October 1927, 20; 15 October 1927, 23.
26 *Nottingham Evening News*, 1 August 1929.
27 *Montgomery Express and Radnor Times*, 9 August 1921.
28 Somerville-Large, 356.
29 *Manchester Guardian*, 26 August 1926, 16.
30 Ibid., 25 January 1926, 5.
31 Ibid., 30 August 1929, 9.
32 Ibid., 1 September 1929.
33 Ibid., 24 February 1928, 7 (Lupton House, Devon); 15 September 1926, 8 (Summerford Park, Cheshire); 18 January 1926, 7 (Rolleston Hall, Staffordshire).

CHAPTER TWO

The King's Houses

Appearing between pages 34 and 51

1 *Times*, 15 June 1927, 16.
2 Windsor, *A King's Story*, 186.
3 Ibid.
4 W. A. R., 27.
5 Ibid.
6 *Builder*, 28 August 1847, 405.
7 Lord Stamfordham to Lionel Earle, 10 November 1912, PRO WORK 19/52; in Dungavell, 279.
8 *Times*, 12 November 1918, 11.
9 Fortescue, 97–8; quoted in Rose, *King George V*, 296.
10 Ibid., 295.
11 *Times*, 1 June 1927, 16.
12 *Observer*, 18 September 1927, 20.
13 Sandringham guide book, Jarrolds, n.d., introduction.
14 Windsor, 32.
15 https://www.sandringhamestate.co.uk/house-museum-and-gardens/history/
16 Pevsner and Wilson, 627. Humbert retained a conservatory by S. S. Teulon which had been added to the eighteenth-century house in 1852; it was turned into a billiard room, and a bowling alley was built on beside it.
17 Alan Powers, *ODNB* entry for Edis.
18 Pope-Hennessy, 279.
19 Windsor, *A King's Story*, 74.
20 Quoted in Rose, *King George V*, 97.
21 Ponsonby, 279.
22 Rose, *King George V*, 291.
23 Matson, *Sandringham Days*, chapter 12.
24 Ibid.
25 Transcript at http://www.bl.uk/onlinegallery/onlineex/voiceshist/georgev/

CHAPTER THREE

The Old Order Passing?

Appearing between pages 52 and 68

1 *Country Life*, 21 April 1906, 558.
2 Portland, 104.
3 Ibid., 247.
4 *Times*, 5 August 1921, 8.
5 Ibid.
6 Ibid., 14 August 1928, 7.
7 Portland, 65.
8 Ibid., 250.
9 Ibid., 58.
10 *Times*, 6 December 1937, 12.
11 Portland, 63.
12 *Times*, 26 August 1927, 13.
13 *Manchester Guardian*, 11 June 1930, 13.
14 *Times*, 11 May 1937, 4.
15 Ibid., 30 March 1920, 10.
16 Balsan, 148.
17 Ibid., 163.
18 *Country Life*, 19 July 1919, 83.
19 Balsan, 186.
20 *Manchester Guardian*, 23 March 1920, 10.
21 *Times*, 10 November 1920, 9.
22 *Manchester Guardian*, 23 March 1920, 10.
23 Ibid., 24 June 1936, 15.
24 Ibid., 19 June 1928, 21.
25 Ibid., 20 December 1919, 6.
26 Ibid., 26 November 1920.
27 The National Archives TNA J77/2100, quoted in Rose, *The Prince*, 49.
28 *Derby Daily Telegraph*, 30 January 1930, 10.
29 Galsworthy, *Maid in Waiting*, ch. 1.
30 Ibid., ch. 2.
31 Ibid.
32 Galsworthy, *Flowering Wilderness*, ch. 33.
33 Ibid., ch. 36.
34 Galsworthy, *Maid in Waiting*, ch. 2.
35 Galsworthy, *Over the River*, ch. 22.

CHAPTER FOUR

Reinstatement

Appearing between pages 69 and 94

1 Tilden, 11.
2 Ibid., 13.
3 *Country Life*, 4 December 1942, 1,082.
4 Ibid., 4 May 1918, 424.
5 Ibid., 31 March 1928, 438.
6 de Moubray, 80.
7 Conway, 101.
8 Ibid., 99.
9 Tilden, 126.
10 Conway, 102.
11 Weaver, 139; http://www.nationaltrustcollections.org.uk/place/lindisfarne-castle.
12 Anon, *Handbook for Travellers in Kent*, 24.
13 'A Visitor' [William Waldorf Astor], 'Hever Restored', *Pall Mall Magazine*, vol. 39 (January 1907), 15.
14 Aslet, 190.
15 Ibid., 196.
16 Tilden, 114.
17 Musson, 34.
18 Tinniswood, *Historic Houses*, 39.
19 de Moubray, 16.
20 Tilden, 114.
21 de Moubray, 21.
22 Conway, 102, 103.
23 de Moubray, 146.
24 Ibid., 148.
25 Tilden, 164.
26 *Country Life*, 4 December 1942, 1,085.
27 Lucas, 10.
28 *Times*, 17 May 1921, 1.
29 H. H. 'The Rev. F. Meyrick-Jones', *Times*, 20 December 1950, 8.
30 Ibid.
31 Elyard, 15.
32 *Country Life*, 17 May 1924, 783.
33 Ibid., 776.
34 Ibid.
35 Ibid., 780.
36 'Mr. E. G. Lister', obituary, *Times*, 13 July 1956, 14.
37 *Country Life*, 8 March 1924, 379.
38 Conway, 103–4.
39 *Times*, 6 January 1912, 7.
40 Ibid., 7 September 1921, 4.
41 Ibid., 14 June 1923, 15.
42 Ibid., 19 May 1919, 8.
43 Ibid., 13 September 1921, 13.

CHAPTER FIVE

A New Culture

Appearing between pages 95 and 120

1 Quoted in Stansky, 6. I owe much of my account of Sir Philip Sassoon's life to Stansky's thoughtful biography.
2 James, 202.
3 Asquith, 514.
4 Stansky, 46–7.
5 *Country Life*, 26 May 1923, 718.
6 Tilden, 42.
7 *Country Life*, 19 May 1923, 681, 682; 26 May 1923, 722.
8 James, 73.
9 Ibid., 7.
10 Stansky, 153.
11 Nicolson and Trautmann, 47.
12 Nicolson, *Diaries*, 76.
13 Boothby, *I Fight To Live*, 48.
14 James, 7, 24.
15 Ibid., 202.
16 *Country Life*, 10 January 1931, 43.
17 Ibid., 40; *Times*, 17 February 1916, 16.
18 Sassoon, 43.
19 *Country Life*, 10 January 1931, 44.
20 Cecil, 85.
21 Boothby, *Boothby*, 72.

22 *Country Life*, 10 May 1930, 691.
23 Ibid., 19 September 1931, 302.
24 Ibid., 10 May 1930, 691.
25 'Is Modern Architecture on the Right Track?', *Listener*, 26 July 1933, 123.
26 *Times*, 8 July 1937, 30.
27 Tinniswood, *The Art Deco House*, 123.

CHAPTER SIX
Lutyens
Appearing between pages 121 and 136

1 Percy and Ridley, 302.
2 Weaver, 272.
3 'Queen's Dolls House', *Times*, 29 July 1924, 21.
4 Percy and Ridley, 199.
5 Tinniswood, *Historic Houses of the National Trust*, 272.
6 Percy and Ridley, 396.
7 Pevsner and Radcliffe, 220.
8 *Times*, 4 November 1933, 2.
9 Lutyens, 182.
10 Ibid.
11 Ridley, 397.
12 Stamp, 176.
13 *Manchester Guardian*, 3 January 1944, 3.

CHAPTER SEVEN
Making Plans
Appearing between pages 137 and 154

1 Barron, 46.
2 Nicolson, *Diaries,* 112.
3 *Country Life*, 12 June 1920, 841.
4 Ibid., 4 May 1918, 428.
5 Pugin, 61.
6 Scott, 149.
7 Muthesius, 203.
8 Ibid., 205.
9 Girouard, 310.
10 *Country Life*, 4 February 1939, 116.
11 Ibid.
12 Ibid., 118.
13 Ibid., 120.
14 Ibid., 13 February 1937, 172.
15 Ibid., 25 October 1919, 534.
16 Ibid., 15 January 1921, 83.
17 Ibid., 13 February 1937, 176.
18 Memoir by Lady Marjorie Stirling (née Murray) in Waterson, 58.
19 Smith, 20.
20 Hill, 461.
21 *Country Life*, 25 February 1939, xxxvii.
22 *Times*, 31 May 1938, 22.
23 Waugh, *Decline and Fall*, 128.
24 Binney, ch. 1.
25 *Times*, 24 February 1921, 5.
26 *Country Life*, 4 February 1939, xxxii.
27 Ibid.
28 Ibid., xxxiii.
29 'Historic Monuments and Buildings Illuminated by Flood-Lighting', *Illustrated London News*, 5 September 1931, 346.
30 Ibid.
31 *Times*, 2 September 1931, 12.
32 *British Journal of Ophthalmology*, no. 15 (November 1931), 654.
33 *Times*, 8 May 1935, 15.
34 James, 205.
35 *Country Life*, 3 April 1937, 348.

CHAPTER EIGHT
Home Decorating
Appearing between pages 155 and 171

1 Fisher, 18.
2 This paragraph draws heavily on Brooks, Appendix 4, 'Charles Carrick Allom (1865–1947) and White Allom & Co.'
3 Woolf to Gwen Raverat, 1 May 1925, in Pryor, 181.
4 Nicolson, *Diaries*, 264.
5 Sibyl Colefax Ltd business card, Bodleian MS Eng.c.3184, fol. 18.
6 Beaton, *The Glass of Fashion*, 210.
7 McLeod, 145.
8 Hamlin, x.
9 *Country Life*, 25 October 1919, 525.
10 McLeod, 49.
11 Waugh, *The Best Wine Last*, 57.
12 'We Salute . . .' *Vogue*, 1 November 1932, 34.
13 *Sunday Times*, 20 January 1929, 13; 22 July 1928, 13.
14 Malacrida, 98.
15 Ibid., 122.
16 Ibid.
17 'Upper Brook Street: North Side', *Survey of London*: vol. 40, 'The Grosvenor Estate in Mayfair, Part 2 (The Buildings) (1980)', 200–10.
18 'The Marchese Malacrida's Apartment', *Vogue*, 23 November 1929, 70.
19 Hibbert et al., 271.
20 Aslet, 'An interview with the late Paul Paget', 20.
21 *Country Life*, 29 May 1937, 594.
22 *Observer*, 12 January 1936.
23 Aslet, 'An interview with the late Paul Paget', 20.
24 *Country Life*, 29 May 1937, 598.
25 Aslet, 'An interview with the late Paul Paget', 20.

CHAPTER NINE
The New Georgians
Appearing between pages 172 and 185

1 Andrews, vol. 3, 314–15.
2 Calloway, 240.
3 Wood, 41.
4 Ibid., 57.
5 *Times*, 5 July 1933, 28.
6 Wood, 57.
7 James, 39.
8 Hardy, v.
9 *Manchester Guardian*, 6 February 1926, 10.
10 *Times*, 5 March 1929, 19.
11 Ibid., 18 March 1929, 12.
12 Ibid., 4 March 1930, 12.
13 *Country Life*, 18 February 1930, 264.
14 *Times*, 26 March 1930, 14.
15 Ibid., 23 February 1931, 15.
16 Ibid., 27 May 1937, 12.
17 Tree, 43.
18 Wood, 60.
19 Tilden, 162.
20 Westminster, 199.

CHAPTER TEN
The Princess Bride and her Brothers
Appearing between pages 186 and 208

1 Rose, *King George V*, 311.
2 Graham, 243.
3 Ibid., 212.
4 Ibid., 213.
5 *Manchester Guardian*, 27 October 1931, 8.
6 Pevsner and Cherry, 182.
7 Windsor, *A King's Story*, 239.
8 *Manchester Guardian*, 3 January 1936, 8.
9 Ibid., 18 April 1938, 8.
10 *Times*, 26 July 1939, 3.
11 Ibid., 6 June 1939, 28.
12 Windsor, *A King's Story*, 333.
13 Bradford, 105.
14 Ibid., 110.
15 *Manchester Guardian*, 27 April 1923, 9.
16 Ibid.
17 Bradford, 114.
18 Ibid.
19 Ibid., 114–15.
20 Ibid., 129.
21 *Country Life*, 2 November 1929, 616.
22 Ibid., 618.
23 Windsor, *A King's Story* 235.
24 *Country Life*, 19 November 1959, 899.
25 Windsor, *A King's Story* 236.
26 Ibid., 235.
27 Ibid., 237.
28 Ibid.
29 Cooper, ch. 8.
30 Tilden, 99.
31 http://www.telegraph.co.uk/property/3297140/A-dainty-dish-to-set-before-the-Prince.html.
32 Vanderbilt and Furness, 282.
33 Ibid., 283–4.
34 Ibid., 306.
35 Bloch, 294.
36 *Cairns Post*, 15 December 1936, 5.
37 Windsor, *A King's Story*, 380.
38 Ibid., 401.
39 Nicolson, *Diaries*, 282–3.
40 Windsor, *A King's Story*, 413.
41 Ibid., 412.

CHAPTER ELEVEN
Getting About
Appearing between pages 209 and 221

1 Bedford, 8.
2 Bowden and Turner, *passim.*
3 Windsor, *A King's Story*, 241.
4 Stansky, 127.
5 Ibid.
6 http://www.airclark.plus.com/RatAerodrome/Rataero.htm
7 http://www.airfieldinformationexchange.org/community/showthread.php?2030–Automobile-association-landing-fields/page3
8 Baedeker, *Switzerland,* xx.
9 Holguín, 1,404.
10 Waterson, 232.
11 Elston, 1.
12 *Baedeker's Riviera*, xxii.
13 F. M. De Borring, 'Riviera Prospects and Proposals', *Illustrated London News*, 14 January 1922, 60.
14 Waterson, 230.
15 Ibid., 231.
16 Ibid., 233.
17 Rose, *King George V*, 322.
18 Ibid., 323.
19 Waterson, 230.
20 Coward, *Private Lives, an Intimate Comedy in Three Acts*, Heinemann (1930). In 1927, referring excitedly to the rumour that the duke's affair with Coco Chanel might end in marriage, the *Milwaukee Sentinel* noted that 'Mme Chanel was soon recognised as second in command aboard *The Flying Cloud*, which left Deauville waters for a tour of romance in the Mediterranean' (30 October 1927). Although Westminster married Loelia Ponsonby instead, he didn't allow that to interrupt his affair with Coco.

21 Bloch, 134.
22 Marx, 260.
23 *Kagorlie Miner*, 30 December 1931, 4; *Adelaide News*, 5 January 1932, 1; *Hobart Mercury*, 8 January 1932, 2.
24 'Chartered by the King for His Holiday Cruise', *Illustrated London News*, 8 August 1936, 224–5.
25 *Adelaide News*, 5 January 1932, 1.

CHAPTER TWELVE

My New-Found-Land, My Kingdom

Appearing between pages 222 and 248

1 Balsan, 37.
2 Ibid., 40.
3 Davis, 148.
4 Balsan, 44.
5 Ibid., 41.
6 *New York Times*, 19 April 1893.
7 Davis, 158.
8 Ibid., *passim*.
9 *Times*, 24 June 1921, 13.
10 *Manchester Guardian*, 14 June 1923, 6.
11 Hugo Vickers, 'Gladys, Duchess of Marlborough', http://www.telegraph.co.uk/culture/art/art-features/8303256/Gladys-Duchess-of-Marlborough-the-aristocrat-with-attitude.html
12 de Moubray, 103.
13 Windsor, *A King's Story*, 237.
14 Harris, 255–6.
15 *Manchester Guardian*, 27 January 1926, 12; 24 February 1926, 8.
16 *Basildon Park*, 2. This George Ferdinando may or may not have been the same George Ferdinando who was gaoled for twelve months in Dublin in 1894 for a stockbroking fraud.
17 http://www.waldorfnewyork.com/events/venues-and-floor-plans/third-floor.html
18 *Manchester Guardian*, 30 December 1920, 6.
19 Harris, 61.
20 Tilden, 53.
21 Ibid., 57.
22 de Moubray, 134.
23 Tilden, 58.
24 Ibid., 54.
25 Ibid., 56.
26 de Moubray, 134.
27 Tilden, 59.
28 http://query.nytimes.com/gst/abstract.html?res=9C06E5DB133AEF3ABC4E52DFBE66838E639EDE
29 Denning, 69.
30 http://www.coffmanbooks.com/TAMpdfs/TAMChapter07–v4.pdf
31 *Observer*, 12 May 1929, 17.
32 *Times*, 10 May 1929, 13.
33 A. R. Powys, Secretary to the Society for the Protection of Ancient Buildings, in *The Times*, 4 October 1930, 6.
34 Levkoff, 94.
35 Ibid.
36 Denning, 75.
37 Ibid.
38 *Manchester Guardian*, 3 August 1934, 8.
39 *New York Tribune*, 20 May 1909, 3.
40 *New York Times*, 19 September 1907.
41 Broughton, 49.
42 *Times*, 31 January 1929, 14.
43 Ibid., 15 June 1923, 28.
44 https://www.thegazette.co.uk/Edinburgh/issue/14931/page/59/data.pdf
45 Purcell, Hale and Pearson, 8.
46 Lees-Milne, 239, 238.
47 Fedden, 31.
48 A point which is well made by Purcell, Hale and Pearson, whose book I have pillaged ruthlessly in my remarks on Fairhaven and Anglesey Abbey.

CHAPTER THIRTEEN

A Queer Streak

Appearing between pages 249 and 267

1 Amory, chapter 6.
2 Beaton, *Ashcombe*, 44.
3 Ibid., 69.
4 Ibid., 55.
5 Ibid.
6 Ibid., 72.
7 Beaton, 'Suggestions for Fancy Dress', 116.
8 Beaton, *Ashcombe*, 72.
9 Ibid., 74.
10 'Its ultimate fate is unknown', says Matthew Parris, in the account of the affair he included in *Great Parliamentary Scandals*, Robson Books (1995).
11 Byrne, 131.
12 Aberconway, 127.
13 *Times*, 31 March 1931, 17.
14 Byrne, 144.
15 *Manchester Guardian*, 15 May 1931, 10.
16 Byrne, 149.
17 Coward, 283.
18 Ibid., 284.
19 *Observer*, 18 October 1931, 15.
20 Coward, 309.
21 *Country Life*, 10–17 September 1932; quoted in Cornforth, 237. The Messels' architects were Walter Tapper and Norman Evill. Unfortunately the house was partly destroyed by fire in 1947.
22 Amory, chapter 10.
23 Andrews, vol. 1, 254.
24 Amory, chapter 10.
25 Amory, chapter 11.
26 *Sunday Times*, 11 August 1935, 16.
27 Ibid., 7 August 1938, 16.
28 Quoted in the *Daily Telegraph* obituary of Zita James, 23 February 2006.

CHAPTER FOURTEEN

The House Party

Appearing between pages 268 and 289

1 Galsworthy, *Maid in Waiting*, ch. 11.
2 James, 21.
3 Nicolson, *Vita and Harold*, 285.
4 James, 21.
5 *Notes and Queries*, 5th Series, vol. 12, 428.
6 Waterson, 77.
7 Westminster, 90.
8 Cooke, 83.
9 Bodleian Library, Colefax Papers, MS Eng. c.3170, fols. 46–61.
10 Troubridge, 11.
11 Ibid., 9.
12 Waterson, 58, 59.
13 Westminster, 148, 149.
14 Troubridge, 134.
15 James, 37.
16 Waterson, 58.
17 Windsor, *The Heart Has Its Reasons*, 174.
18 Ibid., 175.
19 Ibid., 177.
20 *Manchester Guardian*, 17 December 1928, 6.
21 *Manners and Rules*, 47.
22 Craig, 8.
23 Waterson, 63.
24 *Manners and Rules*, 119, 121.
25 Ibid., 119, 216.
26 Westminster, 149.
27 Waterson, 80.
28 *Manchester Guardian*, 9 April 1928, 6.
29 Waterson, 69.
30 *Manners and Rules*, 213–14.
31 Westminster, 91–2.
32 Tilden, 48.
33 Taylor, 217.
34 Stansky, 163.
35 Waterson, 132.
36 *Country Life*, 21 March 1931, 369.
37 Waterson, 92.
38 Harrison, *Rose*, 31.

39 *Dundee Evening Telegraph*, 12 November 1926, 4.
40 Ibid.
41 *Daily Sketch*, 15 March 1923, 2; Hume-Williams, 157.
42 Lord Stamfordham, 15 July 1922; PRO, Lord Chancellor's Office, 2/775.
43 *Portsmouth Evening News*, 19 September 1924, 6.
44 Troubridge, 186.

CHAPTER FIFTEEN

Field Sports

Appearing between pages 290 and 304

1 Portland, 229.
2 The figure comes from Martin, 'British Game Shooting', 204–24. For what follows I have drawn on Martin's article.
3 *The Land: The Report of the Land Enquiry Committee*, 3rd edition (1913), vol. 1, 260.
4 Tennyson, 2.
5 Ibid., 31.
6 *Manners and Rules*, 217.
7 Westminster, 210.
8 Ibid.
9 *Manners and Rules*, 223.
10 Beaton, *Ashcombe*, 46.
11 Ibid., 47.
12 *Manchester Guardian*, 28 May 1931, 9.
13 Windsor, 196.
14 *Ludington Daily News*, Michigan, 22 January 1936, 6.
15 *Times*, 29 December 1934, 19.
16 Thomson, 150.
17 Ibid., 152.

CHAPTER SIXTEEN

In Which We Serve

Appearing between pages 305 and 324

1 Martin, *The Small House*, 82.
2 Todd, 195.
3 Dawes, 159.
4 Harrison, *Gentlemen's Gentlemen*, 39.
5 *Times*, 17 March 1919, 7.
6 Dawes, 152–3.
7 *Times*, 18 March 1919, 7.
8 Thompson, interview 388.
9 Ibid.
10 Ibid.
11 Tyack, 67.
12 The domestic side of life at Cliveden is particularly well documented. The 1970s saw the appearance of the autobiography of Rosina Harrison, who was in service with the Astors for thirty-five years from 1928; followed by a valuable oral history of the indoor and outdoor staff between the wars by Geoffrey Tyack. In what follows I have drawn on both sources.
13 Harrison, *Rose*, 48.
14 Tyack, 82.
15 Ibid., 68.
16 Harrison, *Rose*, 163–4.
17 Ibid., 118.
18 Ibid., 126.
19 Ibid., 121.
20 Ibid., 124.
21 Tyack, 71.
22 Harrison, *Rose*, 151.
23 Ibid., 105.
24 Ibid., 64.
25 Ibid., 210.
26 Ibid., 85.
27 Ibid., 86.
28 Ibid., 95.
29 Newman and Tate, ch. 3.
30 Harrison, *Rose*, 137.
31 Tyack, 69.
32 Harrison, *Rose*, 115.

33 Ibid., 119.
34 Waterson, 172.
35 Harrison, *Rose*, 120–1.
36 Ibid., 131.
37 Tyack, 81.

CHAPTER SEVENTEEN
Serving Top Society
Appearing between pages 325 and 338

1 Parker, 4.
2 Ibid., 5.
3 Waterson, 184.
4 Parker, 15.
5 Ibid., 17.
6 Ibid., 18.
7 Rennie, 103.
8 Harrison, *Rose*, 24.
9 Ibid., 24.
10 *Times*, 2 March 1925, 3.
11 Ibid., 1 July 1926, 3.
12 Ibid., 13 January 1925, 4.
13 Parker, 21.
14 *Times*, 30 January 1918, 4.
15 Parker, 29.
16 Ibid., 38.
17 Ibid., 53.
18 Ibid., 43.
19 Ibid., 47.
20 Todd, 198.
21 Parker, 39.
22 Ibid., 55.
23 Ibid., 59.

CHAPTER EIGHTEEN
The Political House
Appearing between pages 339 and 365

1 Morris, 172.
2 Ibid., 173.
3 Ibid., 192.
4 *Times*, 4 August 1936, 10.
5 Ibid., 11.
6 Stansky, 87.
7 Ibid., 92.
8 Ibid.
9 *Hansard*, 8 February 1922.
10 Mosley, *My Life*.
11 *Times*, 15 May 1920, 14.
12 *Manchester Guardian*, 25 April 1921, 7. The film was *Shoulder Arms*, Chaplin's 1918 war comedy.
13 Stansky, 118.
14 Tilden, 77.
15 Ibid., 75.
16 Ibid., 81.
17 Taylor, 284.
18 Churchill to John Leaning & Sons Ltd (his chartered surveyors), 4 September 1926; quoted in Buczacki, 141.
19 Tilden to Clarice Fisher, Churchill's secretary, 17 March 1927; quoted in Buczacki, 151.
20 Major, 111, 70.
21 *Times*, 5 October 1917, 3.
22 Ibid.
23 Ibid.
24 Ibid.
25 Major, 99.
26 Ibid., 104.
27 Major, 166.
28 *Manchester Guardian*, 20 October 1923, 10.
29 Baldwin Papers 123/58, 19 August 1937; quoted in Roberts, chapter 7.
30 Roberts, chapter 7.
31 *Manchester Guardian*, 31 December 1938, 11.
32 *Times*, 5 May 1938, 17.
33 Nicolson, *Diaries*, 266.

34 Ibid.
35 Harrison, *Rose*, 181.
36 *Manchester Guardian*, 28 March 1938, 9.
37 Reported in *Western Daily Press*, 17 December 1938, 7.
38 *Manchester Guardian*, 23 May 1939, 8.
39 Rose, *The Cliveden Set*, chapter 8.
40 Harrison, *Rose*, 244.
41 Nicolson, *Diaries*, 396.
42 http://hansard.millbanksystems.com/lords/1939/apr/13/the-international-situation#S5LV0112P0_19390413_HOL_15

POSTSCRIPT

The Old Order Doomed

Appearing between pages 365 and 378

1 *Times*, 26 May 1939, 11.
2 Ibid., 25 May 1939, 17.
3 *Table Talk*, 10 August 1939, 10.
4 *Lancashire Evening Post*, 15 July 1939, 4.
5 *Bucks Herald*, 21 July 1939, 3.
6 *Dundee Courier*, 8 August 1939, 7.
7 *Hull Daily Mail*, 26 August 1939, 5.
8 *Country Life*, 22 July 1939, 56.
9 Ibid., 4 March 1939, xxxiii.
10 Anon., *Some Things You Should Know if War Should Come*, Civil Defence Public Information Leaflet No. 1, Lord Privy Seal's Office (July 1939).
11 Ibid.
12 *Country Life*, 30 September 1939, 325.
13 Strong, 130.
14 *Times*, 20 July 1934, 9.
15 Ibid., 26 February 1936, 9.
16 *Observer*, 11 July 1937, 32.
17 *Manchester Guardian*, 19 November 1937, 12.
18 *Observer*, 11 July 1937, 32.
19 Robinson, 120.
20 Strong, 134.
21 Ibid., 128.
22 Amory, chapter 16.
23 *Western Daily Press*, 22 October 1934, 7.
24 *Manchester Guardian*, 15 June 1935, 14.
25 *Gloucester Citizen*, 17 June 1940, 7.

BIBLIOGRAPHY

Aberconway, Christobel, *A Wiser Woman?*, Hutchinson (1966).

Adelaide News.

Amory, Mark, *Lord Berners: The Last Eccentric*, Faber Finds (2012), Kindle file.

Andrews, C. Bruyn (ed.), *The Torrington Diaries*, Methuen Library Reprints, 4 vols. (1970).

Anon., *Handbook for Travellers in Kent*, John Murray (1892).

Aslet, Clive, 'An interview with the late Paul Paget', *The Thirties Society Journal*, no. 6 (1987), 16–25.

Aslet, Clive, *The Last Country Houses*, Yale University Press (1982).

Asquith, H. H., *Letters to Venetia Stanley*, ed. Michael Brock and Eleanor Brock, Oxford University Press (1982).

[Astor, William Waldorf], 'Hever Restored', *Pall Mall Magazine*, vol. 39 (January 1907), 15–16.

Baedeker, *Switzerland, Together with Chamonix and the Italian Lakes* (1922).

Baedeker's Riviera (1931).

Balsan, Consuelo Vanderbilt, *The Glitter and the Gold*, George Mann (1973).

Barron, P. A., *The House Desirable*, Methuen & Co. (1929).

Basildon Park, National Trust (2004).

Beaton, Cecil, *Ashcombe: The Story of a Fifteen-Year Lease*, Dovecote Press (2014).

Beaton, Cecil, *The Glass of Fashion*, Weidenfeld & Nicolson (1954).

Beaton, Cecil, 'Suggestions for Fancy Dress', *Vogue*, 15 December 1937, 116.

Bedford, John, Duke of, *A Silver-Plated Spoon*, Cassell (1959).

Binney, Ruth, *Wise Words and Country House Ways*, David & Charles (2012), Kindle file.

Bloch, Michael (ed.), *Wallis and Edward: Letters 1931–1937*, Weidenfeld & Nicolson (1986).

Boothby, Robert, *Boothby: Recollections of a Rebel*, Hutchinson (1978).

Boothby, Robert, *I Fight To Live*, Victor Gollancz (1947).

Bowden, Sue and Turner, Paul, 'The Demand for Consumer Durables in the United Kingdom in the Interwar Period', *Journal of Economic History*, vol. 53, no. 2 (June 1993), 244–58.

Bradford, Sarah, *King George VI*, Weidenfeld & Nicolson (1989).

Brooks, Diana, *Thomas Allom*, Heinz Gallery (1998).

Broughton, Urban Hanlon, *A Winter Cruise and Some Mental Ramblings*, Edinburgh University Press (1922).

Buchan, John, *Memory Hold-The-Door*, Hodder & Stoughton (1940).

Bucks Herald.

Buczacki, Stefan, *Churchill and Chartwell*, Frances Lincoln (2007).

Builder.

Byrne, Paula, *Mad World: Evelyn Waugh and the Secrets of Brideshead*, HarperPress (2009).

Cairns Post.

Calloway, Stephen, *Twentieth Century Decoration*, Weidenfeld & Nicolson (1988).

Cecil, Hugh and Mirabel, *In Search of Rex Whistler*, Frances Lincoln (2012).

Colefax Papers.

Conway, Sir Martin, *Episodes in a Varied Life* (1932).

Cooke, Maud C., *Social Etiquette: or Manners and Customs of Polite Society*, McDermid & Logan (1896).

Cooper, Diana, *The Light of Common Day* (1959), Kindle file.

Cornforth, John, *The Search for a Style: Country Life and Architecture 1897–1933*, André Deutsch (1988).

Country Life.

Coward, Noël, *Present Indicative*, William Heinemann (1937).
Craig, Elizabeth, *Entertaining With Elizabeth Craig*, Collins (1933).

Daily Sketch.
Davis, Richard W., '"We Are All Americans Now!" Anglo-American Marriages in the Later Nineteenth Century', *Proceedings of the American Philosophical Society*, vol. 135, no. 2 (June 1991), 140–99.
Dawes, Frank Victor, *Not in Front of the Servants*, Hutchinson (1984).
de Moubray, Amicia, *Twentieth Century Castles in Britain*, Frances Lincoln (2013).
Denning, Roy (ed.), *The Story of St Donat's Castle and Atlantic College*, D. Brown (1983).
Derby Daily Telegraph.
Dundee Courier.
Dundee Evening Telegraph.
Dungavell, Ian, 'The Architectural Career of Sir Aston Webb (1849–1930)', PhD thesis, University of London (1999).

Elston, Roy, *The Traveller's Handbook to the Rivieras of France and Italy*, Simpkin, Marshall, Hamilton, Kent & Co. (1927).
Elyard, S. John, *Some Old Wiltshire Homes* (1894).

Fedden, Robin, *Anglesey Abbey*, National Trust (1990).
Fisher, Richard B., *Syrie Maugham*, Duckworth (1978).
Forbes, Lady Angela, *Memories and Base Details*, Hutchinson (n.d.)
Fortescue, Sir John, *Author and Creator*, Blackwood (1933).

Galsworthy, John, *Flowering Wilderness* (1932), Kindle file.
Galsworthy, John, *Maid in Waiting* (1931), Kindle file.
Galsworthy, John, *Over the River* (1932), Kindle file.
Girouard, Mark, *Life in the English Country House*, Yale University Press (1978).
Gloucester Citizen.
[Graham, Evelyn], *Princess Mary, Viscountess Lascelles: An Intimate and Authoritative Life-Story*, Hutchinson (1929).
Hamlin, A. D. F., *A History of Ornament Ancient and Medieval*, vol. 1, Batsford (1916).
Hardy, Thomas, *Late Lyrics and Earlier*, Macmillan (1922).
Harris, John, *Moving Rooms: The Trade in Architectural Salvages*, Yale University Press (2007).
Harrison, Rosina, *Rose: My Life in Service*, Book Club Associates (1975).
Harrison, Rosina (ed.), *Gentlemen's Gentlemen: My Friends in Service*, Arlington Books (1976).
Hibbert, Christopher et al., *The London Encyclopaedia*, Macmillan (2008).
Hill, Oliver, 'The Modern Movement', *Architectural Design and Construction*, 1 September 1931, 461.
Hobart Mercury.
Holguín, Sandie, '"National Spain Invites You": Battlefield Tourism during the Spanish Civil War', *American Historical Review*, vol. 110 (2005), 1399–1426.
Hull Daily Mail.
Hume-Williams, Sir Ellis, *The World, the House and the Bar*, John Murray (1930).

Illustrated London News.

James, Robert Rhodes (ed.), *Chips: The Diaries of Sir Henry Channon*, Weidenfeld & Nicolson (1967).

Kagorlie Miner.

Lancashire Evening Post.
Lees-Milne, James, *Ancestral Voices*, Faber & Faber (1987).
Levkoff, Mary L., *Hearst The Collector*, Abrams (2008).
Listener.
Lucas, E. V., 'A Wanderer's Notebook', *Sunday Times*, 19 July 1931, 10.
Ludington Daily News.
Lutyens, Robert, *Six Great Architects*, Hamilton (1959).

Major, Norma, *Chequers: The Prime Minister's*

Country House and its History, HarperCollins (1996).
Malacrida, Peter, 'Modernist Tendencies in Decoration', *Vogue*, 13 October 1928, 98–122.
Manchester Guardian.
Manners and Rules of Good Society, 'A Member of the Aristocracy', 38th edition, Frederick Warne & Co. (1916).
Martin, Arthur, *The Small House: Its Architecture and Surroundings*, A. Rivers (1906).
Martin, John, 'British Game Shooting in Transition, 1900–1945', *Agricultural History* (Spring 2011), 204–24.
Marx, Harpo with Barber, Rowland, *Harpo Speaks*, Victor Gollancz (1961).
Matson, John, *Sandringham Days: The Domestic Life of the Royal Family in Norfolk, 1862–1952*, History Press (2012), Kindle file.
McLeod, Kirsty, *A Passion for Friendship: Sibyl Colefax and Her Circle*, Michael Joseph (1991).
Montgomery Express and Radnor Times.
Morris, A. J. A., *C. P. Trevelyan 1870–1958: Portrait of a Radical*, Blackstaff Press (1977).
Mosley, Nicholas, *Julian Grenfell: His Life and the Times of His Death 1888–1915*, Holt, Rinehart and Winston (1976).
Mosley, Oswald, *My Life*, Black House Publishing (2011), Kindle file.
Musson, Jeremy, 'To Me the Past is Sacred', *Country Life*, 8 January 1998, 34.
Muthesius, Hermann, *The English House*, BSP Professional Books (1987).

New York Times.
New York Tribune.
Newman, Hilda with Tate, Tim, *Diamonds at Dinner: My Life as a Lady's Maid in a 1930s Stately Home*, John Blake (2013), Kindle file.
Nicolson, Harold, *Diaries and Letters 1930–1939*, Collins (1966).
Nicolson, Nigel (ed.), *Vita and Harold: The Letters of Vita Sackville-West and Harold Nicolson*, Weidenfeld & Nicolson (1992).
Nicolson, Nigel and Trautmann, Joanne (eds.), *The Letters of Virginia Woolf*, vol. 4, Mariner Books (1981).
Nottingham Evening News.

Observer.

Parker, D. H., *The Story of My Life in Gentlemen's Service*, privately printed (n.d.).
Percy, Clayre and Ridley, Jane (eds.), *The Letters of Edwin Lutyens to His Wife, Lady Emily*, Collins (1985).
Pevsner, Sir Nikolaus and Cherry, Bridget, *Buildings of England: London 1*, Penguin Books (1985).
Pevsner, Sir Nikolaus and Radcliffe, Enid, *The Buildings of England: Yorkshire, The West Riding*, Penguin Books (2001).
Pevsner, Sir Nikolaus and Wilson, Bill, *The Buildings of England: Norfolk 2*, Penguin Books (2000).
Ponsonby, Sir Frederick, *Recollections of Three Reigns*, Eyre & Spottiswoode (1951).
Pope-Hennessy, J., *Queen Mary*, Allen & Unwin (1959).
Portland, W. Cavendish-Bentinck, Duke of, *Men, Women and Things: Memories of the Duke of Portland*, Faber & Faber (1937).
Portsmouth Evening News.
Pryor, William (ed.), *Virginia Woolf and the Raverats*, Clear Books (2003).
Pugin, A. Welby, *The True Principles of Pointed or Christian Architecture* (1841).
Purcell, Mark, Hale, William and Pearson, David, *Treasures from Lord Fairhaven's Library at Anglesey Abbey*, National Trust (2013).

Rennie, Jean, *Every Other Sunday*, Coronet (1977).
Ridley, Jane, *Edwin Lutyens: His Life, His Wife, His Work*, Pimlico (2003).
Roberts, Andrew, *The Holy Fox: The Life of Lord Halifax*, Head of Zeus (2014), Kindle file.
Robinson, John Martin, *Requisitioned: The British Country House in the Second World War*, Aurum Press (2014).
Rose, Andrew, *The Prince, The Princess and the Perfect Murder*, Coronet (2014).
Rose, Kenneth, *King George V*, Weidenfeld & Nicolson (1983).
Rose, Norman, *The Cliveden Set*, Jonathan Cape (2000), Kindle file.

Sassoon, Siegfried, *Selected Poems*, Faber & Faber (1968).

Scott, George Gilbert, *Remarks on Secular and Domestic Architecture* (1857).

Smith, Janet, *Liquid Assets: The Lidos and Open Air Swimming Pools of Britain*, English Heritage (2008).

Somerville-Large, Peter, *The Irish Country House: A Social History*, Sinclair-Stevenson (1995).

Stamp, Gavin, *Edwin Lutyens' Country Houses*, Aurum (2012).

Stansky, Peter, *Sassoon: The Worlds of Philip and Sybil*, Yale University Press (2003).

'Stourhead Annals', MSS NT 3027141, Stourhead, Wiltshire.

Strong, Roy, *Country Life 1897–1997: The English Arcadia*, Boxtree (1996).

Sunday Times.

Table Talk.

Taylor, A. J. P. (ed.), *Lloyd George: A Diary by Frances Stevenson*, Harper & Row (1971).

Tennyson, Julian, *Rough Shooting* (1938).

Thompson, P., *Family Life and Work Experience before 1918, Middle and Upper Class Families in the Early 20th Century, 1870–1977*, 7th edition, UK Data Archive (2009).

Thomson, George Malcolm, *Lord Castlerosse: His Life and Times*, Weidenfeld & Nicolson (1973).

Tilden, Philip, *True Remembrances: The Memoirs of an Architect*, Country Life (1954).

Times.

Times Literary Supplement.

Tinniswood, Adrian, *The Art Deco House*, Mitchell Beazley (2002).

Tinniswood, Adrian, *Historic Houses of the National Trust*, National Trust (1991).

Todd, Selina, 'Domestic Service and Class Relations in Britain 1900–1950', *Past and Present*, no. 203 (May 2009), 181–204.

Tree, Ronald, *When the Moon Was High: Memoirs of Peace and War*, Macmillan (1975).

Troubridge, Lady, *Etiquette and Entertaining*, Amalgamated Press (n.d. [1939]).

Tyack, Geoffrey, 'Service on the Cliveden Estate Between the Wars', *Oral History*, vol. 5, no. 1 (Spring 1977), 63–87.

Vanderbilt, Gloria and Furness, Thelma Lady, *Double Exposure: A Twin Autobiography*, David McKay Company, (1958).

Vogue.

Walpole, Horace, *The Letters of Horace Walpole, Earl of Orford, London* (1840).

W. A. R., 'Autobiographical Passages in the Life of Mr Nash', *Mechanics' Magazine*, vol. 24 (1836), 26–9.

Waterson, Merlin (ed.), *The Country House Remembered*, Routledge & Kegan Paul (1985).

Waugh, Alec, *The Best Wine Last*, W. H. Allen (1978).

Waugh, Evelyn, *Decline and Fall*, Penguin Books (1937).

Weaver, Lawrence, *Houses and Gardens by E. L. Lutyens* (1913).

Western Daily Press.

Westminster, Loelia, Duchess of, *Grace and Favour*, Weidenfeld & Nicolson (1961).

Windsor, Duchess of, *The Heart Has Its Reasons*, David McKay Company, (1956).

Windsor, Edward, Duke of, *A King's Story: The Memoirs of HRH the Duke of Windsor*, Cassell (1951).

Wood, Martin, *Nancy Lancaster: English Country House Style*, Frances Lincoln (2005).

PICTURE CREDITS

pp. xi, 293 © PA/PA Archive/PA Images; p. 2 © National Trust; pp. 10, 16, 20–21, 25, 28, 59, 71, 78, 86, 97, 99, 100-101, 102-103, 106, 110, 116, 126-7, 130, 133, 136-7, 144, 146 150, 153, 168, 174, 178, 182, 229, 231, 240, 246, 269, 309, 350, 369 and 370 © *Country Life*; p. 18 – from *Vita and Harold: The Letters of Vita Sackville-West and Harold Nicolson*; p. 30 © Associated Newspapers/REX Shutterstock; p. 70 © RIBA Collections; p. 84 © Trustees of Leeds Castle Foundation, Maidstone, Kent, UK/Bridgeman Images; pp. 95, 191 © National Portrait Gallery, London; p. 107 © Rex Whistler/Private Collection/Bridgeman Images; p. 120 © Punch Limited; p. 124–5 © National Trust Images/Dennis Gilbert; p. 158 © Colefax and Fowler. Photography: Millar & Harris/English Heritage Collection; p. 162 © Francis Lincoln Ltd./Felix Rosenstiel's Widow and Son, Ltd., London on behalf of the estate of Sir John Lavery; p. 170 reproduced by permission of Historic England; p. 187 © Popperfoto/Getty Images; p. 197 © National Trust/Richard Holttum; p. 202 photo by The Print Collector/Print Collector/ Getty Images; pp. 234-5 RIBA Collections; p. 247 © National Trust Images/John Hammond; p. 249 photo by Sasha/Getty Images p. 254 photo by ullstein bild/ullstein bild via Getty Images; p. 265 © Hulton-Deutsch Collection/CORBIS; p. 271 © Rex Whistler/Plas Newydd, Anglesey, UK/The Collection of the Marquess of Anglesey/ National Trust Photographic Library/John Hammond/Bridgeman Images; p. 277 from the Duchess of Windsor's private collection; p. 283 from a private collection; p. 303 photo by Central Press/Getty Images; p. 309 © National Trust Images/Derek Croucher; p. 311 photo by Topical Press Agency/Hulton Archive/Getty Images; p. 341 © National Trust/Trustees of the Trevelyan family; p. 352 © National Trust/Anthony Lambert; p. 357 © The Chequers Trust

The author and publishers have made every effort to trace and contact copyright holders. The publishers will be pleased to correct any mistakes or omissions in future editions.

INDEX

Note: page numbers in *italic* refer to illustrations.